Carnival Kingdom

Biblical Justice for Global Communities

Carnival Kingdom

Biblical Justice for Global Communities

Edited by
Marijke Hoek
Jonathan Ingleby
Andy Kingston-Smith
Carol Kingston-Smith

Wide Margin
Academical

Published in 2013 by Wide Margin,
90 Sandyleaze, Gloucester, GL2 0PX, UK

http://www.wide-margin.co.uk/

ISBN 978-1-908860-02-6

Printed and bound in Great Britain by
Lightning Source, Milton Keynes

Colophon

This book is set in Espinosa Nova, by Cristóbal Henestrosa of the Mexican type foundry Estudio CH. It was cut to commemorate Antonio de Espinosa, the first punchcutter on the American continent and the most important Mexican printer of the sixteenth century.

The cover image, by kind permission of the well-known Bolivian artist, Roberto Mamani Mamani, depicts the carnival figure, Ch'uta. The masked Ch'uta, between two pretty 'cholita' girls represents the subversive carnival energy of the indigenous and *mestizo* culture in Bolivia. Complete with an extravagant colonial moustache and beard and dressed in an eclectic array of bullfighter bolero and contemporary urban clothing, the Ch'uta mimics the colonial master and at the same time represents the hybrid mixing of cultures, times and spaces. The Ch'uta's jovial 'devil-may-care' and flirtatious manner subverts the petty rules and regulations of the formal elite and promotes the fertile capacity to be both doubly (re)productive and to resist the oppressive injustice of the colonial master.

Contents

Acknowledgements

Carnival Kingdom has been a hugely exciting project, and the editors would like to warmly acknowledge those who have made it possible.

Our heartfelt thanks go especially to all the contributing authors without whom *Carnival Kingdom* would not have materialised!

We are also indebted to Sylvia Hathaway for translating so swiftly and ably the chapter written by Dr Dario Lopez.

We are very grateful to our publisher, Simon Cozens at Wide Margin, for his distinctive and refreshing brand of grassroots professionalism. His enthusiasm and his creative guidance have been invaluable.

We are grateful to Roberto Mamani Mamani for granting us permission to use an image of one of his paintings as part of the cover design of the book.

There have been, of course, many others, too many to mention, who have contributed through their writing, their example and their material support.

Our final acknowledgement is to the leading, guiding and inspiration of the Spirit of God who continues to teach us. The vision of this book is that we might all grasp a wider and deeper understanding of God's loving justice in a world that desperately needs the manifest hope of the Carnival Kingdom.

The jusTice initiative

All of the profits from sales of *Carnival Kingdom* will go towards the work of the jusTice initiative.

The initiative was founded in 2010 by Andy & Carol Kingston-Smith with the aim of encouraging and inspiring others to apply their Christian faith to the important work of creating and contributing to just communities around the world.

As people of faith we need to understand the life-enhancing vision of our faith in God in the light of the key socio-political, economic and environmental issues of our time and be able to reflect on what that means for the Christian community.

We hope that the jusTice initiative will play a part in extending your vision and encourage you to formulate responses to the injustices you encounter, through developing a creative and robust theology and living that out as agents of God's Kingdom. As Lecturers in Justice and Mission at Redcliffe College, our work through the initiative is closely tied in with the undergraduate, and in particular, postgraduate programmes at Redcliffe, including the new Masters course *Justice, Advocacy & Reconciliation in Intercultural Contexts* which commenced in September 2012. (http://www.redcliffe.org/Study/PostgraduateCourses/JusticeandMission).

You can engage with the jusTice initiative online through one of the following media:-

- Web: http://www.justice-initiative.com
- Facebook: http://www.facebook.com/pages/Justice-Advocacy-and-Mission/148143665240215
- Twitter: @just_mission
- Blog: http://justiceadvocacyandmission.wordpress.com/

Further information on the initiative can also be found on Redcliffe College's website at:-http://www.redcliffe.org/SpecialistCentres/JusticeAdvocacyandReconciliationinMission

Thank you for your support!

Andy & Carol Kingston-Smith

Foreword

When black slaves stared at each other across the campfire and sung, 'Steal away to Jesus' within earshot of their slave masters, a carnival was taking place.

What we now call 'Negro Spirituals' were often subversive emancipation songs, which celebrated the hope of escape and freedom in the presence of the oppressor. In the subversion of an eschatological theme, black slaves were working with God to do something about their sufferings in the here and now. And what appeared to the oppressor as a song about contentment and containment, turned out to be an act of defiant hope.

In biblical terms, Christians are called to sing the Lord's songs in a strange land. We may choose to do so in predictable lamentations about falling church numbers, the erosion of Christendom, or the decline of marriage. We may even be prompted by our nervous premonitions about human rights and the loss of Christian influence in the wider culture.

Or we could—as this book suggests—become positive subversives whose passion for a spiritual and moral revolution never gets in the way of the Gospel's power to change the 'habits of the heart' for men and women in our world.

Quite frankly, it is generally easy to spot a Christian devotee: we are the disapprovers. We have a tendency to panic and be very 'concerned'. We show up with the humour of undertakers at a birthday party. We talk about justification, but seldom about justice. People are more likely to associate us with 'sin' than 'redemption' and generally we prefer it that way.

For most of us heaven really will be a culture shock.

But imagine a community of believers who refuse to tip-toe around the twenty-first century; who feel the pain of the world more acutely than anyone else; who are passionate about everyone coming to a knowledge of God through the transforming work of the Cross, and who bear the enormity of God's mission in the very core of their being; who hunger and thirst for righteousness, but who, nonetheless look at the world through spectacles of hope and evidently serve a God who turns sorrow into dancing and puts a song into the heart of a slave.

Only then are we likely to truly comprehend what it means to belong to a Carnival Kingdom.

Rev Joel Edwards is the International Director for Micah Challenge, a global Christian response to extreme poverty. He was also co-Chair of Micah Challenge from 2004-2007. Prior to his role within Micah Challenge, he was General Director of the Evangelical Alliance UK, a post he held for over 10 years. He is committed to harmonise matters of faith in the public square, and to advocate on behalf of the world's poor. He continues to hold a number of other roles, including serving as an Advisory Member of Tony Blair's Faith Foundation, and was formerly a Commissioner on the Equality and Human Rights Commission for the UK. A regular broadcaster with the BBC and other UK and international media channels, he is often asked to bring a Christian perspective to current issues. He also serves as a member of the Advisory Board on Human Rights & Religious Freedom with the British Foreign & Commonwealth Office. He is an Honorary Canon of St Paul's Cathedral, London, and has an honorary doctorate from St Andrews University, Scotland.

Introduction

In his book about aspects of C. S. Lewis's fiction, *The Lion's World, A Journey into the Heart of Narnia*, Rowan Williams refers to Lewis's approval of the term 'an ordered state of sin', which Lewis picked up from a student's essay on Paradise Lost. Williams comments:

> The orderliness of a world focussed on the self is doomed to be disrupted by grace, and we can't appreciate quite what Aslan [the Christ figure in the Narnia stories] is about unless and until we see him in action against this kind of order.

The action, however, is not more order, but a sort of free-for-all revel. Here is Williams again:

> It shouldn't surprise us then, if Aslan's freedom is so often depicted as riotous—literally at one point in Prince Caspian 'bacchanalian'.

This brings us, of course, directly to the link that the Carnival Kingdom has with the wider theme of Biblical justice. In brief, the 'ordered sense of sin' is challenged by feasting, singing, dancing and irreverence: a party or revel in fact.

All this might seem rather lightweight, almost frivolous. Can we really confront the 'big battalions' of the world system with a party? What, after all, is the connection between the Carnival Kingdom and Biblical justice? Let me try to write an *apologia* for the logic which lies behind the chapters collected here.

First of all, the idea of a carnivalesque kingdom, in the form of a party or feast, has a surprisingly long tradition behind it. It certainly goes back to the Bible, where, in both Old and New Testaments, the rule of God is ushered in by a feast. It is continued within Christendom by a variety of means: the practice of carnival itself in medieval (and modern) times; the 'fool' or jester at the nobleman's court; the ribald, even scandalous drawings in the margins of medieval manuscripts; the gargoyles on churches and cathedrals; the Ship of Fools—a pilotless ship populated by passengers who are mad or careless or simply indifferent. Later there were the more serious revellers, as we might describe them, such as the Levellers and the Diggers in seventeenth century England, who wanted a party at which everybody sat down together as equals at the same table. The idea never completely disappeared. Think of the harvest supper on a great agricultural estate or the village cricket match and the tea that followed. Even today's notorious office party might be included.

Second, if we go back to C. S. Lewis's Narnia and the bacchanalian revel in *Prince Caspian*, this has not simply to do with people having a good time, but is a breaking down of long-experienced oppression. In the story all sorts of oppressed people (and not just people) are set free. After the original romp featuring Bacchus and Silenus and the feast that went with it, Aslan declares that he will 'make holiday'; rather like Jesus proclaiming the Jubilee at the end of the Nazareth Manifesto in Luke 4. The river god at the ford of Berunna is released from his chains (the bridge); the Narnian girl, Gwendolen, gets a permanent holiday from her tyrannical school, as does the tired teacher from her tyrannical students! Abused animals are set free and a boy is delivered from the man who is beating him with a stick—the man turns into a sort of stick-tree. A woman on her deathbed is restored to health. There are some nice touches here. In the old order, history lessons are deadly dull and clothes are uncomfortable. (Gwendolen is encouraged to take them off.) In the new dispensation there are flowers and bushes and vines everywhere and water gets turned into wine. As Rowan Williams puts it: '"the ordered state of sin"... is whatever makes drab and oppressive the flow of joy and energy in the world of animals, humans—and even rivers'. Aslan has come along to release the flow.

Thirdly, it is important to say something about the theological and philosophical underpinnings of all this. Aslan's party may still sound like time off (as parties in our day-to-day lives generally are) not, so to speak, a way of life. What I think can be permanent, however, is the actual release from oppression in our thinking. We humans are not as straight thinking as we believe ourselves to be. Some years ago I gave a lecture on postcolonialism in which I was trying to make the point that the Enlightenment's 'rage for order' (based on 'Western' scientific rationalism) was experienced by many as an oppressive colonialism. I also wanted to say that this was sometimes best countered by confusion. Here is the relevant passage:

> Somehow we have to accept that the rule of God is a place where we do not know as clearly as we would like to. We see through a glass darkly. Rowan Williams in a tribute to the late Gillian Rose[1] in December last year [2005] called it 'joyful erring'. 'We do not know what our interests are', he said, 'I must fictionalise a version of my interests because I do

not recognise myself.' He argued that Rose's commitment to the 'mutual recognition of misrecognition' is a fruitful flight away from foundation-alism. It is the hybridity that is so confused and confusing that every statement is a mis-statement, every sighting a mis-recognition. We can no longer work out, for example, what it means to be British. That is a good thing. All the forms of foundationalism—based on denomination, kinship, locality, ethnicity, credal orthodoxy, gender, easily identifiable allies—are becoming confusingly muddled. Rejoice! The kingdom of God is near.

In this extract I mention Rowan Williams' idea of 'joyful erring'. It is not just on holidays but every day that we do well to understand that we are not so 'serious' as we thought we were, and that when we claim the seriousness of the structures we build, they easily become oppressive. Indeed, as Andrew Shanks points out in his book *Against Innocence*, our claim to be 'serious' is really a claim to an 'I'm right and you're wrong' sort of innocence[2], the very opposite of 'joyful erring'. This applies to us all, Christians included. We think we know who the enemies of the Kingdom are, but too often we are the enemy, only in the most deadly form of disguise: a presumption of our own innocence.

Where Christians do score is that they know they need God's help. God's deliverance is top-down, that is to say He intervenes in situations of injustice in which we are otherwise helpless. His justice, however, is usually made effective through the revolutionary principle that the world (the old order) is being turned upside down. We are invited to join the revolution so long as we 'play by the rules', and the first rule is that we do not claim our own innocence. There must be no utopianism. Everything is 'speculative' in the sense that all the rules have been cancelled so that they can be refreshed and re-established on a new basis.

The chapters of this book are largely written from this perspective—we might call it 'revolutionary Biblical justice'. The customary order by which the rich and the powerful rule to their own advantage and the poor and the weak take what scraps they can get, is called into question. Justice, it is maintained, does not assume that everyone is treated the same. It assumes rather that God is on the side of the poor, and that we must be also. This is a scandal, of course, but then so is the whole idea of a Carnival Kingdom.

'Revolutionary Biblical justice' is examined as a concept in our first three chapters, using the lens of the Carnival itself (chapter one), Shire justice (chapter two) and the seventeenth century Levellers and Diggers and their kin (chapter three). Elsewhere this justice is derived from and brought to bear on a number of different contexts. It is recognised that there are formidable obstacles to justice in our world today, whether the context is the strife-torn history of Peru (chapter four), the ugly fate of minorities in India (chapter five), the vulnerabilities of border people—migrants, refugees and asylum seekers (chapter six), or the lack of climate justice (chapter seven). Nevertheless the news is not all bad. We are not without witnesses. The Protestant tradition speaks of better things (chapter eight) as does the postcolonial discourse (chapter nine) and the practice of good development theory (chapter ten). Finally we can look to the future and begin to build. The media is one place where much more can be done to infiltrate the good news (chapter eleven). 'Business as mission' can create a world in which justice is available to more and more poor people as they find new ways to earn a living (chapter twelve).

These chapters may seem rather diverse—they certainly originate in many different parts of the world. But that is one aspect of the Carnival Kingdom. Where might you find the English, Peruvians, Indians, Philippinos, Americans, Swedes and the Dutch all agreeing with each other, or agreeing to disagree if they don't? In the Carnival Kingdom, of course.

Jonathan Ingleby

Notes

1. Gillian Rose, who died in 1995, was a philosopher who left behind her a considerable body of work. Though her work is perhaps not as well known as it ought to be, there is no doubt about her influence on a number of contemporary writers, notably Rowan Williams. Her best known work of philosophy is *The Broken Middle* published by Blackwells in 1992.

2. Andrew Shanks, *Against Innocence*, London: SCM Press, 2008.

Imagine a Carnival

Prophetic Image-in-a(c)tion for Just Communities

The Medieval Carnival legitimated revolutionary imagination–if only for a few days. However, when the last laugh had subsided and the last feast was cleared away the question lingered: 'is the alternative reality possible?' **Carol Kingston-Smith** *suggests that the creativity and critique of power embedded in the Carnival may have something to teach us about the promotion and sustaining of justice which reflects the biblical vision of the Kingdom of God.*

When the late Martin Luther King Jr. began his famous speech with the words 'I have a dream', he was sharing a vision of an alternative reality not yet manifestly available to the people of the USA in the 1960s. It was available neither to the black communities who were being denied the right to a dignified life, nor to the white communities, who as a result of unjust racist structures were also denied and denying themselves the dignity which comes from being a part of a just community. Martin Luther King's speech was not, however, an idealised vision plucked out of the air, but rather, one which was forged in direct response to the destructive and harsh experience of dehumanising injustice; injustice observed and experienced both corporately and individually. His dream became an important catalyst for the American Civil Rights Movement.

When we think of justice, we often shape our thoughts and indeed our emotions around what are, in fact, examples of *injustice*. Justice is frequently a concept viscerally interpreted by the anxious knot in our stomach or the dull ache of a long-clenched jaw; by the lingering pain, sadness and anger of broken relationships or the shattering memories of a sequence of events which 'should never have happened'. That is to say, we often find ourselves relating or reacting to justice's shadow, injustice; the events and places where justice was best interpreted as being absent or in some way blocked, perverted or side-lined.

If our context is the soil in which we observe and interpret the contours of injustice and justice, then it becomes critical that we both observe our context carefully and make time to interpret what we find. Martin Luther King judged the impacts of racial divisions in his context to be an unjust state of affairs because he moved from accepting the *status quo*, that is, the existing state of affairs, to critically observing it, then to critically interpreting it before finally rejecting unjust elements in favour of a new vision of reality.

During this process of interpretation, multifarious explanations may emerge and it would be naïve to suggest that this step is anything other than complex. Paolo Freire, the Brazilian educationalist, makes clear distinctions between the value of judgements of a 'naive consciousness' and a 'critical consciousness'[1] which echo Jesus' own frustration with the lack of critical vision of the Jewish leaders of his time. These leaders, it seems, rather than providing the community of faith with tools of resistance to life-denying injustices under the grinding oppressions of Roman imperial rule, had become complicit with the *status quo* and lost their critical vision rooted in their identity as a 'called out' people (Matthew 15:14 & Matthew 16:3).

Importantly, Jesus identifies which critical faculty had been lost to the religious leaders; they themselves had lost the vision or image of the contours which defined Kingdom-community and had 'shut the door of the kingdom of heaven in people's faces.' Jesus diagnosed their inability to encourage the 'image-in-action' of the just community because they themselves 'did not enter' into the life of the Kingdom and in addition they prevented others from entering into the critical image-in-a(c)tion[2] of the Kingdom (Matthew 23:13).

> **I**n order to live faithfully in accordance with the Good News of the Kingdom, we need to develop this 'image-in-a(c)tion' of the Kingdom in the very contexts we find ourselves.

Thus, it seems clear that in order to live faithfully in accordance with the Good News of the Kingdom, we need to develop this 'image-in-a(c)tion' of the Kingdom in the very contexts in which we find ourselves. By this, I mean that as people of faith we need to grasp the images of the Kingdom we find embedded in the whole of Scripture, but most clearly enacted by Jesus himself, and then we need to interpret them in and to our contexts. In this way the image of the Kingdom moves from internal revelation and transformation to external revelation and transformation and *vice versa* through our actions

2

and lives lived in humble and often vulnerable testimony to 'that which we have seen and heard.'

In this chapter, I want to focus in particular on carving out a sacred space in which to attempt to capture something of the enormously liberating imagination of the Christian justice tradition. I will attempt to do this by interacting with what may seem an unlikely source: themes from the Medieval Carnival. These themes present an alternative vision of social reality which, I suggest, may offer some creative images for us to ponder as we evaluate our witness to the Kingdom of God in our communities today. It is a vision which may also help equip us with tools of imaginative and hope-filled action with regards to injustice in our families, communities, nations and world.

The Medieval Carnival was, at its heart, a revolutionary and alternative view of reality; a way of representing, if only for a short time, a new reality in which the present order was turned on its head in

> *The Medieval Carnival was, at its heart, a revolutionary and alternative view of reality.*

favour of those from the underside of history; the peasant, the poor, in short, the non-elite. As such, the Carnival represents a creative interplay between the way things are, that is, the present *status quo*—which for many of the time was harsh and oppressive—and the ways things could be. This envisioning, interpretation and enactment (if only at Carnival time) of an alternative energy and reality was conceived at the interface between 'the *stasis* imposed from above and a desire for change from below, between old and new, official and unofficial.'[3] The Carnival became a showcase of this alternative conception of power from below, where the elite power-holders of the day were clownishly aped by costumed peasants. Grand, public carnival feasts were held to mimic civic ceremonies, 'uncrown' the gentry elite and 'crown' the peasant instead. Humour, satire, dramatic enactments, feasting and laughter were core elements of this time of festive revolutionary imagination.

For a short time at least, the Carnival was a celebration which levelled all in a grand mockery of pomp and status and peasant baseness at one and the same time. But it also carried more subtle themes, such as the exposure of the inside panel of the cloth of culture; the exposure of those things commonly hidden and unseen which became un-seamed and exposed in grotesque caricature. The Carnivalesque revealed the fabric of a society found to be wanting and unseemly. In short, the Carnival deeply critiqued both religious and civil structures. Whilst we may stand aside from the extreme libertinism and debauchery embedded in the Carnival, we might also find some helpful pointers in its passionately-creative contestations against patterns of injustice which are still so often lining the fabrics of our cultures. The Carnival invites us to be bold and to dare to turn our cultural clothes 'inside out' and examine carefully the workmanship of the fabric of our societies, be they European, Asian, Latin American, African or otherwise.

The Christian conception of the reign or Kingdom of God, like the Carnival, presents a profound challenge to the present fallen order of society, both in the prophetic, scriptural tradition of the Old Testament and by the incarnational revelation of the life and teachings of Jesus. Understanding in what ways the Kingdom of God speaks into and calls for the renewal and restoration of our societies is a core task for those of us who consider Kingdom justice to be the path to peace for global communities.

Like the Carnival, the Kingdom is described as an 'upside down Kingdom'—radically different to the *status quo* of earthly kingdoms where power and privilege coalesce in the hands of a few, often at the expense of the majority. At the heart of the vision of the reign of God is the belief that this reign will result in *shalom*; the delightful and convivial energy of a community at one and at peace with itself in purposeful service to God and the greater good of the rest of creation. Nicholas Wolterstorff in his recent book *Hearing the Call; Liturgy, Justice, Church and World*, notes the attributes of *shalom* as being: the absence of hostility and the highest enjoyment of relationships with God, with oneself, with others and with the environment.[4] The prophet Isaiah depicts this joy-filled state as living in the 'tranquil country, dwelling in *shalom*, in houses full of ease' (Isaiah 32:18). *Shalom* ultimately speaks of an extraordinary flourishing which lies beyond the reconciliation of all things (Colossians 1:20); a dramatic shift in the relational patterns of the community of creation which the prophet Isaiah depicts allegorically as a time when:

> The wolf will live with the lamb,
> the leopard will lie down with the goat,
> the calf and the lion and the yearling together;
> and a little child will lead them.

> The cow will feed with the bear,
> their young will lie down together,
> and the lion will eat straw like the ox.

> *At the heart of the vision of the reign of God is the belief that this reign will result in shalom; the delightful and convivial energy of a community at one and at peace with itself.*

4

The infant will play near the cobra's den,
 and the young child will put its hand into the viper's nest (Isaiah
 11:6-8)

This is a metaphorically-rich vision of flattened hierarchies of power, where the once predatory and death-inducing powers at large in the world cease to be a threat and are at peace with the once vulnerable, who now no longer flee in fear but find rest and unexpected new friendships in the new order of life. It also describes a fundamental shift in patterns of consumption to meet our physical needs which are seemingly radically different to the present and which will uproot current hierarchies of power to give way to a new social and material ecology of the Kingdom.

Central to Jesus' teaching on the Kingdom is his continuity with the prophetic tradition which promoted a social corrective mechanism which is also prominent in the Medieval Carnival: the theme of social inversion. This parody of social inversion is typified by the peasant becoming lord for a day and the lord becoming a peasant, and it resonates with biblical themes in both the Old and the New Testaments which remind the rich and the powerful that they will be brought low whilst the poor and op-pressed will be raised up.[5] Even before Jesus' birth, his mother, Mary, inspired by the hope of a renewed and just social reality, rejoiced that the Lord God:

...has scattered those who are proud in their inmost thoughts.
 He has brought down rulers from their thrones
 but has lifted up the humble.
 He has filled the hungry with good things
 but has sent the rich away empty (Luke 1:51-53)

Jesus echoes these sentiments in his own words and actions many times during the course of his ministry, reminding us once again that the Kingdom is one which scatters and brings low the proud and lifts up the humble in a radical re-ordering of society into egalitarian and just relationships which are fundamental to the Kingdom where the delight of *shalom* can rest. Jesus describes this new reality thus:

Blessed are you who are poor,
 for yours is the kingdom of God.

Blessed are you who hunger now,
 for you will be satisfied.

Blessed are you who weep now,
 for you will laugh.

Blessed are you when men hate you,
 when they exclude you and insult you

and reject your name as evil,
because of the Son of Man...

But woe to you who are rich,
for you have already received your comfort.

Woe to you who are well fed now,
for you will go hungry.

Woe to you who laugh now,
for you will mourn and weep.

Woe to you when all men speak well of you,
for that is how their fathers treated the false prophets. (Luke 6:20-26)

The Carnival was recognised for its revolutionary characteristics of resistance to the current order. These were expressed and (ironically) tolerated on officially-permitted occasions when everyone participated—as distinct from the theatre—for the Carnival had no observers, only participants. The Kingdom of God narrative, like the Carnival, permits no footlights; we are all history's 'players' working, as Jesus said, either for the Kingdom or against it (Luke 11:23). In more recent times, Archbishop Desmond Tutu captured this sense of 'no footlights' and thus no observers in the Kingdom, with this observation: 'there is no neutrality in a situation of injustice and oppression. If you say you are neutral you are a liar, for you have already taken sides with the powerful.'[6]

The Carnival Kingdom, as I conceive it here, unlike the Medieval Carnival, is not officially permitted and tolerated as a necessary cathartic release of the pent-up frustrations of both history's downtrodden, and tight-laced sombre elites. It is, rather, a way of life which requires those who enter it to let go of their pride, their fear and their idolatries and become trusting and humble, like children. Early Christians in the Roman Empire were persecuted, not because their cult was illegal (religious cults were legal under the *pax romana*), but rather because they 'overstepped' the boundaries of permissible privatised religion and were explicitly political in their challenge to the sovereignty of Caesar by declaring that Jesus, rather than Caesar, was Lord. That is to say, early Christianity was not 'in bed with power' but rather it testified to another way of living, based around the Lordship and teachings of Jesus, which at a number of points contested the *status quo* of the Empire of their time. The consequence of their resistance was in many cases imprisonment, torture and death.

The Scriptures point towards the Kingdom of God as a reign of justice which will ultimately bring about the reconciliation of all things; where the powers which currently lord it over each other for dominance are restored to a truly amicable relationship without fear and pride which can then be put to the service of God for the purposes of the common good.[7]

Jesus modelled the path which leads to reconciliation at the inception of his formal, recorded ministry in the Gospels. This commenced with an inter-power dialogue during his wilderness temptation. There he spoke truth to the power which sought to coerce both his allegiance and his service. In doing this he set his compass uncompromisingly against the same principles which lay at the roots of the Roman Empire; power through the coercion of military might. Following his death on a Roman cross, His resurrection was the closure of that dialogue.

Importantly, whatever the Carnival may have to teach us about identifying and resisting the oppressive order of fallen powers, it cannot teach us how to nurture and sustain the fruits of the new convivial society after the Carnival has ended. To achieve this we need that deeper narrative of the Kingdom which requires us to take up our cross and follow Jesus (Luke 9:23). The cross symbolises the heart of the character of the King of this Kingdom who was himself the 'suffering servant'. Jesus brought liberty and healing to others but did not seek to preserve his own life in his contestation for justice and reconciliation for all, because he recognised that self-interest and self-preservation lie at the nexus of the fallen powers which breed fear, pride and selfish ambition. The cross reminds us that change begins in a changed perception of ourselves as agents of a powerful and non-violent resistance to an order manipulated by fallen powers. These powers thrive simply because few actually do resist them 'unto death' (whether literal or metaphorical) with the clear-sighted vision and wisdom of the resurrection power of God's Kingdom.

The cross opens the way to the hope of resurrection.[8] It represents Christ's ultimate negation of the fallen powers in their attempt to script his final destiny. Many of us forget that Jesus called us to share in his struggle for justice, which inevitably brings suffering as we take up our own cross. The apostle Peter reminds us that in order for the glory of this just Kingdom to be manifest, we are required to labour and share in the sufferings of Christ (1 Peter 4:13). This powerful Kingdom truth could be seen to represent the ultimate Carnivalesque in that it inverts even life and death in the new order of the Kingdom, where those who seek to preserve their lives will lose them and those who lose their lives for the sake of this Kingdom will find them restored (Luke 9:24). Where the 'whitewashed' tomb of the teachers of the law spoke only of death under the aegis of fallen powers, the tomb under God's grace is the womb of resurrection life; the old has gone and the new has come (2 Corinthians 5:17). Thus, we see that the cross is the ultimate inversion of the present order of reality as it guarantees both our death and resurrection. As such it represents the real hope for a new and enduring Kingdom. This Kingdom is not shaped by the fallen powers, where fear and death are the ultimate predators in the hierarchies of power, but rather, the kenotic power of self-emptying which gives way to resurrection and fullness of life.

As we examine our contexts, like Martin Luther King, we need to remember Jesus' special concern for the needs of the vulnerable, marginalised and oppressed in our communities. In seeking to lift them up to a proper place of dignity and worth in society, we who are rich may have to share our wealth and our power in ways we have not done before in order to see God's Carnival Kingdom flourish. We might need to remind ourselves that, important though they are, our race, our culture, our class or our nation are not in fact the primary basis of our identity, but that rather our identity as children of the Kingdom should set us apart to stand alongside those from any race, culture, class or nation who testify to the good news of the Kingdom—only then can we join the Carnival banquet.

Is injustice a laughing matter?

Then our mouth was filled with laughter, and our tongue with shouts of joy; then they said among the nations, "The Lord has done great things for them." (Psalm 126:2)

He will yet fill your mouth with laughter, and your lips with shouting (Job 8:21)

True ambivalent and universal laughter does not deny seriousness but purifies and completes it... (Bakhtin, 1984, 123)

Figure 1: The Laughing Christ

When we think about justice, laughter is not usually at the forefront of our mind. So what has laughter got to do with justice? We can probably grasp more readily the role of lament in marking solidarity with the loss and pain of injustice...but laughter?

The image of 'The laughing Christ'[9] is a powerful portrayal of the embodied, incarnational laughter of a Christ who liberates and brings freedom; a Christ whose own life of resistance to the powers even 'unto death' results/resulted in the joyful eruption of resurrection laughter. It is this resurrection laughter which is capable of rupturing the tyranny of despair, as we dare to envision creative new ways of living in freedom in subversion to the unjust *status quo*. Laughter is important because, like weeping, it is an embodied response; it affirms our material bodies as worthy bearers of both the image and emotions of God.[10] In Pentecostal and Charismatic spirituality, laughter has often been identified as a central feature of the work of the Holy Spirit and often accompanies a deep sense of vision of restoration and joy. Biblical scholar J. William Whedbee, in his fascinating book *The Bible and the Comic Vision,* uncovers in a number of biblical narratives the presence of subversive laughter which belongs to a 'special power of comedy' of the marginalised and oppressed. Furthermore, he notes in particular that recent studies of women reveal that 'their special kinds of humour and comedy may suggest there is nothing accidental about such notable women of comic wit amongst the stories and poems which are so fundamental to biblical literature.' This congenial humour of biblical women is both 'life-giving and life-saving' precisely because, in 'standing on the margins of society, women are able to deconstruct the dominant power structures and to recharge the forces of life'.[11]

Laughter undeniably lies at the heart of the Medieval Carnival. It was officially expelled from formal, polite society where 'an intolerant, one-sided tone of seriousness' prevailed to maintain the 'sombre providentialism...[and] character of the feudal regime, with its oppression and intimidation'. For the ruling elites of Medieval times 'this tone of icy petrified seriousness [was] supposedly the only tone fit to express the true, the good, and all that was essential and meaningful.'[12]

Carnival laughter is highly nuanced and subversive, capable of producing spaces of freedom and hope under tyranny and adversity; encouraging the imagining, envisioning and enacting of a way of life beyond the limitations

Carnival laughter is highly nuanced and subversive, capable of producing spaces of freedom and hope under tyranny and adversity

and absurdities of the current unjust *status quo*. Laughter releases the implicit humour of unpicking rigid social and political structures and 'disembowelling' and exposing the truths which are indeed often stranger than fiction and which are often hidden behind the pretence of well-used scripts of power. Laughter is so powerful that the humourist author Mark Twain is said to have acknowledged it as the human race's only 'effective weapon'.

Laughter's interpretive power is described by Peter Lewis who notes in his examination of the theory of laughter of the 19th Century pessimist,

Schopenhauer, that the latter regards the 'humorous mood' as erupting in a transitory interpretive space which 'derives from a conflict with the external world.'[13] As such, for even those of us who are pessimists, laughter can, as Lewis summarises, enable us to 'laugh at the very things that cause pain, thereby enabling us to bear what would otherwise be unbearable.'[14] However, for other social critics, this very use of laughter can play into the hands of oppressive powers and become structurally-complicit laughter which consolidates injustice rather than subverting it. One such critic is Slovenian philosopher Slavoj Žižek, who forcefully challenges the notion of emancipatory laughter as being naïve and who even goes as far as linking laughter with totalitarianism directly, as '...laughing transgressions are always already part of the internal power relations that constitute our postmodern condition.'[15]

Clearly, there are many different types of laughter and it may help at this point to explore Paolo Freire's taxonomy of laughter and how it resonates with biblical themes of laughter. Freire noted in his famous *Pedagogy of the Oppressed* how laughter is a critical element to self-emancipation. However, he does concur with Žižek in that he recognises that not all laughter is emancipatory.

Freire categorises laughter as resulting from three states of human consciousness. The first state is described as the naïve consciousness which, he judges, tends to over-simplify problems, to be over nostalgic for the 'good old days' and tends to underestimate the ability of the average citizen to play a meaningful role in their own emancipation. In addition, the naïve consciousness avoids deeper analysis and careful argumentation, tending towards polemic, fanciful and even magical explanations at the expense of mature and reflective dialogue.[16] Laughter from this state of naïve consciousness lacks a critical capacity and becomes trivially positive, numbing us from harsh realities and helping us to 'laugh it off' or 'just relax' in the face of the growing injustices, exploitation and even environmental catastrophes around us.

The second state, Freire describes as the superstitious consciousness. In this frame, the disorder in the world is viewed through the paranoid lens of conspiracy theory. The laughter evoked is the cynical laughter of 'those in the know' who have superior knowledge of the web of conspiracies of power. However, Lewis contends that this laughter stops short of agency and emancipation[17] as it often becomes an end in itself rather than producing the energy and motivation for real change. In fact it only:

> ...results in more isolation, or perhaps the illusion of individual liberation through new age spirituality, virtual reality gaming, or the occasional

work-place transgression. The cynical and or ironic postmodern laugh becomes a poor substitute for political action, a cathartic moment of release that simultaneously 'affirms' one's superiority over the system while also indexing ones complacency with this modicum of reassurance. Stated differently, the cynic or postmodern conspiracy buff receives too much dirty pleasure from his/her privileged insider knowledge, and as such this pleasure sustains political inaction. In other words, if there is a critical dimension to this laugh, it has always already been co-opted by a cynical cultural logic that anticipates and feeds off of the very tendencies toward superstition that constitute the cognitive backdrop of the laugh.[18]

Freire's third and final (and preferred) state of human consciousness is called the critical consciousness. Fatalism and cynicism are replaced by a new vision of realistic, collective possibilities for social transformation. The hopeful dialogue replaces both cynicism and fatalism and is characterised by a:

> ...depth in the interpretation of problems; by the substitution of causal principles for magical explanations; by the testing of one's "findings" and by openness to revision; by the attempt to avoid distortion when perceiving problems and to avoid preconceived notions when analyzing them; by refusing to transfer responsibility; by rejecting passive positions; by soundness of argumentation; by the practice of dialogue rather than polemics.[19]

Within this critical consciousness, laughter can then legitimately become both transformative and revolutionary in that it can call for a fresh examination of society's

Laughter... can call for a fresh examination of society's norms.

norms alongside others who are disempowered or mistreated under those norms. Freire stresses the importance of laughing (and weeping) with the oppressed as crucial to engaging in a transformative relationship which is neither cynical and hierarchical, nor naively self-interested.

So then, it is important to locate laughter within the various states of human consciousness as being multi-faceted and multi-motivated. Nonetheless, I concur with Edward Lewis's conclusion of laughter's potential transformative power:

> ... critical laughter is transformative because it embodies the r(u/a)pture of joy accompanying any verification of equality. The joy of the transformative laugh is the experience of an egalitarian community whose flesh has not yet been made into words. The laugh is therefore not so much the proclamation of a wrong (spoken through argumentative reason which gives the noise of pain a *logos*) but rather the affective verification of a surplus equality—it is the sensual pleasure of democracy.[20]

Freire summarises the critical laugh as being conscious of the shared vision of the exodus from under the tyranny of power into spaces of freedom; a 'pedagogy of happiness, laughter, of questioning, or curiosity, of seeing the future through the present, a pedagogy that believes in the possibility of the transformation of the world'. [21]

Carnival Kingdom Laughter

I want to present three forms of Carnival Kingdom laughter here which offer us both a means of resistance to injustice ever present around us in the world, and a renewal of our vision of the Carnival Kingdom.

The first form of Carnival laughter is linked with the second but in many ways it may properly be located as God's own laughter. We can only laugh with God, because God, who has the ultimate critical consciousness, laughed first. His own laughter reveals to us its place in the order of the universe. It may indeed unsettle some of us to realise that this laughter might accurately be called a laughter of supreme derision. This is no politically-correct or socially-polite laughter, but rather the full-bellied laugh of a Creator God who doubles over at the supreme insolence and high-minded affront of the 'little ones.' The Psalmist David brings this laughter into sharp focus at the end of the passage below from Psalm 37:

[1] Do not fret because of those who are evil
  or be envious of those who do wrong;

[2] for like the grass they will soon wither,
  like green plants they will soon die away.

[10] A little while, and the wicked will be no more;
  though you look for them, they will not be found.

[11] But the meek will inherit the land
  and enjoy peace and prosperity.

[12] The wicked plot against the righteous
  and gnash their teeth at them;

[13] but the Lord laughs at the wicked,
  for he knows their day is coming

In Psalm 2, God's laughter in the face of the pretence of the ruling powers of the day is described as 'scoffing'. We might well wonder whether there is a proper place for us to join God in this type of laughter but regardless we *can* enjoy the hope which emerges in the ensuing landscape depicted by the Psalmist.

The second form of Carnival Kingdom laughter I shall call anticipatory laughter, which erupts in joyful realisation, through revelation, of a new reality breaking in but as yet beyond the present reality with its strictures of oppression and injustice. There is a thread of laughter which runs through Scripture in the concept of anticipatory rejoicing. In the Psalms, lament in the face of real suffering and injustice is often interposed with the words 'yet I will rejoice'. Some might regard it as the 'laughter of madness', in that there are often no apparent visible reasons for such abandoned rejoicing to the onlooker. Habakkuk takes this 'mad rejoicing' into the heartland of injustice and destruction, where fear has 'crept into his bones' and there is no immediate prospect of release from oppression and the consequences of injustice:

I heard and my heart pounded,
my lips quivered at the sound;

decay crept into my bones,
and my legs trembled.

Yet I will wait patiently for the day of calamity
to come on the nation invading us.

Though the fig tree does not bud
and there are no grapes on the vines,

though the olive crop fails
and the fields produce no food,

though there are no sheep in the pen
and no cattle in the stalls,

yet I will rejoice in the Lord,
I will be joyful in God my Saviour.

The Sovereign Lord is my strength;
he makes my feet like the feet of a deer,
he enables me to tread on the heights (Habakkuk 3:16-19)

For Habakkuk, like the Psalmist who recognised that the joy of the Lord is our strength, laughter, rejoicing and joy are gifts which enable, envision and strengthen us in times of chaos and trial. Luke Bretherton proffers that Carnival laughter both 'mocks the madness of the world unredeemed' and reminds us that in order to truly understand and enter into the 'true joy and celebratory laughter of resurrection' we first need to 'understand the nature of chaos and laugh at it' for the grotesque distortion that it in actuality is. This then frames laughter in the context of 'scatological humour'[22] which enjoins Christians to laugh, 'rather than weep', in recognition that the present state of things is 'not the ultimate truth...we can deride it because it is not the eschatological transformation, the transfiguration of creation into its fulfilment, into an over-abundant new creation.'[23]

This theme of the renewal of rejoicing and laughter is acknowledged as being intrinsic to both the revelation and presence of the Kingdom in Isaiah 61, which Jesus reminds his hearers in the Synagogue was coupled with a remit to bring justice to the people. We can experience the oil of gladness and wear the garments of praise, we can laugh and rejoice because we can see beyond the current challenges to a day that is coming when 'every tear will be wiped away' (Revelation 21:4) and when, in the words of Michael Bakhtin, we can anticipate 'the return of happier times, abundance, and justice for all the people.'[24] In this anticipatory laughter, born out of revelation and sustained by faith, we resist and invert the poisoned fruits of injustice which are sorrow, vengeance and misery with a profound and 'new awareness [which has] been initiated and [has]...found its most radical expression in laughter.'[25]

But laughter does not only have an anticipatory function, it also erupts reactively and spontaneously in the material presence of the Kingdom which has come on earth (as it is in heaven). Laughter and rejoicing break out when the hungry *are* fed, when the blind *can* see and when the lame *can* walk again. We laugh when the river of justice waters the dry plain and we can feed our young; we laugh when we enjoy the fruits of our labour in freedom and without undue and unfair cost to others; we laugh when our children are able to mature and flourish and play meaningful roles in society without the pump of selfish, greedy ambition and striving which is so characteristic of the fallen order of things. We laugh, in short, because we have tasted and we have seen that 'the Lord is good and his mercy endures' (Psalm 100:5) in the here and now, the material present. We laugh when we have enjoyed the evidence of promises brought to fruition because of the faithful labour of those who have preceded us and who have declared through their lives and their witness (even unto death) that God's Kingdom will come and His will shall be done on earth as it is in heaven. This is the third type of biblical laughter which will endure into eternity.

So then, firstly, laughter derides the power of injustice under the eschatological premise that the powers of this age are passing away ('He who sits in the heavens laughs; the Lord holds them in derision'–Psalm 2:4). Secondly, laughter liberates the vision of the Just Community of the Carnival Kingdom; it recognises and denounces the caricatures and 'the pretensions of power and the tendency of church, state and academy to self-aggrandisement to the point of idolatry' and reveals them for 'what they are: foolishness.'[26] Laughter also carries a liberating, birthing, envisioning function. In the community of the Carnival Kingdom, laughter releases strength and vision to build a new world which takes courage to establish and tenacious creativity to maintain. Thirdly, at its core, Carnival laughter announces that justice has come and in this way it has an 'indissoluble and essential relation to freedom'[27] and recognises the

> victory of this future over the past....the birth of the new...is as indispensable and as inevitable as the death of the old...in the whole of the world and of the people there is no room for fear. For fear can only enter a part that has been separated from the whole, the dying link torn from the link that is being born.[28]

Bakhtin goes on to expand the power of laughter as having:

> ...deep philosophical meaning [which] is one of the essential forms of the truth concerning the world as a whole, concerning history and man; it is a peculiar point of view relative to the world; the world is seen anew, no less (and perhaps more) profoundly than what was seen from the serious standpoint... Certain essential aspects of the world are accessible only to laughter.[29]

Whilst the ancients observed the enormous significance of laughter,[30] Church Fathers such as Tertullian, Cyprian and John Chrysostom were antagonised by unseemly laughter, which was regarded to be part of a wider culture of debasement and debauchery to the extent that John Chrysostom regarded jest and laughter to be ungodly and from the devil. In official religious circles laughter came to be regarded as degenerate and part of what the Carnivalesque writers termed the 'lower order material second nature'. However, significantly, in the context of our focus on justice, laughter was officially permissible at Easter as a signal of the closing of lenten mourning and the renewal of resurrection rejoicing and hopefulness. This *risus paschalis*, or Easter laughter, is a legitimate bursting forth of a viscerally-experienced and newly-awakened relief born of a new vision into a new reality; a resurrection of hope in regeneration which lies at the heart of the gospel of the Kingdom of God. As such it is a wholly appropriate holy laughter! Most powerfully, Easter laughter celebrates the 'return of...abundance and justice for all the people'. A new resurrection awareness had been initiated and 'had found its most radical expression in laughter.' A laughter which 'does not deny seriousness but purifies and completes it... purifies from dogmatism, from the intolerant and the petrified; it liberates from fanaticism and pedantry, from fear and intimidation, from didacticism, naïveté and illusion.'[31]

The words of the prophet Isaiah remind us that the day of the Lord's favour is a day when joy and laughter replace the despair and mourning of the oppressed, a day when new vision and strength is released to rebuild and restore places and cities long devastated. It is in this day we are called to participate again and again as followers of Jesus' Way.

As such, in the same way in which Jesus presenced his Kingdom on earth by tackling unjust powers at work to oppress the people by exposing them publically, so also laughter exposes the 'non-sense' of injustice and turns it 'inside out' in a sort of confessional liturgy which unpicks the cloth of unjust powers and caricatures their ultimate impotence. Jesus promoted the characteristics of the Kingdom community through his envisioning teaching and parables which inspired hope in his hearers. In the same way laughter releases hope, conceived as it is around the seed of a vision of a new way of living which bursts forth beyond the restrictions of 'life-as-it-is', that is, the unjust *status quo*. In a powerful way laughter breaches petty rules of legalism and breaks open a new liturgical space in which the imagination, inspired by the seeds of Kingdom joy, can re-create the divine *perichoresis* (that is, the divine dance of unity) which unifies the story of justice.

As laughter tears down, so it re-builds a new, fresh vision of being. This is a new way of relating beyond the hitherto known and experienced, beyond even the signposts of the law. Like grace-filled splashes of colour which bear the mark of the fundamentally joyful delight of *shalom*, so utterly intrinsic to the justice of God, laughter embodies and gives birth to resurrection hope.

The Carnival Banquet

The final Carnival theme I want to examine in relation to justice is that of the Carnival banquet. The banquet brings together the themes already discussed of solidarity and social equality and laughter around a table of plenty; a banquet for the entire world. The banquet is a fitting culmination of the work for justice—plentiful provision in community for all. In her book *A Place at the Table: Justice for the poor in a land of plenty*, Judith Ann Brady makes the theme of 'a place at the table' a guiding metaphor for achieving justice for the poor and the oppressed. The table represents friendship, provision and nurture and it also represents inclusivity and agency, in that all who sit at the table can join in the conversation and decision-making which flows from that.[32]

For people of faith, working for God's Kingdom to come on earth as it is in heaven, there are two stages of the biblical banquet feast. The first, the Eucharist, anticipates the second, the wedding feast of the Lamb (Revelation 19:9).

Jesus' recasting of the Passover feast with his disciples in the lead up to his own death links the justice themes of the people of Israel's liberation from Egypt with his own work of liberation and justice as King of the new Kingdom and his anticipated culmination of that work on the cross. The Carnival banquet always contains an 'element of victory and triumph'[33] which provides the symbolic pause between the celebration and completion of one cycle of labour for justice and the invigorated new beginning of another cycle of labour for justice. In a completely material way the literal 'death' of the food 'wrested from the world' gave renewed life to those who consumed it at the feast. For the people of Israel, the Passover feast was a somewhat hurried celebration of an end of an era of slavery-forced work, which marked and energised a new beginning as the 'called out' and liberated people of YHWH. Even as we work for his justice and *shalom*, we need to remind ourselves frequently ('for as often as you eat this bread and drink this wine') both of the lament and suffering of the 'whole of creation which groans' and of the joy and thankfulness of the freedom we can taste in anticipation. The Eucharist is truly 'food and sustenance for the journey' and, in addition, it marks out and reminds us that there is also material provision in true fellowship.

There is a second biblical focus on the banquet theme which is that of the 'marriage feast of the lamb' in Revelation 19:6-9. This banquet is the ultimate celebratory closure of all cycles of work for the justice of God's Kingdom and it acknowledges, interestingly, both the work of Jesus and of all of those who have taken up their cross and followed him:

Hallelujah!
 For our Lord God Almighty reigns.
Let us rejoice and be glad
 and give him glory!
For the wedding of the Lamb has come,
 and his bride has made herself ready.
Fine linen, bright and clean,
 was given her to wear.

(Fine linen stands for the righteous acts of God's holy people)

Bakhtin notes the additional power of the wedding feast imagery where the two epilogues of a feast and a wedding bring about a cycle of completion which opens the door to the 'potentiality of a new beginning instead of the abstract and bare ending.'[34] For the person of faith, the Eucharist is a symbolic feast which celebrates repeated cycles of work for justice in God's Kingdom.[35] Yet it also points beyond the immediate travail for God's Kingdom and recognises, in solidarity with 'all who suffer the pains of childbirth' (Romans 8:22) that there will come a time when the permanent and outrageous plenty of the wedding feast will replace the transitory nature of the Eucharist feast. This Eucharist itself marks the move beyond slavery to the world's unjust systems, towards the liberation and laughter of pilgrim communion and feasting. Importantly too, the banquet table also reminds us of the concrete value of our material lives. In the words of Bakhtin: 'This victory over the world in the act of eating was concrete, tangible, bodily. It gave the very taste of the defeated world, which had fed and would feed mankind. In this image there was no trace of mysticism, no abstract-idealistic sublimation.'[36]

When we consider a world where hunger and starvation remain all too common, where food prices are soaring and where even those in developed nations like the UK are increasingly having to rely on the charity of food banks in order to put food on their tables, the metaphor of the banqueting table of the Carnival Kingdom is a sobering one. It calls us to realise that what blocks the meeting of basic human needs also blocks the coming of the Kingdom.[37] The banquet table reminds us to work for the justice of provision of the material well-being for all of humanity, but it also reminds us to open our lives to the hospitality of the Kingdom, which calls us to share so that those who have little have enough and those who have much, have less; the redistribution economics of the Carnival Kingdom which are a powerful reminder of our ultimate place within the context of a human family of faith.

There are times when history unveils particular opportunities for us to examine afresh our trajectory as an extended global family.

So, in conclusion, there are times when history unveils particular opportunities for us to examine afresh our trajectory as an extended global family. These 'unusual periods' are times when the certainties of past Golden Ages seem at best tarnished and those things previously taken for granted are now fiercely contested. These periods unveil both unusual dangers and unique opportunities to let go of what might be regarded as being, at best, sterile and at worst death-inducing patterns of life, in exchange for new birthings; new ways of being which release a new fullness of life. In Scripture these historical opportunities are linked at a personal level to what Paul says in 2 Corinthians 5:17 of Christians, who at a profound level of crisis and turning, have been born again into a new way of living and presencing themselves in human history. This new way of living bears the hallmark of freedom from manipulation, coercion and the unjust imbalances of power and alienation which contribute to what Paul calls the 'yoke of slavery' (Galatians 5:1).

The Carnival Kingdom invites us all afresh to examine where our primary allegiances lie; it invites us to turn away from the divisive and transitory comforts of idols made of worldly honours and gold and instead, to enter fully into its life as a child, with hopeful and critical emancipatory laughter, and with generous hands which help lay up the banqueting table with all those who live and love the image-in-a(c)tion of God's Carnival Kingdom for all.

Carol Kingston-Smith spent her early years in Brazil as the child of missionary parents. Following a brief career in health working in preventative health of marginalised inner city communities, she and her husband and 4 children went with Latin Link to La Paz, Bolivia, where they were involved in discipleship in a Bolivian street children's project called Alalay. Following completion of her MA thesis, which examined the impact of liberation theology in the Bolivian context, Carol has taught a number of courses at Redcliffe College. She and her husband, Andy, co-founded the jusTice Initiative and recently launched a new MA course, Justice, Advocacy and Reconciliation in Intercultural Contexts.

Notes

1. Freire, P. *Education for Critical Consciousness*, New York: Continuum, 1998.

2. Jesus Christ is the Word made flesh (image) and his actions translate or represent to us the character of God and his Kingdom. As Christians we need firstly the biblical and Spirit-empowered imagination to embrace what that Kingdom could/should look like in our contexts today and secondly, the actions which deliver that image into reality by the power of the Spirit. I use the term image-in-a(c)tion to attempt to translate this process into words.

3. Holquist, in Bakhtin, M. *Rabelais and his World*, Bloomington: Indiana University Press, 1984. (Prologue xvi)

4. Wolterstorff, N. *Hearing the Call; Liturgy, Justice, Church and World*, Grand Rapids: William B. Eerdmans Publishing Company, 2011, p.110.

5. Biblical social inversion metaphors were equalising in their intent rather than revolutionary. The proud needed to be humbled and the downtrodden encouraged and lifted up in order to re-establish mutually respectful egalitarian relationships which more properly reflected the image of God.

6. Tutu, D. *God Has a Dream: A Vision of Hope for our Time*, London: Rider Publishing, 2004, pp65-66.

7. This extraordinary shift in the power dynamics is described in Isaiah's vision in 11:6.

8. Jürgen Moltmann in his recent book *Sun of Righteousness Arise! God's future for humanity and the earth* (London: SCM Press, 2010), notes that in the light of the failure of the Enlightenment vision of progress to avoid the annihilations of the previous century of wars, which so particularly marked his own life, the Christian message of resurrection is ever more pertinent: 'Today the essential thing is to believe in the power of the resurrection, and to prepare the way for the kingdom of God in the context of today's apocalyptic horizons.' (p.39) His vision of resurrection life is one which gives birth to a love of life in the midst of despair: 'The origin of the Christian faith is once and for all the victory of

the divine life over death: the resurrection of Christ. 'Death is swallowed up in victory': that is the heart of the Christian gospel. It is the gospel of life... Jesus didn't found a new religion; he brings new life into the world, the modern world too. So we do not so much need interfaith dialogues, interesting though they are. What we need is a common struggle for life, for loved and loving life, for life that communicates itself and is shared, life that is human and natural – in short, life that is worth living in the fruitful living space of this earth.' (p.77) I suggest that the all-embracing focus on resurrecting life and hope in the midst of the impacts of the many death-producing systems in the world is a core testimony to the Kingdom of life, love, justice and laughter.

9.   This anonymous image forms part of collection of images of Christ from around the World collated by the Church Mission Society (CMS) as part of a resource for mission pack called 'The Christ we Share'.

10.   Open theism develops the possibility of God having emotions as a personal God, unlike classical theism where divine impassibility denies changing emotional states.

11.   Whedbee, J. W. *The Bible and the Comic Vision*, Minneapolis: Fortress Press, 2010, pp282 & 283.

12.   Bakhtin, M. *Rabelais and his World*, Bloomington: Indiana University Press, 1984, p.73.

13.   Lewis, P.B. "Schopenhauer's Laughter" *The Monist*, 88:1, 2005, p.47.

14.   Lewis, P.B. 2005, p.50.

15.   Lewis, T.E. "Paulo Freire's Last Laugh: Rethinking critical pedagogy's funny bone through Jacques Rancière" *Educational Philosophy and Theory*, 42:5-6, 2010, p.638.

16.   Freire, 1998, p.18.

17.   *Agency* refers to an individual's ability to autonomously reflect and act in order to bring about change.

18.   Lewis, T.E. 2010, pp.639-640.

19.   Freire, 1998, p.18.

20.   Lewis, T.E. 2010, p.643.

21.   Freire cited in Lewis, T.E. 2010, p.646.

22.   Scatological humour is embedded in the *Carnivalesque* and refers to grotesque carica-ture and focus on fæces and 'lower bodily functions' not usually discussed in polite society but which are nevertheless critical components of material life.

23.   Bretherton, L. "Puritanical Darwinism and sacred laughter" *ABC Religion and Ethics* 12 Apr 2012.

24.   Bakhtin, 1984, p.99.

25.   Bakhtin, 1984, p.99.

26.   Bretherton, 2012.

27.   Bakhtin, 1984, p.89.

28.   Bakhtin, 1984, p.256.

29.   Bakhtin, 1984, p.66.

30.   Hippocrates was an early observer on the therapeutic power of laughter and Aristotle believed that only when a child began to laugh did he become a human being. Homer also recognised the extraordinary power of laughter when he spoke of the 'indestructible, eternal laughter of the gods.'

31.   Bakhtin, 1984, p.123.

32.   Brady, J.A. *A Place at the table: Justice for the poor in a land of plenty*, New London, CT: Twenty-Third Publications, 2008, p.10.

33.   Bakhtin, 1984, p.283.

34.   Bakhtin, 1984, p.283.

35.   In emphasising the link with the cycles of work for justice represented by the Eucharist I am not ignoring Christ's *a priori* work of redemption which the Eucharist represents, but rather, I am including an element which I believe is often overlooked in its celebration; the material and spiritual reality that private/personal cycles of repentance and forgiveness also have public/community manifestations and consequences. These horizontal cycles of redemption we might describe as working for justice in our families, communities, workplaces etc. (in the spirit described throughout this chapter) and they find their source, sustenance and conclusion in the Eucharist which sustains them spiritually but also materially in the acknowledgement of the solidarity of the body of Christ on earth–the Kingdom community.

36.   Bakhtin, 1984, p.285.

37.   Jesus drew attention to this truth in many ways during his ministry, not least in the parable of the final judgement in Matthew 25:31-4.

Shire Justice

What hobbits can teach us about *Shalom*

Reading Tolkien's Lord of the Rings gives us a picture of another world, near enough to our own for it to inspire us to think again about how we order our lives in the twenty-first century. One example of this is the Shire and its justice. **David McIlroy** *claims that 'shire justice' is akin to the Biblical idea of* shalom, *something that every society needs if it is to flourish.*

The greatest work of imaginative fiction in the twentieth century begins with a birthday party. Tolkien starts *The Lord of the Rings* in the rural idyll of the Shire, and in the opening pages of *The Fellowship of the Ring* gives us a picture of a community which is in harmony with itself and its environment. But, as the readers soon discover, the peace of this community is threatened by the shadow of Mordor. Four hobbits, Frodo, Sam, Merry and Pippin, set out from the Shire to destroy the Ring of Power. In the penultimate chapter of *The Return of the King*, having accomplished their mission, they return to find the Shire ruined and despoiled by Sharkey (the white wizard Saruman, now stripped of his powers) and his men. Armed with the courage and wisdom which they have learned on their journey, the four hobbits liberate the Shire and restore its rightful order.

Tolkien's fiction did not intend his writings to be an allegory. We are not supposed to be able to draw one-to-one correspondences between the details in his work and aspects of our world. Instead, Tolkien intends to evoke feelings and responses within his readers, to awaken our imaginations so that we discover new possibilities and recover old wisdom that we are in danger of losing.[1] What Tolkien shows us in his descriptions of the Shire at the beginning and end of *The Lord of the Rings* is what a just community could look like, how it could be corrupted, and how it might be restored. He asks us to dare to imagine "Shire Justice".

The Shape of Shire Justice

Tolkien feeds our imagination with a description of the Shire in the Prologue to The Lord of the Rings.

> The Shire at this time had hardly any "government". Families for the most part managed their own affairs. Growing food and eating it occupied most of their time. In other matters they were, as a rule, generous and not greedy, but contented and moderate, so that estates, farms, workshops, and small trades tended to remain unchanged for generations. ... The only real official in the Shire at this date was the Mayor of Michel Delving ... [and] almost his own duty was to preside at banquets, given on the Shire-holidays, which occurred at frequent intervals.

The only government services run by the Mayor are the Messenger Service and the Watch. The Watch was made up of Shirriffs, who were the closest thing the Hobbits had to a police force, but Tolkien describes them as

> in practice rather haywards than policemen, more concerned with the strayings of beasts than of people. There were in all the Shire only twelve of them, three in each Farthing, for Inside Work. A rather larger body, varying at need was employed ... to see that Outsiders of any kind, great or small, did not make themselves a nuisance.[2]

There was one other official post in the Shire: the Thain. The Thain had the power to call a shire-moot in times of emergency. The shire-moot was a *parlement*, a general assembly of the hobbits to decide what to do in response to a threat. The shire-moot could call for a shire-muster, it could summon all the hobbits to unite in defence of their land. The Shire is therefore a 'yeoman republic',[3] in which strong extended families live prosperously but modestly in accordance with common values.

Particular social conditions in the Shire make such limited government a possibility. Christian theologians, from Thomas Aquinas to Oliver O'Donovan, have long taught that the virtue of the citizens is the most important factor in a polity.[4] The functions the government of the Shire is called upon to perform are minimal both because family bonds among the hobbits are strong and because its people are law-abiding, co-operative and generous. The hobbits live in large families, sometimes in extended family groups, and always with a keen sense of their place in the network of relationships in their family and clan.[5] It is in these family groups that the values of the hobbits are taught and hobbits learn how to relate rightly to one another.

The hobbits need no police force because their general disposition is to act justly towards one another. Tolkien tells us that 'usually they kept the laws of free will, because they were The Rules (as they said), both ancient and just.'[6] In the Shire, the Hobbits are typically law-abiding, because they own their own laws. They have judged for themselves that their laws are both representative of the community's tradition (ancient) and right and fair (just).[7] Given the virtue of Hobbit society, which is at peace with itself, a strong police force is redundant.

There is a 'radical nostalgia'[8] to Tolkien's description of the Shire. It calls to mind a vision of a society 'in which men and women feel at home with themselves, with each other and with nature, a world in which harmony reigns.'[9] By this means he creates images of how things 'ought to be', and perhaps, how they once were. But the Shire is not Eden. Some of its inhabitants, and in particular the Sackville-Bagginses and Ted Sandyman, display the objectionable qualities and the petty attempts at superiority which can characterise close-knit communities.

In many respects, the Shire represents an idealised version of a mediaeval English village, governed by a common law in harmony with the customs of the people, bonded together by frequent festivals, and in need only of protection against external enemies. More than one commentator has suggested that it is modelled on Warwickshire or Worcestershire,[10] or possibly even Herefordshire.[11] Given that J.R.R. Tolkien was Professor of Anglo-Saxon, Norse and Celtic at Oxford University, there may well be elements drawn from a vision of a Saxon village before the Norman Conquest.[12]

There is, however, another intriguing analogy to be drawn. The book of Deuteronomy offers an account of a harmonious, agrarian, egalitarian society, whose people live in spontaneous obedience to their laws, enjoy frequent festivals, and live in close-knit communities built around strong family ties. In the Shire, Tolkien offers us an imaginative picture of what ancient Israel could have been like, if only its people had lived justly.

> *In the Shire, Tolkien offers us an imaginative picture of what ancient Israel could have been like, if only its people had lived justly.*

The key to Deuteronomy's social vision is the idea of *shalom*. *Shalom* is an idea which encapsulates order, justice and peace. In Isaiah's vision of *shalom*, the community of *shalom* is a place of peace, security and undisturbed rest (Isaiah 32:16-18). It is 'not simply the absence of hostilities', but 'true harmony, that is, people living together in the right order that

God intended'.[13] Where there is *shalom*, society is rightly ordered, everyone enjoys what is justly theirs, and peace reigns because personal relationships are good. *Shalom* is given its shape by the laws set out in Deuteronomy (which means in Greek, 'second law'). *Shalom* is a goal which is pursued by actions which are just (*tsedeqah*) and by just judgments (*mishpatim*).

There are three secrets to *shalom*. The first is that *shalom* is built around good relationships between people. The second is that *shalom* requires an intimate understanding of what God wants. The third is that *shalom* demands that no-one is excluded from participating in society.

The first secret of *shalom* is that *shalom* is built around good relationships. *Shalom* is a state of affairs that exists between people. Just actions and just judgments promote and restore right relationships within the community. Deuteronomy is clear that material security and prosperity is the result of right relationships and not vice versa. In Micah's vision of the Day of the Lord, when swords are beaten into ploughshares, "Every man will sit under his own vine and under his own fig tree, and no one will make them afraid" (Micah 4:4; see also Isaiah 65:21). In the Shire, it is eating together and exchanging presents which sustain good relationships.

The second secret of *shalom* is having an intimate understanding of what God requires. Deuteronomy urges the Israelites to know God's rules intimately. They are to take them to heart, to teach them to their children, to think and talk about them at home and in the streets, in the morning and at night-time (Deuteronomy 6:6-9). Justice involves everyone in the community. Each community in a particular location and each household within that community should know for itself how to behave justly towards its neighbours, meaning that law-enforcement would be a last resort. Like the Rules which the hobbits followed, Deuteronomy's laws were supposed to be a way of life for the Jews.

The third secret of *shalom* is that no-one is excluded from participating as a dignified member of society. *Shalom* does not necessarily demand total equality, but it does require that each person and family has enough access to basic resources such as land, money and education, so that they can contribute to and receive from others without feeling ashamed.[14] We see this in the Shire. Sam is the gardener for Bilbo and Frodo but his family own their own house, 'Number 3 Bagshot Row just below Bag End'.[15] The difference in social status between the two is not so vast as to prevent Sam and Frodo from sustaining a reciprocal friendship in which both give and receive to the other.

Deuteronomy's laws are designed to prevent the creation of a permanent under-class. Each family was given its allotment of land and that allotment of land could not be sold permanently. Once every 50 years, the Jubilee legislation provided that land which had been leased had to be returned to its original owners. The idea was that each family group should have a relatively equal share of the land, and even if one group prospered and another struggled, no-one should be trapped in intergenerational poverty with no hope of social mobility. Up until the time of *The Lord of the Rings*, the Shire had no call for such legislation because each hobbit family held no more land than they needed and no family sought to acquire an inordinately large estate.

The Shire is a place of *shalom* because it is 'well-ordered' and because the hobbits act justly towards one another.[16] The *shalom* which the hobbits enjoy is the consequence of the virtues which they display, the virtues of enjoyment, contentment and hospitality.

Enjoyment of Things without Enslavement to Things

The hobbits love good beer and smoking pipe-weed. They enjoy eating, six meals a day if possible. They will find any excuse for a party, and for giving and receiving presents. These, their chief pleasures, are communal rather than solitary activities. The things which they enjoy bring them together as a community rather than dividing them and isolating them.

When Tolkien says that the hobbits spend most of their time growing and eating food it is easy to think of them as being just like us, workaholic consumers. However, the hobbits have learned the habit of enjoying things without being enslaved by them. Their consumption is moderated by their generosity. They have learned not just to consume things but also to give them away. Their frequent festivals show that they prioritise community over profit. They know that things are given to us to be looked after and to be shared with others. The hobbits find delight in simple pleasures—or, to put it more accurately, they have never lost that child-like ability to revel in the gifts of ordinary life.[17] Tolkien gives us the secret of being able to enjoy things without being enslaved to them. The hobbits were 'so unwearyingly fond of good things not least because they could, when put to it, do without them'.[18]

> **T**olkien gives us the secret of being able to enjoy things without being enslaved to them.

The hobbits show us that depending on God, the great giver, protects us from becoming possessed by our possessions, and enables us to delight again and again in the gifts which God gives.

How do we tell whether we are able to enjoy things without being enslaved by them? We tell by whether we are able to let go of them if necessary. Of the four hobbits who leave the Shire, Pippin and Merry are the ones who are most obsessed with food, forever thinking about breakfast, second breakfast, or another meal.[19] Through their experiences in Rohan and Gondor respectively they learn what it is to focus on the well-being of a wider community rather than their own comforts. Frodo and Sam take a different journey. On their way to Mordor, bit by bit, all the things to which they were attached are stripped away from them. In the end, even the orc-gear and weapons, which they were using to disguise and protect themselves, have to be thrown away. Like Job, they end up losing all their material protections. At this point, the readers see that relationships matter more than possessions, as Sam carries Frodo up Mount Doom.[20] It is only when people are put first that things can be rightly enjoyed.

Contentment

The social stability of the Shire is the sign that its people are content. They are at peace with one another, with themselves, and with their environment. The Shire is contrasted with the Wild. Nature has been domesticated but not destroyed, it is cultivated not exploited.

Like chastity, contentment is a virtue which our age defies. Our economic system requires that we constantly consume more, that we chase endlessly after new gadgets or experiences which we must discard tomorrow or come to recognise as 'so last year'. The hobbits, by contrast, are enabled to maintain a harmonious, fraternal social order because each individual and family recognises when they have got enough, and that is why 'estates, farms, workshops, and small trades tended to remain unchanged for generations'.[21]

It is because Sam has been formed in a culture which has taught him to be content that he is able to resist the temptation of the Ring in Cirith Ungol. The Ring presents Sam with a vision of 'Samwise the Strong, Hero of the Age, striding with a flaming sword across the darkened land, and armies flocking to his call as he marched to the overthrow of Barad-dûr.'[22] Sam is able to see through this mirage. He overcomes the temptation because of his love for Frodo and also because of what Tolkien calls

> his plain hobbit-sense: he knew in the core of his heart that he was not large enough to bear such a burden, even if such visions were not a mere cheat to betray him. The one small garden of a free gardener was all his need and due, not a garden swollen to a realm; his own hands to use, not the hands of others to command.[23]

Sam rejects the allure of power because he knows that he will be content to be a free gardener tending a small garden. He has no inflated sense of his own self-worth, no artificial idea of his own needs, and no exaggerated claim about his own rights. We need to learn from Sam how to reject the advertiser's claims that we need more or newer things to vindicate our worth. In our overcrowded, overworked, overheating planet we urgently need to discover the virtue of voluntary simplicity[24] and the self-discipline to renounce the destructive attempt to 'keep up with the Joneses'.

Hospitality

The hospitality of the hobbits is shown in their free gifts of presents. At birthday parties, the custom of the hobbits is that the person whose birthday it is gives presents rather than receiving them.[25] This custom encourages the hobbits to be constantly generous. Bilbo is the ideal example of this. His eleventy-first birthday party is open to everyone.[26]

Although Bilbo's adventures to the Lone Mountain had made him wealthy, he was 'generous with his money'. His home was open to all of his relatives (with the significant exception of the Sackville-Bagginses who constantly coveted Bag End) and also to hobbits from 'poor and unimportant families'.[27] Most significantly of all, for the purposes of the story, after Frodo's parents drown in a boating accident, Bilbo adopts his nephew as his heir and raises him.[28] Bilbo's actions show us what it means to follow the God who puts the lonely into families (Psalm 68:6). Shire hospitality is far more than throwing the occasional dinner party. It is a lifestyle which involves opening our homes to the homeless, the friendless and those cut off from their relations. Bilbo's hospitality to Frodo proves to be an enormous blessing to them both, to the Shire, and to the whole of Middle-Earth.

The three hobbit virtues are essential to Shire Justice. Such justice has the shape of a virtuous circle: enjoyment leads to contentment which leads to hospitality which leads to enjoyment.

Threats to Shire Justice

Although the great enemy in *The Lord of the Rings* is Sauron, Tolkien shows how the threats to Shire Justice arise in the hearts of the hobbits themselves. They are the tendency to insularity, the temptation of avarice and the lust for power which results in tyranny.

Insularity

One of the chief dangers which the hobbits face is that of turning their backs on the wider world.[29] Having created such a cosy, homely, community, there is the constant temptation to insulate it against the disruptions and interruptions of the world outside. It is all too easy to retreat into the gated community or to close the front door and to refuse to interact with those who are different from us, those who have problems, those whose behaviour will challenge our prejudices and our way of doing things.

This is a danger which two of Tolkien's best-loved characters have to wrestle with. For Bilbo, the temptation to reject or to resent the outsider is illustrated at the beginning of *The Hobbit*. His tranquillity in Bag End is disrupted as dwarf after dwarf knocks on the door, expecting entry. As Bilbo scurries to and fro, getting more tea and beer and cakes for the dwarfs, he becomes increasingly resentful. The limitations of Bilbo's willingness to show hospitality are exposed. He is challenged about whether his door is open to all who seek refreshment or just to other hobbits. In the final scene of the book we are shown that Bilbo has learned his lesson. When Gandalf and Balin pay him a visit, they find a Bilbo who no longer worries about whether his guests will eat him out of house and home but who is happy to share his possessions. The very last words of the book have Bilbo laughing and passing the tobacco jar to Gandalf so that they can enjoy the companionship of a good smoke together.[30]

For Sam, the issue is not practical but intellectual. At the beginning of *The Lord of the Rings*, Sam's thinking is entirely parochial in nature. He cannot imagine 'thinking outside the box'. He has no conception that folk outside the Shire could see things differently and that he might be enriched by their perspectives. But when Sam is in Lothlórien, he starts to understand the world-view of the Elves.[31] The way in which Sam's horizons have been enlarged is embodied in the name given to his daughter, born just before the end of *The Lord of the Rings*. She is called Elanor, after a yellow winter flower which Sam had seen in Lothlórien.[32]

Like the Shire, Deuteronomy's vision of social harmony is built around strong extended family groups. In such a society, those who are marginalised are those without close family relations. Time and again, Deuteronomy and other passages in the Hebrew Scriptures emphasise the importance of including the widow, the orphan and the foreigner within the blessings of *shalom* (Deuteronomy 27:19; Exodus 22:21-23). In our world today, widows, orphans, refugees and minority groups remain amongst the most vulnerable. In *The Lord of the Rings*, we see Bilbo demonstrating

Shire Justice to the orphan (by adopting Frodo) and to the foreigners (by hosting the dwarfs). As we will consider later, Frodo shows mercy to the widow (in his dealings with Lobelia Sackville-Baggins). Shire Justice includes within a community who have been ignored by it, shunned, or excluded from it.

> Shire Justice includes within a community those who have been ignored by it, shunned, or excluded from it.

Avarice

The second threat to the *shalom* of the Shire is avarice. The most dramatic illustration of this is Sméagol-Gollum, a hobbit who has been totally corrupted by the Ring. Sméagol allows his desire to possess the Ring to overpower his friendship with his cousin Déagol. Avarice leads him to murder Déagol and isolates him from all other hobbits. Sméagol loses everything in his obsession with the Ring. He abandons the world of daylight for damp, dark caves. He becomes unable to enjoy cooked food, preferring the taste of raw fish. In the end, he loses his own identity, as Sméagol is replaced by Gollum. The Latin word for avarice is *cupiditas*. It is a distorted form of love, a disordered, disproportionate attachment to something. The result, for Gollum, is that Gollum ends up not possessing the Ring but becoming enslaved by it. Tolkien's message to us is that greed is an addiction.[33] Gollum stands as a solemn warning of what happens to a person when they cannot hold lightly to those gifts and things which they have been given but instead ascribe ultimate value to them.

The destructive power of avarice is also what leads to the ruin of the Shire. Bilbo's house at Bag End is coveted by his cousin Otho Sackville-Baggins and Otho's wife, Lobelia. The acquisitiveness of the Sackville-Bagginses is highlighted at the end of *The Hobbit*. Bilbo returns home to discover that he has been presumed dead, that all his furniture is being auctioned off, and that the Sackville-Bagginses are already measuring up his rooms to see if their furniture will fit. Tolkien tells us that they never did give Bilbo back all of his silver spoons.[34]

In *The Lord of the Rings*, we find that Otho and Lobelia's greed has been inherited by their only son, Lotho. His greed did not stop at the acquisition of Bag End, which Lobelia buys from Frodo before he leaves on his adventures.[35] Farmer Cotton tells the returning party that it seemed that Lotho

> wanted to own everything himself, and then order other folk about.
> It soon came out that he already did own a sight more than was good

for him; and he was always grabbing more, though where he got the money was a mystery: mills and malt-houses and inns, and farms, and leaf-plantations.[36]

The key commentary on Lotho's actions is that he owned 'a sight more than was good for him.' Tolkien is making an important point here. Not only is Lotho's greed bad for his neighbours, who are disempowered and disinherited as he expands his portfolio of land, it is also bad for Lotho's soul.

Although Tolkien does not labour the point, it is Lotho's greed which invites Sharkey's interference in the Shire. Lotho's speculations in land are financed on borrowed money, money lent by Sharkey. To repay the interest on his loans, Lotho has to start sending away pipe-leaf and other goods. In the end, Sharkey demands an account. Like bailiffs, his ruffians come into the Shire with their 'great wagons, some to carry off the goods south-away, and others to stay.' Lotho discovers that a borrower is a slave to the lender (Proverbs 22:7). Although Lotho's hard-bought position enables him to become 'The Chief', he soon discovers that the true power lies with Sharkey's ruffians. He is nothing more than a puppet ruler.

Like Gollum, Lotho ultimately falls prey to his own greed. Whereas Gollum ends up destroying himself and the Ring in Mount Doom, Lotho meets an ignominious end, imprisoned in Bag End, the house which his parents had coveted for so long, and murdered there in his sleep by Sharkey's lieutenant, Wormtongue.[37]

Tyranny

In Farmer Cotton's explanation of what has happened to the Shire he identifies two motivations of Lotho which have had disastrous consequences. We have already looked at one, Lotho's avarice, his desire to 'own everything himself'. The other is Lotho's lust for power, his wish to 'order other folk about'. The result is tyranny, as Lotho first becomes Chief Shirriff, then usurps power by deposing the Mayor, Will Whitfoot. As 'the Chief', Lotho behaves as if he owns the place, seizing whatever he desires, making endless lists of new rules and pushing people about through his shirriffs and ruffians.[38] He treats his fellow hobbits as being of no account, overriding their rights and imprisoning anyone who attempts to stand up to him.[39]

Lotho was corrupted by the same lust for power which had corrupted Sauron. In one of his letters, Tolkien describes how Sauron had begun by thinking that he knew better than all others how to organise the world, and ended by forging a Ruling Ring, which would rule and bind others.[40] The lust for power results in tyranny, the lawless use of power for its own sake. In forging the Ring, Sauron was following in the footsteps of his master Melkor, who in *The Silmarillion* rebels against Eru because 'he wished himself to have subjects and servants, and to be called Lord, and to be a master over other wills.'[41] The Ring gives Sauron 'the power to dominate other wills'.[42]

This is exactly the opposite of Tolkien's Christian understanding of power as service. The contrast between tyranny and service is revealed in the careers of the two wizards, Saruman and Gandalf. Saruman's desire for power leads to his alliance with Sauron and to his expulsion from the order of wizards. Gandalf, by contrast, never dominates but always facilitates. Whereas Saruman builds a fortress at Isengard and gathers an army of orcs, Gandalf travels among the free peoples, encouraging and equipping others for leadership.[43]

Tolkien's antidote to tyranny is to distribute power to the lowest reasonable level. Stratford Caldecott sees Tolkien's social philosophy as part of 'a tradition of Catholic social thought known as "Distributism", whose most eloquent exponents in the previous generation were Hilaire Belloc and Gilbert Keith Chesterton.'[44]

> Distributists saw the family as the only solid basis for civil society and of any sustainable civilisation. They believed in a society of households, and were suspicious of top-down government. Power, they held, should be devolved to the lowest level compatible with a reasonable degree of order (the principle of "subsidiarity"). Social order flows from the natural bonds of friendship, co-operation and family loyalty, within the context of a local culture possessing a strong sense of right and wrong. It cannot be imposed by force, and indeed force should never be employed except as a last resort and in self-defence.[45]

The key to distributism is that power is distributed and that local community is valued. It involves principles of subsidiarity and sphere sovereignty,[46] which distribute power between different levels and organisations within society. It is a social vision of what Tolkien called in one of his letters 'moderated freedom with consent.'[47]

Distributing power does not, however, entirely dissolve the lust for power. The tyranny of Lotho and Sharkey in the Shire is still dangerous, even if it is not on the scale of Sauron's threat to Middle-Earth. An important part of the message of *The Lord of the Rings* is that the Ruling Ring is able to corrupt both the important and powerful on the one hand, as well as the small and powerless on the other. Throughout the book, Tolkien describes how, through carrying the Ruling Ring, Frodo battles with constant temptation to let it wield him rather than *vice versa*. Frodo fails at the last. When he arrives at the Crack of Doom, he finds himself unable to relinquish the Ring. Only when Gollum bites off his finger is he free of it.

Restoring Shire Justice

Frodo, Sam, Merry and Pippin return to a Shire which is unrecognisable from the one which they left. The pubs have all been closed. There are food shortages because the harvest is now confiscated by the 'gatherers' and only a small proportion of it re-distributed by the 'sharers'.[48] The law is no longer an instrument of justice which embodies the best values of the community; it is now an ever-growing list of rules which are used to oppress them.[49] Both the architecture and the landscape reflect the inversion in the Shire's values. The old mills and farm-houses have been knocked down and replaced with ugly, purely functional, industrial units and hovels. The trees have been cut down and the gardens left untended.[50]

In 'The Scouring of the Shire', Tolkien shows how the *shalom* of the Shire is restored once again. Three features are especially significant in this account: restraint, restoration and repentance.

Restraint

The first thing which has to be done by the four returning hobbits is to deal with the ruffians who are terrorising the population.

Frodo's response is the model of restraint. He makes it clear that:

> there is to be no slaying of hobbits, not even if they have gone over to the other side. Really gone over, I mean; not just obeying ruffians' orders because they are frightened. No hobbit has ever killed another on purpose in the Shire, and it is not to begin now. And nobody is to be killed at all, if it can be helped. Keep your tempers and hold your hands to the last possible moment![51]

Shire Justice is remarkably restrained. Frodo has learnt that it must be applied not only to hobbits but even to those who have invaded their land. As they are preparing for the battle of Bywater, he makes it clear to everyone within ear-shot that there is to be 'no killing, not even of the ruffians, unless it must be done, to prevent them from hurting hobbits.'[52]

When Saruman is cornered at Bag End, the hobbits from the villages call for him to be killed as a villain and a murderer. Frodo replies: 'I will not have him slain. It is useless to meet revenge with revenge: it will heal nothing.'[53] Shire Justice does not condone wrongdoing. It is not morally indifferent. But it does recognise that revenge leads only to a vicious cycle of killing and it seeks to break that cycle through the power of mercy.[54]

If the ruffians' behaviour has all the hallmarks of police brutality, shire justice, by contrast, uses the minimum force necessary to restore order and *shalom*. In the battle of Bywater, Frodo does not fight but intervenes to prevent angry hobbits from killing those enemies who have dropped their weapons.[55] Shire justice makes possible the reconciliation of those who have laid down their weapons. Nonetheless, shire justice must deal with those who will not be reconciled. Evil must be opposed and banished from the Shire.

The returning hobbits also show us that Shire Justice involves self-restraint. Once the ruffians have been defeated, Frodo, Sam, Merry and Pippin release from the Lockholes all who had been imprisoned. All the prisoners have been ill-treated. Amongst them is the Mayor, Old Will Whitfoot. He is too ill to resume his duties immediately and so Frodo steps in as Deputy Mayor. If Frodo were intent on seizing power, the situation presents an ideal opportunity. In many a fairy story, Frodo would have returned to the Shire and become its king. That is not the way in which *The Lord of the Rings* ends. Instead, we are told that Frodo's only action as Deputy Mayor is 'to reduce the Shirriffs to their proper functions and numbers',[56] thereby restoring the right ordering of the Shire.

It is Sam who will, one day, be elected as Mayor. But there is no suggestion in *The Lord of the Rings* that Sam will usher in a 'new world order'. We know that Sam will not misuse his power as Mayor because he has already resisted the vision of what it would be like to wield power when he put on the Ring outside Shelob's Lair. Sam will not seek to exploit his status as a hero to overturn the egalitarian character of the Shire. Instead, Sam will use his position, his experience, and his gifts to serve. The very last words in *The Lord of the Rings* are Sam's. He does not use them to announce a vast programme for social improvement. Instead, he simply says: 'I'm back', signalling to us and to his wife, Rosie, that the *shalom* of the Shire has been restored. Whereas the Shire was ruined by Lotho's avarice and lust for power, it will be restored under Sam's empowering stewardship.

Restoration

'The Scouring of the Shire' is not something done by Frodo, Sam, Merry, and Pippin *to* their fellow hobbits, it is something done by them *with* their fellow hobbits. Their restoration of the Shire involves three things: a restoration of hope, a restoration of empowerment, and a restoration of the land.

The Chief rules by fear. The number of shirriffs has increased dramatically. Ruffians from outside the Shire have been hired to intimidate the local population.[57] The Shire has become a police state. The number of laws have multiplied; all sorts of things have been forbidden. The possibility of arrest or worse has paralysed the hobbits in the same way that the Capitol uses the Peace-Keepers and the Hunger Games to subdue the Districts in Suzanne Collins's dystopian fantasy.[58]

The four hobbits restore hope through open acts of defiance. Just as Christ used the symbolic power of overturning the tables of the money-changers in the Temple, so the returning party climb over the gate at the Brandywine Bridge,[59] refuse to co-operate with the shirriffs who arrest them at Frogmorton,[60] and rout the ruffians at Bywater.[61] These actions show that things could be different.

Fear paralyses. People resign themselves to their situation and adopt coping strategies. Their oppression becomes normalised. Shire Justice empowers. Merry mobilises the hobbits by blowing the Horn of Rohan.[62] He calls a shire-muster and reveals the truth that no regime is strong enough to retain power against a united uprising of its citizens. Shire Justice inspires. Without being told to, the hobbits mustering at Bywater light a fire, in defiance of the Chief's Rules.[63] Farmer Cotton joins Merry in organising the popular resistance which traps the first group of ruffians sent to break it.

The third restoration is the restoration of the land. Sharkey has ruined the Shire, first by cutting down its trees and tearing down its beautiful buildings in order to construct utilitarian factories and mills but, then, once that was done, purely for the sake of it.[64] The Shire is poisoned in a deliberate act of Sharkey's malice.[65]

In the midst of this devastation, Sam remembers that he has been given some grey dust by the elves. Merry suggests that Sam should choose one spot as a nursery and use it all there. No doubt if he had done so the nursery would have been beautiful. But Sam chooses not to do so. He thinks first of the community, saying: 'But I'm sure the Lady would not like me to keep it all for my own garden, now so many folk have suffered'.[66] Everywhere that he plants new trees to replace those which have been destroyed, he places a grain of the dust. Sam does not tend exclusively to his own affairs; he actively seeks to restore the land as a whole. His actions exemplify what Ralph C. Wood calls the 'self-giving communality' which is the essence of Shire Justice.[67] The fruit of Sam's generosity of spirit is the prosperity of 1420, a year when the weather was perfect, the children born were all beautiful and strong, the harvest was plentiful, the beer had the best taste ever and everyone enjoyed good health.[68]

> *The 'self-giving communality' is the essence of Shire Justice.*

Repentance

The final thing which is needed to restore Shire Justice is repentance. The restraint shown by Frodo makes it possible for the shirriffs to lay down their badges and to re-integrate into the community. Frodo also sees even Lotho as someone who should be given the opportunity to repent. He perceives that Lotho has become a prisoner of the new regime, just like everyone else. He sees it as the moral duty of those who have returned to try to rescue him,[69] even though it was Lotho's actions which paved the way for the Shire's ruin.

However, Lotho is already dead. What repentance looks like is, instead, revealed in the figure of Lotho's mother, Lobelia. Lobelia, who had spent her entire life climbing the social ladder, fell foul of Sharkey's men when she failed to realise that Sharkey had the real power, even over Bag End.[70] The final chapter of *The Lord of the Rings* begins with her release from the Lockholes. When she is released, she is cheered and clapped, and welcomed back into the community. Her restoration is confirmed by the fact that she gives Bag End back to Frodo and when she died, 'Frodo was surprised and much moved: she had left all that remained of her money and of Lotho's for him to use in helping hobbits made homeless by the troubles. So that feud was ended.'[71]

Lobelia's actions show how repentance is integral to reconciliation. The enmity between the Sackville-Bagginses and the Bagginses of Bag End is brought to an end by her actions which make clear the changes which have taken place in her heart. In leaving her wealth to be used to assist those who were harmed by the actions of her son and of Sharkey's ruffians, Lobelia's actions echo those of Zacchaeus. Her actions after her release acknowledge her part in the wrongs which have occurred and her willingness to do what she can to help put them right.

Conclusions

Shire Justice is an inspiring vision of what community life could be like. It is a community of *shalom* where relationships are good, where people live in accordance with an intimate, and shared, understanding of right and wrong, and where no-one is excluded. It is a community which combats the temptation of insularity with the virtue of hospitality, the allurement of avarice with the virtue of contentment, and the tyrannous lust for power with an emphasis on the enjoyment of community. When disorder and injustice occurs, the minimal force necessary is used to restore order and *shalom*, and wrongdoers are invited to repent and be reconciled to those they have oppressed. It is a community where hope is constantly being reinvigorated, where empowerment is continually being encouraged, and where the land is continuously being restored and tended.

However, such a vision seems to be so far from our existence in this unjust world. The difficult question for readers of Tolkien is: How is the virtuous community which Tolkien depicts in the Shire to be fostered and nurtured under contemporary conditions?

> **S**hire Justice begins with a proper attention to our own selves.

Shire Justice begins with a proper attention to our own selves. We need to work at becoming 'the kind of selves we need to be in order to live in harmony with others'.[72] We need to adopt the disciplines of fasting and feasting, of giving and receiving, of contentment and hospitality, which cultivate the hobbit virtues of Shire Justice.

Shire Justice perseveres in the knowledge that God's greatest work has always been done away from the spotlight of history. Sauron discovered that his power was undone not on the battlefield before the Black Gate before the massed armies of the West, but through the quiet, unseen work of two insignificant hobbits. In our world too, Shire Justice will be achieved through the lives of many unsung Frodos and Sams whose quiet pilgrimages are full of the just actions and just judgments which build *shalom*.

Finally, Shire Justice is realistic about the potential cost. For some, restoring the Shire may result in the earthly happiness enjoyed by Sam, Merry and Pippin. But for others, it may cost them their reputation, their health and even their lives. The just sharing of Shire Justice will only be brought about through people who are prepared to make sacrifices. That is why Shire Justice is a work for those who, like Frodo, know that even if Shire Justice eludes us in this life-time, there is a place of perfect *shalom*, where there are no more tears, there is everlasting peace, never-ending justice, and undisturbed rest, and that one day a ship will sail out of the Grey Havens to take us there.

Dr **David McIlroy** is a barrister and theologian. He holds Master's degrees in Law from the Universities of Cambridge, UK, and Toulouse, France, and a PhD in the Theology of Law from Spurgeon's College, University of Wales. David practises as a barrister in the fields of employment law and banking law from 3 Paper Buildings, Temple, London. David teaches the Mission of Justice and the Theology of Law course at Spurgeon's College, and is a Visiting Senior Lecturer in Banking Law at the School of Oriental and African Studies (SOAS), University of London. He is Vice-Chairman of Governors at Spurgeon's College, and is on the editorial board of Law & Justice and Political Theology. He preaches regularly at his home church, Mitcham Lane Baptist Church in London and has spoken about justice in the UK, the USA, Denmark, Germany, Hungary, Albania, Uganda and South Africa. He is passionate about helping lawyers to see their work as a vocation through which they can serve God and others. Through his books (A Biblical View of Law and Justice, A Trinitarian Theology of Law) and many articles, David seeks to deepen people's reflections on justice and to inspire others to take up the challenge of acting justly, loving mercy, and walking humbly with God (Micah 6:8). Further details about David's work can be found on his website http://www.theologyoflaw.org.

Notes

1. Wood, R. C. *The Gospel according to Tolkien: Visions of the Kingdom in Middle-earth*, Louisville: Westminster John Knox Press, 2003), p.5; Curry, P. *Defending Middle-Earth, Tolkien: Myth & Modernity*, London: Harper Collins, 1998, p.18.

2. *The Lord of the Rings*, London: George Allen & Unwin Ltd, 1966, pp.21-22. *The Lord of the Rings* has been published in numerous different editions, sometimes in one volume and other times in three volumes. Corresponding page numbers in the different editions can be found in Foster, R. *The Complete Guide to Middle-Earth*, Hemel Hempstead: Unwin, 1978.

3. Curry, *Defending Middle-Earth*, pp.50-51.

4. Aquinas *Summa Theologiae* II-II.64.6; O'Donovan, O. *The Ways of Judgment*, Grand Rapids: Eerdmans, 2005, p.138.

5. *The Lord of the Rings*, p.19.

6. *The Lord of the Rings*, p.22.

7. Oliver O'Donovan has argued that political authority rests on the combination of power, tradition and judgment. Power is necessary to support the other two pillars, but where they are strong, it fades into the background: *Resurrection and Moral Order: An Outline for Evangelical Ethics*, 2nd edn; Leicester: Apollos, 1994, p. 129; *The Desire of the Nations: Rediscovering the Roots of Political Theology*, Cambridge: Cambridge University Press, 1996,

pp.46, 233; *The Just War Revisited* , Cambridge: CUP, 2003, p.121; *The Ways of Judgment*, p.142.

8.   The title of chapter 1 of Patrick Curry's *Defending Middle-Earth*, see also pp.53-54.

9.   Harrison, F. 'England, Home and Beauty', in Richard Mabey with Susan Clifford and Angela King (eds.), *Second Nature*, London: Jonathan Cape, 1984, p. 171.

10.   Duriez, C. *The Tolkien and Middle-Earth Handbook,* Tunbridge Wells: Monarch, 1992, p.230; Curry, *Defending Middle-Earth*, p.37.

11.   Shippey, T. *The Road to Middle-Earth: How J.R.R. Tolkien created a new mythology*, revd. edn., London: Harper Collins, 2005, p.48.

12.   Shippey, *The Road to Middle-Earth*, pp.114-117.

13.   Colson, C. *Justice that Restores*, Leicester: IVP, 2000, p.101.

14.   Ronald A. Sider, *Rich Christians in an Age of Hunger*, 4th edn., London: Hodder, 1997, p.xii.

15.   *The Lord of the Rings*, p.34.

16.   *The Lord of the Rings*, p.17.

17.   Wood, *The Gospel according to Tolkien*, pp.23-25.

18.   *The Lord of the Rings*, p.18.

19.   *The Lord of the Rings*, pp.84-87.

20.   Wood, *The Gospel according to Tolkien*, p.110.

21.   *The Lord of the Rings*, p.21.

22.   *The Lord of the Rings*, p.935.

23.   *The Lord of the Rings*, p.935.

24.   Curry, *Defending Middle-Earth*, p.51.

25.   *The Lord of the Rings*, pp.36, 39.

26.   *The Lord of the Rings*, p.39.

27.   *The Lord of the Rings*, p.33.

28.   *The Lord of the Rings*, pp.33-35.

29.   Nitzsche, J. C. *Tolkien's Art: 'A Mythology for England'*, London: The Macmillan Press Ltd, 1979, pp.104-106; *The Lord of the Rings*, p.17.

30.   *The Hobbit*, London: George Allen & Unwin, 1937, p.285. Nitzsche, *Tolkien's Art*, p.40, compares Bilbo's attitude at the beginning of *The Hobbit* to Smaug, hoarding his wealth instead of sharing it with others.

31.   *The Lord of the Rings*, p.369.

32.   *The Lord of the Rings* pp.1064, 368-370.

33.   Wood, *The Gospel according to Tolkien*, pp.55-56.

34.   *The Hobbit*, p.282.

35.   *The Lord of the Rings*, p.79.

36.   *The Lord of the Rings*, p.1049.

37.   *The Lord of the Rings*, p.1057.

38.   *The Lord of the Rings*, pp.1049-50.

39.   *The Lord of the Rings*, pp.1039, 1050.

40.   Carpenter, H. (ed.), *The Letters of J.R.R. Tolkien*, London: George Allen & Unwin, 1981, p.243.

41. *The Silmarillion*, London: George Allen & Unwin, 1977, p.8; Dickerson, *Following Gandalf: Epic Battles and Moral Victory in the Lord of the Rings*, Grand Rapids: Brazos Press, 2003, pp.97, 113.

42. Dickerson, *Following Gandalf*, pp.95, 143; Caldecott, *Secret Fire: The Spiritual Vision of J.R.R. Tolkien*, London: Darton, Longman and Todd, 2003, p.39.

43. Dickerson, *Following Gandalf*, p.43.

44. Caldecott, *Secret Fire*, pp.124-26.

45. Caldecott, *Secret Fire*, p.125.

46. McIlroy, 'Subsidiarity and Sphere Sovereignty: Christian Reflections on the Size, Shape and Scope of Government', *Journal of Church & State* (2003) pp.739-64.

47. *Letters*, pp.178-79.

48. *The Lord of the Rings*, pp.1036-37.

49. *The Lord of the Rings*, p.1050.

50. *The Lord of the Rings*, pp.1041, 1054.

51. *The Lord of the Rings*, p.1043.

52. *The Lord of the Rings*, p.1047.

53. *The Lord of the Rings*, p.1056.

54. Wood, *The Gospel according to Tolkien*, pp.152-153.

55. *The Lord of the Rings*, p.1054.

56. *The Lord of the Rings*, p.1059.

57. *The Lord of the Rings*, p.1036.

58. Suzanne Collins, *The Hunger Games*, London: Scholastic, 2009.

59. *The Lord of the Rings*, p.1036.

60. *The Lord of the Rings*, pp.1038-40.

61. *The Lord of the Rings*, p.1041-43.

62. *The Lord of the Rings*, p.1044.

63. *The Lord of the Rings*, p.1046.

64. *The Lord of the Rings*, pp.1050-51.

65. *The Lord of the Rings*, p.1056.

66. *The Lord of the Rings*, p.1061.

67. Wood, *The Gospel according to Tolkien*, p.163.

68. *The Lord of the Rings*, pp.1061-62.

69. *The Lord of the Rings*, p.1043.

70. *The Lord of the Rings*, p.1051.

71. *The Lord of the Rings*, p.1059.

72. Volf, *Exclusion & Embrace: A Theological Exploration of Identity, Otherness, and Reconciliation*, Nashville, TN: Abingdon Press, 1996, p.21.

Turning the World Upside Down

The English Revolution as Inspiration for the Transition to a Sustainable Society

*Injustice creates social tipping points which can spawn reform or revolution. Green economist **Molly Scott Cato** links the spirit of the medieval carnival with the revolutionary period of the English Civil War and asks if there are lessons we can learn from history which can help us navigate the turbulence of our times.*

Freedom is the man that will turn the world upside down ... True freedom lies in the community in spirit and community in the earthly treasury, and this is Christ the true manchild spread abroad in the creation, restoring all things unto himself.

Gerard Winstanley,
A Watch-word to the City of London, 1649

In an era of climate change and economic crisis it becomes clearer every day that human society needs to undertake a rapid and radical transition to a new paradigm for social and economic life. The answers to the small questions all appear to meet with the same answer: the market. But the failure of the market to answer our deepest human needs generates a cry for the raising of deeper questions and the space to raise and debate these with openness, equality and respect. Into a similar era of turbulence and uncertainty fell one of the most shocking and bloody episodes of English history: the English Revolution that has since been labelled the Civil War.

What I seek to do in this chapter is to explore the potential offered

Human society needs to undertake a rapid and radical transition to a new paradigm for social and economic life.

by the concept of carnival to facilitate the urgent transition towards a sustainable paradigm for social and economic life. I do this through drawing on the way that elements of carnival made possible the social and political transition of the English Revolution of 1641-60. The main source material for the ferment of ideas alive at this time were the documents reporting the Putney Debates, a series of heated discussions that were recorded and have become some of the earliest documents representing the English democratic inheritance. The image of UK citizens is as stalwart and loyal inheritors of a noble and longstanding democracy, the descendants of an imperial past about which many still retain residual pride. Yet an equal case could be made for England as the origin of the revolutionary ideal. Some remember that Tom Paine was an instigator of both the US and French revolutions, but fewer recall that England was the scene of the first revolution against the power of an autocratic monarch.

The revolt that became a civil war and then a revolution may have begun with an attempt by wealthy land-owners to defend their rights against an autocratic monarchy, but as the conflict dragged on, more fundamental questions were asked: about who had the right to own land and how that right was justified; about the nature of political authority; and about the balance of political and spiritual authority. These are timeless questions, but what makes this period of English history so interesting is that these questions were being asked by the mass of people, many with only a limited education, and that their opinions and debates have been preserved.

We are in times of crisis and times when dramatic, if not revolutionary change, is called for. Beset by financial and ecological crises it is clear that the human race is threatened, that the dominant global model of economy is broken, and that we have taken a wrong turning. The word most frequently used when describing the change we need to make is 'transition'. We have some clues about the kind of changes that are necessary—a radical reduction in our energy use, a revival of democratic ideals, a renewed commitment to equality, and a reclaiming of the spiritual to balance the dominance of materialism—and yet it can feel like a daunting challenge. What I hope to do in this chapter is to share inspiration from an earlier generation of transformative activists: the 17th-century 'Levellers'. As we challenge the power structures of global capital that are oppressive to both social and

> *The word most frequently used when describing the change we need to make is 'transition'.*

ecological health, I explore how the conception of carnival might help us to find reinforcement in our own radical history.

The English Civil War as an Instantiation of the Spirit of Carnival

Between 28th October and 7th November 1647, some of the most important and revolutionary questions ever raised in the political debates of England were hotly contested in St. Mary's church in what was then the small village of Putney amongst members of The New Model Army who had defeated the King's forces and now demanded the right to decide on the new world they would live in. The debate came at the end of the bloody civil war which had raged since the revolt against the King by parliamentarians in 1642 and would end with the first legally sanctioned beheading of a King by his people two years later in 1649.

The debates at Putney were polarised between the Grandees, the senior officers who were mainly landowners, and the Agitators, the 'common' people who felt the victory was theirs and wanted political rights in return. Their demands were widespread and radical. Army leader Thomas Rainsborough argued a case for radical equality of rights and property. His famous statement 'for really I think that the poorest he that is in England hath a life to live, as the greatest he' was a key step on our road to democratic rights divorced from property, a case made more boldly by 'honest John' Lilburne, the pamphleteer whose words were so incendiary that he spent most of his life in gaol. These were the Levellers, who rejected the idea of a society based on privilege and the inequality that they had been born into.

These radical thinkers were clever enough to foresee that, without a redistribution of resources, political rights would ultimately be eroded. Hence the call for land redistribution so that it could become, in Gerard Winstanley's words, 'a common Treasury.' Like today's radicals many put their words into practice, organising communes that followed the early Christian communes and gave models to later communities of the 1960s. Like many Greens today they had a spiritual connection to the land, as demonstrated by Winstanley's comment that 'True religion and undefiled is to make restitution of the earth.'

So can we make a case for the time of the Civil War as a time of carnival, in the sense intended by the title of this collection? Bakhtin uses the carnival as an image for a challenge to hegemony that is subversive, using humour rather than force. His experience of Russia's revolutionary decade of the 1920s strongly influenced his theory of carnival, a force that offered openness in opposition to the increasing bureaucratisation and ideological closure as the revolution developed.[1] I think we can find examples from the Putney Debates that exemplify this attempt to challenge the existing social order in a playful and satirical way. In his history of this period, whose title I have borrowed and to whose painstaking research I am indebted throughout the chapter, Christopher Hill compares the topsy-turvy world of the Levellers with the traditional English notion of a land of Cockayne, a land similar to Bakhtin's ideas of carnival. Commenting on Coppe's vision of a land flowing with milk and honey and his recollection of the Lord's support for the lilies of the field he writes: 'This is the land of Cockayne, of tipsy topsy-turvydom.'[2]

Bakhtin draws his conception of carnival from the role of religious festivals in feudal Europe, where he identified a duality between the official workaday life constrained by ecclesiastical rules and overshadowed by the fear of damnation, and the anarchic and rebellious humour of the carnival festivities, a life out of time, dominated by laughter and subversion.[3] In her introduction to Bakhtin's development of the concept of carnival, which is largely through this literary criticism, Vice identifies a series of thirteen key features. It is beyond the scope of this chapter to encompass all of these, and some are distinctly not relevant to my theme, however others have a particular relevance in terms of considering the potential offered by performative activity to shift power systems and facilitate the transition from one socio-economic paradigm to another, whether we are thinking of this transition in terms of the replacement of a monarchy with a commonwealth in the 17th century, or the contemporary transition to a sustainable society.

First, and perhaps most important, is the timelessness of the spirit of carnival, and the opportunity this presents to create radical change. Carnival represents a liminal zone in terms of both space and time: carnival time is characterised by 'moments of death and revival, of change and renewal' which was made possible by a 'festive perception of the world'. According to Wettergren, 'In the carnival life as we know it was suspended in favor of a utopia that laughed at hierarchical structures and privileges, ridiculed death, transgressed social norms and taboos. The medieval carnival was "hostile to everything constant, everything accomplished and complete.

> *Carnival time is characterised by moments of death and revival, of change and renewal.*

46

It looked into the unknown future.'"[4] In Medieval times this referred to the period prior to Lent when hierarchies were challenged and strict codes of behaviour transgressed. Carnival challenges social hierarchies, allowing unusual combinations, 'the sacred with the profane, the lofty with the low, the great with the insignificant, the wise with the stupid' and also permits 'free and familiar contact between people.'[5] Such liminal times removed the normal rules governing behaviour and contained the impulse for radical change within socially accepted time-periods. 'Everything completed, fixed, or defined is declared to be dogmatic and repressive; only the destruction of all extant or conceivable norms has value'. This intellectual move culminates in Bakhtin's statement that 'the will to destroy is a creative will.'[6]

For many of those who are attempting to bring about ecologically-focused innovation the ecological crisis is a situation that justifies the challenging of all social rules. The space between two paradigms - the current one based on waste, greed and a profligacy with energy and resources that threatens the future of our species and has already brought the death of many thousands of other species - is one where experimentation unbound by the normal conventions of culture is justified. The importance of the crisis and the urgency of the need to respond bring in their wake a resistance to bureaucratised or oppressive norms. The emergency is seen as an excuse to resist in a playful way. Thus I have characterised the development of the Stroud Pound, and perhaps the other Transition currencies, as a vehicle for learning through play while the all-powerful global economy still meets our provisioning needs, but its demise is seen as inevitable.[7]

There is also an earthiness to carnival which contrasts with the ethereal of the spiritual realm as conceived by Medieval Christianity. Whether this represents a 'profanation', or rather a recognition that the earth-bound existence is authentically human and thus not merely valid but perhaps primary, is unclear. One aspect of this grounding is the recognition of death as a part of life and the acceptance of the inevitable linkage of life and death, in reaction to the Christian notion of earthly struggle to achieve true and eternal life in heaven. In view of my later focus on the English Civil War it is worth noting that Bakhtin drew particular attention to the ceremony of crowning and then ritually dethroning the carnival king. According to Vice, the spirit of carnival also changes the fundamental metaphysical rules about life and death. The challenge of the fear of death is temporarily overcome in carnival. This is reflected both in the everyday reality of death during the Civil War and the sense amongst environmentalists that human survival itself may be at stake as a result of the ecological crisis.

The most important characteristic of carnival, in terms of my topic here, is the potential to perform a novel and counter-cultural social form. The carnival is a performance, but a performance that is all-encompassing and hence facilitates the adoption of changed social personas and perhaps even relationships of power: 'carnival does not know footlights, in the sense that it does not acknowledge any distinction between actors and spectators. Footlights would destroy a carnival, as the absence of footlights would destroy a theatrical performance.'[8] In true carnival the footlights are absent. Vice interprets this as meaning that in carnival 'there is no such thing as a spectator or audience member.'[9] The Levellers in particular were well aware that they were acting on a national, if not an international stage. Their rhetorical performances during the Putney debates make this clear. Shakespeare's dismissal of the world as a stage on which men and women were '*merely*' players is transcended by these men and women just a couple of generations later who took history into their own hands and performed a new way of living that assumed their right to equality of political power and land ownership.

The concept of performativity[9] may be useful here in explaining the revolutionary impulses of the Civil War and the kinds of changes we need to make now. Because our identities are defined by past actions and relationships they are held in place by networks of social and cultural relations and can be hard to change. Behaving 'out of character' can distance us from our friends and leave us with a feeling of inauthenticity, or of behaving like an imposter. The carnival spirit can give us the chance to 'try on' a different mask or character, perhaps in the expectation that when we take off the mask we may find that our face has changed to fit it. Thus performance, and especially the participatory performance that situations of carnival make possible, can facilitate rapid and transformative change.

Finally we should acknowledge the central role of laughter and especially parody as a tool to achieve the social turbulence that was central to the performance of carnival: 'Carnival laughter is directed at exalted objects, and forces them to renew themselves'. Such techniques were also widely used by both the Levellers—we can think of James Naylor's procession into Bristol on a donkey—or the ubiquitous street theatre that has been a central feature of cultural protest since the 1960s. The peace and ecological movements have been at their most effective when they have found a performance that is also a parody of the world they seek to challenge, the Rebel Clown Army being one of the most impressive recent examples. This laughter is only partially an indication of humour or joy; a deeper interpretation might be an expression of the need of the human spirit to reject the despair that both war and crisis can bring, fulfilling the

*Figure 1: The Rebel Clown Army Protect the People
of Faslane against Nuclear Weapons*

deeper psychological function of laughter as a technique to dispel their threat to psychic wholeness.

Making the Connections

To find inspiration in the actions and words of the 17th-century radicals we first need to acknowledge them as worthy forebears and then to seek parallels between their project and our own. In this section, I attempt to describe these parallels as I see them in four different areas: in the need to reclaim the land; in the quest to reclaim the power of the spiritual, however defined, as part of the realm of public discourse; in the demand that the circle of those considered worthy to exercise political power should be extended; and finally, and more tentatively, in the demand for an 'embedded epistemology', a way of making sense of the world that is inherently relational.

Reclaiming the Land

As a green economist I place land right at the heart of my project to restructure and relocalise the global economy: changing our relationship with land is central to the transition to sustainability.[11] The issue of land was also central to the Putney Debates, although it was one of the areas where the agitators were less successful in the negotiations, primarily because the Grandees were large landowners themselves and feared that their personal interests might be threatened.

Gerard Winstanley is the best remembered of those who argued for major land reform, and his arguments are the most coherent. Winstanley's vision was one of shared land and shared labour. He thought that land should be 'a common Treasury of livelihood to whole mankind, without respect of persons.'[12] He saw this as a universal spiritual truth in a way that is familiar from many indigenous communities around the world:

> In the beginning of Time, the great Creator Reason, made the Earth to be a Common Treasury, to preserve Beasts, Birds, Fishes, and Man, the lord that was to govern this Creation; for Man had Domination given to him, over the Beasts, Birds, and Fishes; but not one word was spoken in the beginning, That one branch of mankind should rule over another. (*The True Levellers' Standard Advanced*)

His belief was that an equal relationship with land could form the basis for a just society and could underpin human dignity in work. As he argues later in the same document:

> That we may work in righteousness, and lay the Foundation of making the Earth a Common Treasury for All, both Rich and Poor, That every one that is born in the land, may be fed by the Earth his Mother that brought him forth, according to the Reason that rules in the Creation. Not Inclosing any part into any particular hand, but all as one man, working together, and feeding together as Sons of one Father, members of one Family. (*The True Levellers' Standard Advanced*)

What Hill refers to as 'agrarian communist ideas' had, in his view, circulated in England long before the Civil War period, especially in communities of Anabaptists and other non-conformists who had inherited their ideas from the Lollards of the late 14th century. The crisis and chaos of the 1640s gave these ideas the opportunity to surface, but also meant that traditional forms of provisioning had failed, giving people a practical need for a new understanding of how land might be made available to those who were not just disinherited but actually hungry. Here we may see a link to our present situation of crisis, both in the poorer countries of the world, where displacement and dislocation have led to the breakdown of traditional embedded systems of provisioning, and also in the over-developed societies of the rich world, where peak oil and climate change threaten our energy-intensive supply chains.

The global movement that best expresses this universal demand for land is *La Via Campesina*, the international peasants movement that is opposing the globalisation of food chains and the land grabbing that this process entails.[13] This organisation coined the term 'food sovereignty' to challenge the loss of control over basic provisioning to multinational corporations. It was launched in April 1992 to defend peasant farmers and those across the world who meet their needs directly from the land and found their livelihoods threatened by the actions of institutions of neoliberal domination, and especially by the World Bank and the global trade body that became the World Trade Organisation. Beginning in Central America, *La Via Campesina* has now expanded to include farmers in Asia and Africa, as well as Europe. It now has tens of thousands of farmer members in more than 60 countries.

It has its rational aspect: *La Via Campesina* was active at the Rio+20 conference in 2012, where it argued that a land-based economy and the use of the land as common property would form the basis for a truly green economy.[14] It also has its carnivalesque aspect, of which the best known European examples are the actions of Jose Bové and the French wing of the global peasants movement. Gad Weil's *La Grande Moisson* was a related piece of spectacular street theatre that took place in June 1990. He and fellow street artists planted the Champs Élysées with grain while urban Parisians slept around them.

In the UK context the struggle for land rights is best exemplified in the work that revolves around Chapter 7 and *The Land* magazine. Here the work of the 17th-century radicals is specifically commemorated and celebrated. Issue 7 from the summer of 2009, for example, included a history of enclosure in Britain and included articles on how London's commons were saved by direct action and literary responses to these land 'clearances'. The tradition is continued through support for squatting and for humorous demonstrations on themes of land rights.

The discussion around patterns of land use, efficiency and population is the first echo of the debates following the civil war. Hill identifies the pressure on land as the result of a growing population needing to be fed. Land which had been used inefficiently, left as 'waste' or under woodland, needed to be cleared, manured and cultivated in order to increase its productivity. While wealthy landowners argued for enclosure to increase their holdings and remove the troublesome cotters and com-

Figure 2: The Champs Élysées reclaimed for agriculture

moners, Winstanley saw communal agriculture as a means of improving rural productivity without condemning peasants to servitude. This argument has been modernised but largely unchanged by a recent report from the global consultancy McKinsey.[15] Called *Resource Revolution* it considers the change underway globally in land-ownership and land-use patterns to be 'the next agro-industrial revolution'. Its central argument is that peasant farmers do not use land efficiently and that introducing private property rights and technological agriculture is the only possible way of feeding the world's growing population. As the argument about the need to enclose land gathers strength so does the opposition in the form of land settlement and systems of common land use. In poorer countries this expresses itself through squatting, whether on farmland or homeland. Both are found in Brazil, where the *Movimento dos Trabalhadores Rurais Sem Terra* and *Movimento dos Trabalhadores Sem-Teto* protect the rights of poor people to land for life and livelihood.[16]

> *In the UK we have communities sometimes deliberately modelled on the Digger community founded by Winstanley.*

In the UK we have communities sometimes deliberately modelled on the Digger community founded by Winstanley. Labelled as low-impact living communities, these enable their members to fulfil a large part of their livelihood from the local land, and to build their own homes from local materials. A leading example is the Lammas community in Pembrokeshire, West Wales which is part of the Global Ecovillage movement. The members of the Lammas community have fought and won the right to build their own homes within the Pembrokeshire National Park, on the basis that they will make their livelihood in a low-impact way from the local land.[16]

The Source of Authority: Spiritual or Material?

If Medieval carnival was based in periodic and cathartic rejection of the spiritual authority of the Church, then the situation in the period of the English Civil War was much more complex, with numerous sources of spiritual authority vying with each other. For the more radical groups, freedom from traditional spiritual authorities was justified on the basis of individual response to the spirit, which provided a superior justification for belief and action and an emancipatory approach to freedom.

Freedom is widely interpreted and based in divine inheritance: since God has made all men and women equal, argued John Lilburne, how could any man or woman exercise any authority over any other: 'man and woman... in the world since, who are, and were, by nature all equal and alike in power, dignity, authority, and majesty, none of them having by nature any authority, dominion, or magisterial power one over or above another'. While practical requirements might demand that some are more active in organisation or administration, this could only be permitted with full and explicit consent:

> And unnatural, irrational, sinful, wicked, unjust, devilish, and tyrannical, it is for any man whatsoever, spiritual or temporal, clergyman or layman, to appropriate and assume unto himself a power, authority and jurisdiction, to rule, govern or reign over any sort of men in the world without their free consent. (*The Free-man's Freedom*)

The meaning of the concept of 'sin' was debated in a manner that had a powerful subversive potential. In Winstanley's writing, sin moves from being a tool for ecclesiastical control to a source of liberation and justification for emancipatory socio-economic action:

> Sin itself looked different to the proponents of an upside-down world. Winstanley asked, who were the greatest sinners in the world? He replied that 'the greatest sin against universal love' was 'for a man to lock up the treasuries of the earth in chests and houses, and suffer it to rust and moulder, while others starve for want to whom it belongs—and it belongs to all.'[18]

The sin was private property itself and the exclusion of some from the divine blessing and natural abundance that was their birthright. This understanding of sin also liberated the human conscience to become the primary driver of human action:

> That matters of religion, and the ways of God's worship, are not at all entrusted by us to any human power, because therein we cannot remit or exceed a tittle of what our consciences dictate to be the mind of God, without wilful sin. (*An Agreement of the People*)

Amongst the many sects that emerged during this turbulent decade the Ranters, who turned the idea of 'sin' on its head, perhaps best exemplify the spirit of carnival. They gathered strength once it was clear that the political demands of the Levellers would not be met and represented a form of personal rather than political resistance. The Ranters rejected conventional forms of sin, claiming that since God was 'in dwelling' in each of them, how should an external authority judge their behaviour? They were thus free to engage licentiousness in terms of alcohol, smoking, swearing and free love. In an interesting precursor to current debates about the need for a phenomenological approach to our relationship to each other and the natural world, one group based in London and led by Laurence Clarkson called itself 'My one Flesh' to indicate the unity of creation. This has clear links with contemporary calls for a re-embedding of human communities with the natural world as part of the transition to sustainability.[19]

The seeking for answers within rather than by recourse to an external spiritual authority challenged all forms of temporal authority, enabling democratisation in its most radical sense:

> What rank and file radicals wanted was democratization—of religion by mechanic preachers and abolition of tithes, democratization of law by decentralization of courts, abolition of feed lawyers, democratization of medicine by abolition of the College of Physicians' monopoly and the provision of free or cheap medical remedies for all. In all three spheres their enemy was monopoly.[20]

There is a strong parallel here with the rejection of systems of authority found first in the counter-culture of the 1960s and now inherited by the Transition movement.

If the hegemonic idea against which the 17th Century radicals rebelled was an authoritarian form of Catholic Christianity, then the target of contemporary radicals is the domination of the consumer society, with its commodification of emotions and manipulation to sacrifice social and economic control to the narrow market relationship of buying and selling, with no consideration of the ecological consequences of this activity.

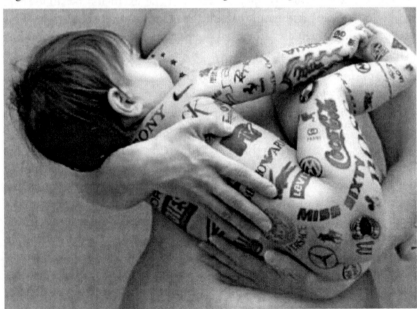

Figure 3: Canadian culture-jammers Adbusters use the powerful medium of the advertising poster to challenge the corporatisation of modern consumer culture

This dominant mode of thought and behaviour is challenged in true carnivalesque style by the culture jammers. Wettergren defines culture jamming as a symbolic form of protest against corporate activity which she links back to the Situationist strategy of *detournement*, a word that directly translates the world-turning of the Levellers and Diggers.[21] Examples of such culture jamming include Reverend Billy and the Church of Stop Shopping. Reverend Billy performs pseudo-Evangelical ceremonies of salvation in shopping centres, where consumers are urged to learn the error of their ways and dispose of the tawdry proofs of their devotion to Mammon. Canadian culture jammers Adbusters similarly use counter-cultural humour to challenge the advertising industry.

Boland provides a Bakhtian account of the way humour has been used to influence the public perception of the Irish financial crisis.[22] The Celtic Tiger, an animal that might itself be part of a cast of carnival characters, already provided the basis for mockery of the state, although Boland sees this as satirical rather than carnivalesque. However, in the wake of the bank failure and the European bailout Boland finds evidence of TV comedy shows breaking the bounds of standard comedy and entering the realm of the carnival, as politicians, interviewers, and audience alike all become part of a farcical performance in which all are ridiculed and the boundaries between performers and observers disappears. The street protests against the incurring of huge debts in supporting 'zombie banks' also demonstrate elements of the carnival.

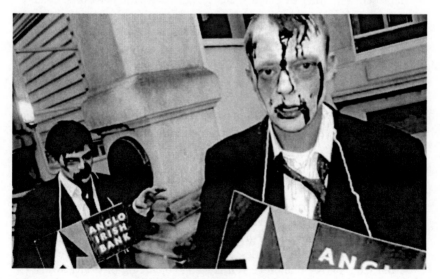

Figure 4: Carnival characters demonstrate against the creation of Ireland's zombie banks

Equality of Representation

A key document presented by the Levellers at the Putney Debates was the *Agreement of the People*. It gave precise details as to how power was to be exercised in the new commonwealth and required: proportional representation; two-year parliaments (elected on the first Thursday of every other March); the power of parliament to be inferior only to those who elected it and responsible for:

> the enacting, altering, and repealing of laws; to the erecting and abolishing of offices and courts; to the appointing, removing, and calling to account magistrates and officers of all degrees; to the making war and peace; to the treating with foreign states; and generally, to whatsoever is not expressly or impliedly reserved by the represented to themselves.

This is a radical platform that goes beyond what any national democracy has yet achieved. It makes explicit a fact that many who live in contemporary democracies have forgotten: that representative democracy requires the consent but also the vigilance of the electorate: electing representatives to serve on your behalf does not absolve you of the right and responsibility of decision-making.

The representatives of the army who engaged in these debates were well aware of how these freedoms might be limited:

> all obstructions to the freedom and equality of the people's choice of their representers, either by patents, charters, or usurpations by pretended customs, be removed by these present Commons in Parliament, and that such a freedom of choice be provided for, as the people may be equally represented. (*The Case of the Army*)

I wonder whether we might consider the first-past-the-post system and the requirement to pay a deposit to be a 'pretended custom'.

Although the sects and strands treated them differently, the upheavals of the post-war years also offered women and opportunity to argue for their equality:

> since we are assured of our creation in the image of God, and of an interest in Christ equal unto men, as also of a proportionable share in the freedoms of this commonwealth, we cannot but wonder and grieve that we should appear so despicable in your eyes as to be thought unworthy to petition or represent our grievances to this honourable House... Are any of our lives, limbs, liberties, or goods to be taken from us more than from men, but by due process of law and conviction of twelve sworn men of the neighbourhood? And can you imagine us to be so sottish or stupid as not to perceive, or not to be sensible when daily those strong

defences of our peace and welfare are broken down and trod underfoot
by force and arbitrary power? (*Petition of Women*)

The Putney Debates were held by many to be the first step on the road
to universal suffrage and democratic rights. The argument for equality
has, in our own time, led to the liberation of women, people of minority
ethnic groups, and of all sexual orientations. While we may celebrate
these demonstrations of social progress, for many ecologists they will not
be complete until they embrace the different species with whom we share
this planet. Thus the call for a 'parliament of all beings' and for 'guardians
for future generations' may feel as radical today as the enfranchisement
of landless peasants and women did in the 17th century and may have a
similarly comical aura for the members of that species that presently holds
all the power.

As a response to the crisis of political legitimacy that is one aspect of
the neoliberal hegemony we find the emergence of a carnival character
with curious echoes of earlier centuries: the Guido Fawkes mask, seen
increasingly at demonstrations by Occupy and other movements protesting
at the inequality resulting from the financial crisis, may be interpreted
in this light. In a feature common to carnival imagery the mask appears
to have taken on a multiple structure of meanings. Initially intended to
replicate the facelessness of the global corporations those wearing the
masks were critical of, ironically the copyright for the image is owned by
Time Warner, which receives a royalty for each mask that is sold. The link
to the original Guy Fawkes, instigator of the 1604 Gunpowder Plot to blow
up the English House of Commons is now only tenuous, although the mask
was worn at demonstrations against MP's expenses in 2009. The mask is
now used as a symbol of the revolt of the people against politicians who
no longer represent them, an impulse very close to that which initiated
the Civil War in 1640. Thus, in spite of the fact that Guy Fawkes aimed
to destroy the English parliament, the mask now represents a demand to
overcome the tyranny of unrepresentative power in a way that has echoes
of the later Civil War.

Embedded Epistemology

We have already seen how many of the sects that emerged during this
radical decade challenged the authority of the Church in matters spiritual
but a similar challenge was made as to what might be the origin of true
knowledge. The radical new idea was that the surest knowledge might arise
not from a text, guaranteed by a metaphysical God, but rather through
a deep knowledge of the natural world. Christopher Hill quotes the Antinomian Henry Pinnell contrasting the way 'a man knows a thing by

reading of it' with 'experimental certainty of it in himself'. In the words of Richard Overton,

> To know the secrets of nature is to know the works of God' or in Gerard Winstanley's words, 'The whole creation . . . is the clothing of God'. 'So that this is the great battle of God Almighty; light fights against darkness, universal love fights against selfish power; life against death; true knowledge against imaginary thoughts'

This was a time when the meaning of truth, what is now studied under the heading of 'epistemology', was a commonplace of political debate. Was one to trust the knowledge derived from one's own senses or were we better off relying on the guarantee of God, even when this seems to sometimes run counter to our observations? This was a question of great political importance, since the interpretation of God's truth was the business of priests and the support for their livelihoods. To suggest that we might find our own way to God was to challenge the whole edifice of the Church. In the field of pedagogy the Moravian Jan Amos Komensky argued for education to enable the 'common people' to leave superstition behind and come to genuine understanding based in observation of objects rather than the study of texts. Meanwhile the English scientist Francis Bacon argued for knowledge derived from observation rather than Scripture. As Hill argues, between them they sought an emancipation of knowledge: 'The Comenian fusion of Baconianism and Hermetic natural philosophy laid great emphasis on the social and democratic possibilities of the new science.'[24]

We may find echoes of the Levellers' epistemology in the growing popularity of permaculture amongst contemporary environmentalists. Permaculture is a form of neo-scientific philosophy which seeks to ground knowledge in natural processes, a way of looking at the world as a system and 'creating sustainable human habitats by following nature's patterns.'[25] Its proponents consider it to be a design philosophy for a sustainable society. Although permaculture arose in the sphere of agriculture, or what its proponents often prefer to call 'gardening', its insights have been generalised into a system of planetary stewardship or 'care for the earth'.

Conclusion

It was the Marxist historian Christopher Hill who revived the energy of the 17th Century radicals and made their thinking available to a modern audience. His interpretation has a highly contemporary feel and one that speaks directly to the theme of this collection. In interpreting Winstanley's conceptualisation of the Fall he presents him as something of a proto-ecologist:

> If we bear in mind that for him the Fall was caused by covetousness and set up kingly power, we may rather think today that this is one of the profoundest of Winstanley's insights. As we contemplate our landscape made hideous by neon signs, advertisements, pylons, wreckages of automobiles; our seas poisoned by atomic waste, their shores littered with plastic and oil; our atmosphere polluted with carbon dioxide and nuclear fall-out, our peace shattered by supersonic planes; as we think of nuclear bombs which can "waste and destroy" to an extent that Winstanley never dreamed of—we recognize that man's greed, competition between men and between states, are really in danger of upsetting the balance of nature, of poisoning and destroying the fabric of the globe.[26]

On Hill's account Winstanley considered that natural disasters resulted from the Fall, the disconnect between people and the divine world of nature, a sentiment that lends itself to a contemporary ecologist updating. Hill also interprets the demands of his radical subjects in a way that would find much in common with today's Eco-warriors and land-right activists:

> Rejecting private property for communism, religion for a rationalistic and materialistic pantheism, the mechanical philosophy for dialectical science, asceticism for unashamed enjoyment of the good things of the flesh, it might have achieved unity through a federation of communities, each based on the fullest respect for the individual. Its ideal would have been economic self-sufficiency, not world trade or world domination.[26]

This tallies very closely with the system of self-reliant local economies that green economists call for to replace the globalised economy. The ongoing crisis of capitalism, in both its financial and ecological aspects, adds to the resonance of the calls made by the radicals of this earlier crisis.

What we may find in the history of the dissenters of 17th Century England is what has been called a 'radical theology of change'. What gave permission for the outburst of outrageous behaviour that deliberately set out to challenge all conventions was the primary and fundamental act of killing a king. The social order of the times had been broken from top to bottom, and anything became possible. How can we relate this to our present times and the urgent need to respond to economic and ecological crises? I would argue

The social order of the times had been broken from top to bottom, and anything became possible.

that our social order has also been radically challenged. The social contract is challenged by a financial system that enables the rich to benefit at the expense of the poor, and the political system has lost all credibility because of its failure to respond. In such a situation anything becomes possible: it is a revolutionary moment. Whether we, the people, respond with violence as did our 17th Century forebears, or with humour and subversion, as did many of their contemporaries remains to be seen.

Molly Scott Cato *is Professor of Strategy and Sustainability at Roehampton University and has worked for several years as a green economist. In 2009 she published* Green Economics: An Introduction to Theory, Policy and Practice *and she has also written widely on themes concerned with mutualism, social enterprise, policy responses to climate change, banking and finance, and local economies. Her new book called* The Bioregional Economy: Land, Liberty and the Pursuit of Happiness *develops ideas for a new model of stable and sustainable economic life. She is an active member of the Green Party, the party's national spokesperson on economics, and leader of the Green group on Stroud District Council. She works with Transition Stroud and was involved in the launch of a local currency in Stroud in 2009. She is also a Director of Stroud Common Wealth.*

Sources

The writings of the 17th Century radicals have been carefully and lovingly archived and are now available online. The sources used here are derived from the online collection at the Online Library of Liberty, which are drawn from the following publications:

Pigott Woodhouse, A. S. (ed.), *Puritanism and Liberty, being the Army Debates (1647-9) from the Clarke Manuscripts with Supplementary Documents* [1938], University of Chicago Press, 1951.

An agreement of the people for a firm and present peace upon grounds of common right and freedom; accessible at: http://www.constitution.org/lev/eng_lev_07.htm

John Lilburne, *The Free-man's Freedom Vindicated*, 1646.

Petition of Women, Affecters and Approvers of the Petition, 1648.

John Wildman, *The Case of the Army, Truly Stated*, 1647.

Richard Overton, *Man Wholly Mortal*, 2nd edn., 1655.

Gerard Winstanley, *The True Levellers' Standard Advanced*, 1649.

Notes

1.   Lachmann, R., Eshelman, R. and Davis, M., 'Bakhtin and Carnival: Culture as Counter-Culture', *Cultural Critique*, No. 11 (Winter, 1988-1989), pp. 115-152.

2.   Hill, C., *The World Turned Upside Down: Radical Ideas During the English Revolution*, 1972, p.340.

3.   Vice, S., *Introducing Bakhtin*, Manchester: University Press, 1997.

4.   Wettergren, Å, 2009 'Fun and Laughter: Culture Jamming and the Emotional Regime of Late Capitalism', *Social Movement Studies*, 8/1, 2009, pp.1-11, quoting Bakhtin, *Rabelais and His World*, The M.I.T. Press, 1968.

5.   Vice, 1997, p.152.

6.   Vice, 1997, p.92.

7.   Cato, M. S. and Suarez, M., 'The Stroud Pound: A Local Currency to Map, Measure and Strengthen the Local Economy', *International Journal of Community Currency Research*, 16(D), 2012, pp. 106-15

8.   Bakhtin, 1968, p.7.

9.   Vice, 1997, p.187.

10.   Butler, J., *Bodies that Matter. On the Discursive Limits of Sex*, London: Routledge, 1993.

11.   Cato, M. S., *The Bioregional Economy: Land, Liberty and the Pursuit of Happiness*, London: Earthscan, 2012.

12.   Corns, T. N., Hughes, A. and Loewenstein, D., *The Complete Works of Gerrard Winstanley*, Oxford: Oxford University Press, 2008, ii, p.80.

13.   Mense, M., 'Transnational Participatory Democracy in Action: The Case of *La Via Campesina*', Journal of Social Philosophy, 9/1, 2008, pp.20-41. The website for La Via Campesina can be found at http://viacampesina.org/en/index.php/organisation-mainmenu-44

14.   More detail can be found at this address: http://viacampesina.org/en/index.php/actions-and-events-mainmenu-26/-climate-change-and-agrofuels-mainmenu-75/1261-rio-20-the-un-and-la-via-campesina-debate-green-economy; accessed on 27 October 2012

15.   Dobbs, R., Oppenheim, J., Thompson, F., Brinkman, M. and Zornes, M., *Meeting the Worlds' Energy, Materials, Food and Water Needs*, Chicago: McKinsey Global Institute, 2011.

16.   Their websites are found respectively at: http://www.mstbrazil.org/ and http://www.mtst.org/; accessed on 27 October 2012.

17.   For more information visit their website: http://www.lammas.org.uk/

18.   Hill, 1972, p.332.

19.   Carolan, M. S., 'I do therefore there is': enlivening socio-environmental theory, *Environmental Politics*, 181, 2009, pp.1-17.

20.   Hill, 1972, p.297.

21.   Wettergren, 2009.

22.   Boland, T., 'Critical Comedy: Satire, Absurdity and Ireland's Economic Crash', *Irish Political Studies*, 27/3, 2012, pp.440-456.

23.   Winstanley quoted in Manuel, F. E. and Manuel, F. P, *Utopian Thought in the Western World*, Cambridge, Mass.: Harvard University Press, 1979, p.355.

24.   Hill, 1972, p.288.

25.   Holmgren, D, *Permaculture: Principles and Pathways Beyond Sustainability,* Hepburn, Vic.: Holmgren Design Services, 2002.

26.   Hill, 1972, p.294.

27.   Hill, 1972, p.341.

The Liberating Dimension of the Kingdom of God

Evangelical community, civil society and political action

Active citizenship informed and motivated by a theology which values and defends the life of every human being as the creation of God and which deepens biblical justice is vital if we want to contribute to a radical transformation of the structures of power and inequality. **Dr Darío López Rodríguez** *presents the relevance of such a citizenship from the context of poverty and marginalisation in Peru.*

From the ends of the earth

This chapter has been written from my Galilee, *Villa Maria del Triunfo*, a marginal urban neighbourhood situated to the south of the city of Lima, Peru, my mission field and area of pastoral service for the past three decades. It has been conceived from the reality of violence, poverty and injustice. Everything I set out here has been incubated in a constant dialogue with the missionary context, and it is this position from which I think, confess and serve the God of life. It has been forged as a response to the day-to-day questions, the diverse human needs of the members of the Church of God of Peru, "Mount Sinai", and the non-evangelical families linked to the social programmes with children and adolescents that this Pentecostal congregation has delivered for the last 20 years. The participants in these programmes have been women who take part in social movements, women who have been attacked physically and verbally, single mothers, immigrant families, children who live in homes where a lack of bread and basic services—water, drainage and electricity—is commonplace, and adolescents who come from homes with worrying indications of domestic violence.

One can weave a theology of life from the periphery of society, which... deepens when the justice of the Kingdom of God is proclaimed in a context of institutionalised injustice.

In my pastoral pilgrimage over 20 years, I have learnt that one can weave a theology of life from the periphery of society, which expresses itself as non-violent active resistance to the forces of anti-life which act with impunity in Latin American societies due to the abuse of power, injustice, corruption and high levels of poverty. This is a theology which values and defends the life of every human being as God's creation, and which deepens when the justice of the Kingdom of God is proclaimed in a context of institutionalised injustice. The thread of this theology, anchored in the good news of the Kingdom of God, is the preferential love of God for the poor and the excluded.[1] Preferential love is a universal theme in the Scriptures which present God as the *go'el* of the underprivileged, who defends the helpless, includes the excluded, humanises that which society treats as an object, and gives dignity to those people treated as leftovers by the powerful.[2]

I have been discovering these central affirmations of the liberating dimension of the good news of the Kingdom of God by examining the Scriptures in constant dialogue with the questions which arise from the missional context. Through this process I have come to understand that, for a disciple of Jesus of Nazareth, there does not have to be a dichotomy between the spiritual and the material, the religious and the secular, the sacred and the profane, the private and the public. Beneath this theological umbrella, which is fundamental for the service of the helpless and the dispossessed, I have also come to understand that the defence of human dignity for the poor and the excluded, the struggle against poverty and extreme poverty, opposition to every form of racism and exclusion, social and political action with the aim of achieving significant social transformation in favour of the poor and the excluded, are evangelical requirements, concrete expressions of living under the impulse of the liberating Spirit. From my perspective, then, the good news of the Kingdom of God has a liberating dimension which must translate into social and political action for the benefit of the helpless of society and for the common good. As a consequence, the inclusion of churches in civil society and the public presence of believers in the political terrain should not be considered a circumstantial or peripheral matter; rather, they are visible and concrete expressions of those churches' own understanding of what it means to be the people of God in mission at a particular time in history.

Having explained the historical reality and the pastoral and urban experience from which my theological proposal is articulated, I shall next examine briefly the current situation of the Latin American evangelical churches, concentrating both on their positive characteristics and on their more obvious negative characteristics. Then, taking into account all of these factors, I shall examine the critical questions that the evangelical churches need to consider as inescapable agenda points for their mission in the world. They must do this if they expect their presence in Latin American societies not to be anecdotal or inconsequential, but rather to be a living sign of the justice of the Kingdom of God within the reality of injustice and violence; a reality which directly affects the most vulnerable sectors of society–children, women, the poor and indigenous people. Finally, by way of conclusion, I shall propose the strategy which needs to be followed and which can be expressed in three concrete social and political actions: (1) knowing the historical reality, (2) insertion into the historical reality, and (3) transforming the historical reality.

The Evangelical Churches

Most well-known positive characteristics

The evangelical churches of Latin America exhibit great diversity in terms of their origins, theology, liturgy, their forms of church government, their degree of involvement in the context of mission, their impact upon society, their social composition, and their numerical size.[3] However, beyond this diversity, they share a common theological foundation which identifies them as evangelical, despite their differences in origin and doctrinal emphasis.[4] Some are churches linked with Protestantism which were transplanted through immigration, such as the Lutheran churches in the south of Brazil and Chile which came as part of migration movements and which established themselves to serve the immigrant communities.[5] Others are the result of independent and interdenominational missionary movements which birthed national denominations, such as the *Iglesia Evangelica Peruana* in Peru. In Latin America, we also see churches which are the result of the missionary efforts by denominations such as the Methodist Church, the Nazarene Church, the Presbyterian Churches or the Baptist Churches; there are also Pentecostal denominations of foreign origin such as the Assemblies of God, or the Church of God, which are quite extensive in Latin America, as well as the indigenous Pentecostal denominations such as the *Iglesia Metodista Pentecostal* in Chile or the *Iglesia Pentecostal Misionera* in Peru.

The evangelical Latin American churches which have seen the most numerical growth are the churches which serve the popular classes.[6] These churches are situated in the poorest and most deprived areas of large cities and in rural areas, and they have connected well with the social and spiritual hopes of the poor and excluded people of Latin America. With a majority of poor people and immigrants, a participative and cheerful liturgy, and the active participation of lay people in the leadership (among other visible characteristics) they have a truly popular character. Samuel Escobar agrees:

> Much of the methodology, the liturgy, the style of these churches reveals precisely the popular origin of their members and their leaders. In this sense they are truly contextual although they have never theorised about contextualisation.[7]

This is the case, for example, for the diverse Pentecostal denominations which together represent the most vigorous, dynamic and growing sector of the Latin American evangelical community. A glance at the religious map of Latin America confirms that it would neither be unusual nor exaggerated to recognise that the Pentecostal denominations are fundamentally churches of popular origin; they constitute the huge majority of the evangelical population and are the ones which show sustained, rapid, and notable numerical growth.

These Latin American evangelical churches are also inclusive and levelling churches. This reality can be seen in the majority of the evangelical churches, regardless of where they are situated. It is not solely, however, a notable feature of the popular churches such as the Pentecostal churches; in churches found in the middle class areas, one can also observe the increased presence of immigrants and poor families who come from popular neighbourhoods, and the same is true in those few evangelical churches which have established themselves in upper class areas. In all of these cases, one notes a heterogeneity in the attendance of the service. However, when one looks at the positions of leadership, the same rule does not apply. In this area, one does observe a certain preference toward people from the middle and upper classes.

The Latin American evangelical churches are moreover missionary churches. The verbal proclamation of the Gospel, through means such as open air preaching or handing out leaflets, is one of their most positive characteristics. For every evangelical Latin American church, whatever its doctrinal emphasis and its particular history, being evangelical implies sharing your faith with other people. In that sense, each believer becomes a missionary who has a testimony to share with his family, neighbours and work colleagues or school/college mates. During the last few years, an increasing missionary awareness has also developed in the area of cross-cultural mission. Denominational and interdenominational missionary agencies have formed in the last two decades and the number of Latin American missionaries who are now serving in other parts of the world is increasing. Additionally, as a result of the process of immigration, many Latin Americans who travelled to European countries or to North America in search of better economic opportunities, because they had a faith to share, became missionaries on the journey. As Samuel Escobar underlines: "Amongst the hundreds of thousands of Latin Americans who go to other parts of the world in voluntary exile or obligation there is a small but significant number of evangelicals who take their vibrant faith and they share it as they travel."[8]

Most well-known negative characteristics

One of the negative characteristics, or rather the most well-known shortfall of the evangelical Latin American churches, is its limited presence in the public life of Latin American countries. This is due to the fact that these churches concentrate largely on the verbal proclamation of the Gospel, which they consider to be the supreme and unique work of the Church. The missionary presence in these lands is marked by a radical separation from the world, based on a very poor comprehension of the relationship between the church and the world, which leads to passivity, indifference and silence in the face of critical issues such as the violation of human rights and the scandalous poverty in which thousands of Latin Americans live. Furthermore, a good part of Latin American evangelical churches, both pastors and members, find it difficult to commit to social and political actions directed at the common good. Three decades ago Orlando Costas explained the problem in this way:

> Talking about hope for the new world without getting involved in making this world a better place to live is to negate the very same hope; surely it is to escape towards a vague and extremely mundane abstraction which paralyses the transformative force of the eschatology of the gospel and ends up consecrating the status quo. Having hope that the world will be redeemed and not undertaking some redeeming action in the world is a blasphemy.[9]

Although this situation has changed a little in recent years, and there are now evangelical congregations which undertake significant work in the areas of health, education, income generation and the fight against poverty,[10] the emphasis nevertheless seems to fall still on the public denunciation of individual sin. There is little mention of social sin, such as the justification of institutionalised violence, and much indifference in the face of problems like exploitation and oppression. Deep-rooted structural sins in Latin America, such as poverty, racism and exclusion, are hardly recognised at all. In other words, the majority of evangelical churches respond to the effects of institutionalised violence, but have little interest in denouncing the structures of sin and in actively participating in the construction of a society which is more inclusive and closer to the programme of the Kingdom of God. This reality explains why there is little desire on the part of these churches to comprehend critical issues on the public agenda, as, amongst other reasons, citizenship is limited to periodic voting in elections, and there is a disconnection between the social and political expectations of citizens on the ground.

In the light of the good news of the Kingdom of God, especially in its liberating dimension, the churches and the evangelical Latin American believers need to respond to such questions as: What do the Scriptures say about caring for one's neighbour and about Christian presence in society? What do they say about the integral care of creation, the defence of human dignity, and the protection of those parts of society which cannot protect themselves? Is the denunciation of social sin and structural sin part of the integral mission of the Church or is it a concealed and disguised way of "politicising" the good news of the Kingdom of God? This contextual theological reflection is both necessary and urgent, particularly for the members of hundreds of evangelical churches which inhabit Latin America's fragile democracies; these societies display many different forms of institutionalised injustice, often characterised by the unlawful use of political and economic power and the unchecked trampling on the human dignity of the poor and the deprived. In this necessary and urgent process, it would be very helpful to keep in mind proposals of integral mission such as those formulated by Samuel Escobar for whom:

> In a broad sense the term *mission* has to do with the presence and testimony of the Church in a society, the way in which the church is a community whose members incarnate a way of life according to the example of Jesus Christ, the service where the community publicly submits to God, the community which is engaged in serving human needs, and the prophetic function of confronting the forces of evil which destroy people and societies.[11]

The evangelical presence in the public arena

Taking into account these most well-known deficiencies of the majority of the Latin American evangelical churches, one of the first problems which has to be corrected for the light of the liberating dimension of the

Kingdom of God be present in the public arena—whether it be socially or politically—is the current practise of converting churches into instruments of political power or apologists for dehumanising ideologies. For a Latin American gospel to be effective, it needs to be clear that the God of life is not limited to any particular theology, to any particular political ideology, or to the interests of the religious bureaucracies and the political parties. No-one can place limits upon His sovereign action on the social and political processes of the people. No-one can suppress His words or silence those prophets who He has called and commissioned to be the defenders of life, which is the gift of God and needs to be loved and defended. This is the case because no-one, whether they be evangelical or non-evangelical, can shut God into a temple, assuming that He is not interested in structural problems and that He neglects critical issues such as legalised violence or the situation of material need in which the poor and deprived find themselves.

Moreover, for the church's presence in the public arena to be in greater conformance with the principles and justice of the Kingdom of God, it needs to be taken into consideration that there have been various cases in Latin America in which religion and religious people have turned into political instruments of the state and state leaders, thereby theologically justifying and legalising their abuses. This happened in Chile (1973-1989) and in Argentina (1976-1985) during those military dictatorships in which many innocent people were assassinated or disappeared. The same can be said with respect to Guatemala during the government of Efrain Rios Mont (1982-1983) and in Peru during the dictatorial regime of Alberto Fujimori (1992-2000). To be fair, it must be remembered that there have also been moments in the history of the evangelical church in which prophetic minorities have changed the course of history, defending law and justice in spite of insults, persecution and death threats by the defenders of the *status quo*. This was the case in Peru during the period of political violence and indiscriminate repression, in which the most politically conscious sectors of the evangelical churches and of the Roman Catholic Church defended human rights and the Rule of Law,[12] as demonstrated by the Truth and Reconciliation Commission.[13] A close look at the history of the Latin American evangelical church indicates that, time and again throughout the years, both routes have been taken both publicly in religion and in the public conduct of the clergy.

An examination of the viewpoint and actual practice of Latin American evangelical believers and churches in respect to the critical themes which affect every ground level citizen (including hundreds of evangelicals) can help us to understand the degree to which evangelicals are following, or not following, the principles of the good news of the Kingdom of God– peace, justice, reconciliation, truth, and solidarity. By 'critical themes' I refer to those themes which challenge the social conscience and the socio-political practice of all those who claim to follow and obey the God of life within the historical context of poverty, injustice, violence, oppression and overt or covert violation of fundamental human rights. These themes are the defence of human rights, and especially the right to a life of dignity; the battle against marginalisation and exclusion, one of whose most extreme consequences is racism; the battle against the scandal of poverty, and the extreme poverty which affects thousands of human beings; the responsible care of our common home in a context where powerful economic interests destroy non-renewable natural resources and carry out violence against indigenous peoples; the incursion into social movements which are supported by the democratic process and the political participation of believers in the light of a growing loss of reputation by politicians and a crisis in the party system. We shall dedicate the following pages to the analysis of theological discourse and the socio-political practice of Latin American Christians in relation to these critical themes from the public agenda.

The Defence of Human Rights

Within the Latin American evangelical churches there are pastors, leaders and members for whom the defence of human dignity, particularly in its political dimension, does not form part of Christian witness. These pastors, leaders and members believe that this is an inappropriate work for Christians, and as such, a "mundane" or "secular" issue which should only be the responsibility of non-evangelical social activists and those of a militant leftist political persuasion. This reductionist theological perspective has a somewhat feeble foundation in the light of the testimony of the Scriptures to the justice of God and the sanctity of human life, and has a directly harmful effect upon the understanding of the practice of mission held by the churches from this sector of the evangelical community. Such a reductionist theological perspective also alienates the churches from their historical reality into which they need to bear witness to their faith in Jesus of Nazareth as Lord of all the universe, and it impedes those social and political actions in defence of human dignity in which the churches should be collectively engaging, such as contributing to the defence of the Rule of Law and to the consolidation of democracy.

The evangelical view regarding the defence of human dignity does not have to follow this route, if one takes into account the biblical teaching of the incalculable value of human life, according to which human life is

70

sacred and no-one has the right to violate it, trample on it, or transgress it with impunity. Despite this, it is argued that the actions of human rights violators are for reasons of national security, due obedience, crimes of office, "excesses" in the battle against subversion, or in defence of the Rule of Law. In fact, these have been the usual justifications used over the years in Latin America by human rights violators, both civil and military, in democratic regimes or in military dictatorships, relying on the silence or the tacit help of corrupt politicians and religious figures who are themselves addicted to power.

The God of life has called us to proclaim the Kingdom of God with words and concrete actions of love for our neighbour within situations of institutionalised violence—racism, exclusion, marginalisation, poverty. As churches and evangelical Latin American believers in contexts of mission where such situations are particularly common, we need to ask ourselves the following questions: How should evangelical communities express their public commitment to the defence of human dignity in today's globalised world—a world in which thousands of human beings are crucified every day upon the altar of the free market and in front of the complacent gaze of those who hold political, economic and religious power in their hands? What means do they have to demonstrate their commitment to life and their direct rejection of all the ways of death? Can they remain silent, indifferent and unfeeling when hundreds of human beings are treated as disposable objects or not necessary to the System? In the light of the biblical affirmation that God is the God of life and that He is a just God who loves justice, the churches and the Latin American evangelical believers, if they seek to be faithful to the God of life and consequently to His message of justice, would need to be first in line in their actions to promote and defend human life, the gift of God, with concrete expressions of His justice.

> *How should evangelical communities express their public commitment to the defence of human dignity in today's globalised world?*

The experience of Peruvian evangelicals in the context of violence and death which devastated the country in the period from 1980-1995, illustrates the point to which, even in extreme political situations, a conscience illuminated by the Scriptures and a commitment to one's helpless neighbour born from the Spirit of life, can generate social and political actions in defence of human life. During this period, the terrorist violence of the "Shining Path" and the "Revolutionary Movement of Tupac Amaru", together with the no less violent and indiscriminate repression by the forces of order, produced a tragic death toll, involving the death of approximately

71

70 thousand Peruvians, especially rural people.[14] About 600 pastors, leaders and evangelical church members were assassinated in armed conflict zones, several churches were forcefully closed or invaded whilst the faithful were having times of prayer and fasting, and tens of evangelical families were forced to leave their land in order to move to safer areas.[15] It was in these critical years that the National Evangelical Council of Peru (CONCEP) acted organically to defend its members, leaders and evangelical pastors, when their citizens' rights were transgressed.[16] This particular experience indicates that, in highly critical political situations, such as a time of subversive violence and indiscriminate repression, expressions of religious faith take on patterns of individual and collective behaviour which are quite different to what might be expected by the traditional stereotypes of passivity and social and political conformity usually associated with the Latin American churches. The experience of CONCEP demonstrates that it is possible to defend human rights, even in their political dimension at a time of armed conflict, without losing at any moment evangelical identity and without converting the evangelical churches into instruments of the State or into defenders of repressive politics.

The battle against marginalisation and exclusion

One of the long term structural problems in the majority of Latin American countries is the considerable incidence of poverty and extreme poverty; this is particularly the case in those countries which have a higher population of indigenous people, who are often marginalised and excluded as a lamentable consequence of racism. This deep social problem with political roots is an unresolved problem from the Spanish and Portuguese colonial past, and not only affects the surrounding society but also the internal relationships of the evangelical churches. One still notes the exclusion and marginalisation of those who come from indigenous groups within those churches situated in urban areas and in churches with mostly mixed social composition, especially when it comes to electing local or national leadership.

In the political sphere, politics in the fragile Latin American democracies has primarily worked to serve the interests of national and international power groups. The vast majority of the marginalised and excluded have, with the exception of their right to vote in periodic elections, been denied power and participation in decision making about structural problems. These large majorities have not been considered as real citizens, but rather as a simple labor force, only useful for validating with their votes the continuity of an unjust, exclusive and precarious democratic regime which works against the common good.

To bring this situation to an end it must be understood that, for all citizens, and especially for the large majorities, the right to participate actively in the construction of a democracy is only really meaningful when it is inclusive and participatory, when social justice more than political discussion is a daily reality for all people and families. The excluded and marginalised, those on or below the poverty line, need to become actors in the construction of a state and of a society radically different to that which we currently have in South America. The hour has come to radically transform the relationships of power, so that power is at the service of all citizens and directed towards the common good!

> *The excluded and marginalised, those on or below the poverty line, need to become actors in the construction of a state and of a society radically different to that which we currently have.*

In reality, as just described, the evangelicals need to understand that if the state is not fulfilling its function in defending the helpless, then the common good will be of little interest to it. In the face of this abdication of the functions of the state for the benefit of powerful economic sectors, the believers then need to fight so that social justice becomes a daily reality, so that every citizen has access to bread, to health, to education, to work, amongst other fundamental human rights; not as a favor, but rather as an inherent right. This is an urgent task which requires that believers and evangelical churches to have a political conscience—not just social emotion, but a better understanding of citizenship. They need to be constantly watchful so that the practices of a good government also apply in the *local* power structures where they find themselves as disciples of the God of life. It also requires an understanding that public life is a common space, in which state policies for the common good are analysed, debated, proposed and approved, and are not there simply to favour a particular religious persuasion.

> *The hour has come to radically transform the relationships of power, so that power is at the service of all citizens and directed towards the common good!*

Acting in this way, individually and collectively, it will be possible to move from discussion to the practice of non-violent action. Analysing the structural causes of violence against the defenceless in society is a necessary and urgent step in the battle against the scourge of exclusion and marginalisation, but a step which will be insufficient if the evangelicals do not seriously enter into the political arena, actively participating in the public square where the common good is legislated for and where laws apply. It will also require that those who become the loudspeakers, or the public faces of the evangelical community, in the spaces of civic and political action—a relatively new arena for evangelicals—understand that there is a process involved which will require theological, political, ethical and technical skill.

The battle against poverty and extreme poverty

The insulting situation of poverty in which millions of human beings find themselves, especially in the southern hemisphere, is considered one of the historical causes or long term factors underlying the reality of violence against the defenceless in society. It is the basis upon which many forms of individual and institutional violence are constructed, and the other forms of violence which constantly torpedo the human dignity of the poor and oppressed derive from this situation. The many wounds which exist in our countries, of which the most visible is the notorious gap which separates rich and poor, are expressed in extremely critical issues such as the enormous social, political and economic difference which exists between those who have the most and those who barely survive every day, as well as the unequal distribution of political power and the asymmetric social relations which, for the main part, characterise Latin American societies—this is especially visible in the treatment given to indigenous people.

These gaps generate situations of inequality, not just in the distribution of income but also in education, in access to health, and in the treatment by the justice system of those who have the least. All this explains the indefensible situation in which thousands of poor families find themselves—families who remain courageous in the face of suffering daily violence, and who illustrate that there is a structural violence which lines up with certain political, social, economic and even religious interests. It must also be underlined that "this issue, however, is not merely a simple knowledge of the condition of the material misery in which millions of human beings find themselves nor an expert use of cold statistical data."[17]

Taking into account all of these issues, experts in the field have signalled that poverty can underpin many critical problems such as sexual exploitation, high rates of school attrition, child malnutrition, exploitation of the workforce, particularly affecting children and adolescents. Other issues, such as heaping together families within scandalous situations of housing poverty, and the marginalisation and exclusion in which thousands of human beings find themselves more by accident or happenstance in Latin

American countries, also have structural causes. These same issues cannot be resolved by indifference and passivity and even less will be resolved by the justification or legitimisation of those kinds of public policy which consider human beings to be disposable objects or cold statistical figures.

In the face of these critical realities, what does the attitude of evangelical believers and churches need to be? In the first place, they will need to conscious of the fact that these situations of poverty and extreme poverty in which thousands of human beings find themselves are due to *structural* causes. In other words, there are situations of institutional violence which explain the conditions of oppression and exploitation in which real human beings live, people whose human rights are currently violated with impunity. Secondly, they will need to understand that to radically change this reality, they will need to insert themselves into spaces of civil action and actively participate in them, discussing, designing and passing pubic policy which can substantially change the unsafe situations in which the most vulnerable sectors of society—such as children and single mothers —find themselves. In other words, evangelicals need to understand that to change these situations, or at least to diminish the destructive effects of these situations upon the poor and oppressed, the integral mission of the churches will also include social and political action geared towards a radical transformation of the structures of power and of asymmetrical social relationships.

The care of the environment

One of the largest problems currently being played out in Latin America, related to the worldwide problem of environmental pollution, is the irrational exploitation of non-renewable natural resources. The big mining, petroleum and timber consortia, with their covetous interest in maximising their profits at all cost, and with the support of corrupt politicians, pollute the sources of water, destroy land dedicated to agriculture, and cause deforestation of large expanses of woodland. These large consortia, allied with corrupt politicians and civil servants, accuse indigenous people of hindering the economic development and modernisation and, often, with the support of public force, strip them of their land. This lamentable situation is a call to action of solidarity for the followers of Jesus of Nazareth, the Messiah who came to free the oppressed and proclaim the jubilee, "the year of the Lord's favour" (Luke 4:18-19). An action of solidarity needs to take into account that: "One of the essential components of the liberating mission of Jesus of Nazareth... was inverting the destiny of the poor and marginalised, radically transforming social and economic relations contrary to the principles of the Kingdom of God."[18]

There are many factors which go to explain the current condition of the natural resources, as well as the real problems like environmental pollution. One of these factors is the voracity of those business people who are solely interested in the material increases to their bank balances. To them the future of millions of human being does not interest them in the slightest. The only thing they care about is recovering their economic investment and obtaining maximum material benefits. For these business people it is not a problem to buy consciences, to finance political campaigns to secure their interests, or to pressure governments so that they submit to international financial organisations. It is not a problem because within their "ethical bases", lying, bribery, corruption of civil servants or applying political pressure are "normal" issues, "necessary" to guarantee their investment. They care little—too little—about the death of millions of human beings or about the slow extinction and destruction of non-renewable natural resources.

Yet there is another factor: it is the passivity and silence of evangelical Christians. Too little has been done to halt the frenetic, destructive path which, step by step, has decimated our natural resources. Those responsible for these deeds are only seldom publicly denounced. In other words, evangelicals are not carrying out their divinely appointed task of responsibly stewarding humanity's common home. This is despite concrete problems such as air pollution which directly affect them—pollution does not distinguish between evangelicals and non-evangelicals! In other words, evangelical Christians are part of the problem, because with our passivity and our complicit silence, we are allowing the irreversible destruction of green areas which are the "lungs" of the world, and the gradual disappearance of non-renewable resources and the extinction of species. These are problems which have as an immediate consequence the alteration of the ecological balance and irreparable damage to our common home which, step by step, is being destroyed.

Realisation of the evangelical presence in civil society and in the political community

In past decades a large number of pastors, leaders and members of the Latin American Evangelical Church have taken serious objection to the concept of participating in public life, because they consider that dealing with profane and secular issues does not form part of Christian testimony in the world. Yet in the last few years, there have been a growing number of pastors, leaders and members of different evangelical churches who have been moving from political abstention to a growing participation in the electoral processes as mayoral candidates, governors and congressmen/ women, including as candidates for President of the Republic.

The new situation in which the evangelical community finds itself is as an organised sector of society with a not insignificant numerical weight. In various countries evangelicals surpass 10% of the population, something unthinkable years ago. This gives rise to concrete challenges which require clear answers from a biblical, theological and socio-political standpoint, as well as a fluid and permanent dialogue with other collective actors who interact with the public space. What are the challenges?

• Understanding that politics is an issue for people who need to know what happens in this public space and know how to act in a world in which the good intentions and good convictions of religious people are not enough.

• Understanding that full citizenship demands that citizens exercise vigilance and demand of politicians and civil servants a transparency in their public management, accountability and access to information.

Within a reality which has generated better spaces for citizens' participation and where the evangelical churches have an obligation to get involved in public matters, one must also ask whether evangelicals bursting onto the public stage will act to strengthen democracy, full citizenship and development, or if indeed by their social and political actions they will be cooperating in the dismantling of democracy and collaborate with corrupt regimes which are the violators of human rights.

To respond to these critical questions one needs to take into account the two ways in which evangelical churches understand political participation and have a civic impact:

• For one sector of pastors and members of the evangelical churches, it is simply about having a presence in the areas of power and gaining a presence in order to defend their religious interests. This sector does not understand that politics is a personal choice which one should not use within the religious community for political partisan ends. It also forgets that politics is concerned with the common good and good government, with sharing power and with education that penetrates the public space.

• For the other sector of pastors and members of evangelical churches, political participation and public impact, rather than to do with specific religious interests, is related to an affirmation of one's citizenship. They intervene in public matters because they believe that citizenship is constituted there and because it is a space where they can focus, negotiate and formulate an agenda for the common good. These pastors and members consider that they need to be present in the spaces of power because those are the places where proposals for the defence and consolidation of democracy are debated, analysed and articulated.

Over and above the reasons and particular interests of these two sectors of the evangelical church, we need to clarify the minimum conditions that are necessary to participate effectively and efficiently in the field of politics. The experience of the last few years in the diverse contexts of Latin America have demonstrated that there have been both light and shade in the political participation of evangelicals,[19] and this warns us moreover that to have a better performance in the public space a minimum of five more conditions must be added:

• The articulation of a basic, biblical-theological basis (and consequent practice) of Christian evangelical faith, so that those believers who step into the public space preserve their identity as members of the people of God and so that, from a platform of evangelical faith, they articulate, formulate and defend public policies orientated towards the common good.

• Some drawing on the previous experience of public management from such people as leaders of neighbourhood committees, milk committees, committees for public vigilance, parents' associations of educational institutions or other social movements linked to organised civic society. In this way novices, improvisers, and the overly ambitious or opportunists could be prevented from entering public roles and thereby giving a poor image of the evangelical community.

• A minimum knowledge of political culture in order that they be suitably prepared to enter the area in which laws and public policies are born by dialogue, negotiation and consensus between all the political players, be they evangelical or non-evangelical.

• A political vocation, with an understanding of the national reality, a mastery of one or various areas of scientific knowledge (administration, law, social sciences, human sciences, engineering etc.) and an aptitude for the work so that they can argue about public policy with party political cadres without suffering an inferiority complex. They also need to be able to efficiently and effectively execute the responsibility which has been entrusted to them by the public vote.

• Proven ethical solidity so that they will not let themselves be seduced by power, and fall into the circle of corruption which is so common in an area where indecent proposals and bribery have become normal practice.

Whatever the route might be in which the public presence of evangelicals is expressed (forming confessional political parties, inserting themselves into political parties of different backgrounds, participating in social movements or being good neighbours) it must be understood that politics is not restricted to the parliamentary confines or to local government, neither to the role of organised civil society, but rather it is a matter that is the responsibility of all citizens. In other words, politics is more than participating in periodical elections and the civic action of consenting to vote for a particular candidate or political party in each electoral process. Rather, politics is a task for all, and requires that all citizens demand accountability, transparency in public management, good use of public funds, as well as equality of opportunities for all those citizens, whatever their religious confessions, their social position or their cultural background.

> *Politics is a task for all, and requires that all citizens demand accountability, transparency in public management, good use of public funds, as well as equality of opportunities for all.*

An integral, contextual ministry

In light of the problematic issues described in the last section with respect to the five critical issues that evangelicals need to confront, and in order that their presence in Latin American society is not peripheral, anecdotal or abstract, a contextual, integral ministry must be articulated and implemented. To do this adequately, ministers require, on one side, a basic knowledge of the context of mission and then, understanding the missionary territory they are standing upon, the ability to responsibly insert themselves into the concrete historical reality. Two issues need to be clear, then:

• *Knowing the historical reality.* Knowing the historical reality implies, amongst other issues, having precise or first-hand information about social problems such as gang membership and people's growing personal insecurity; the effects of migration and problems which migrants face, such as autonomy and gradual loss of cultural identity; the reality of cultural mixing which has visible effects in the social composition and in the structure of the congregations in evangelical churches. Knowing the historical reality also implies being conscious of internal power relationships, of the forms of communication which the different social sectors have, and of the new political practices generated in spaces of public action such as neighbourhood committees and women's organisations.

• *Inserting oneself into the historical reality.* This demands an understanding that Christian mission does not need to limit itself to the religious plan of human life, but rather that it needs to cross multiple social, cultural and political borders. It requires an interdisciplinary team of missionaries, with a basic theological training, with at least some political understanding, with previous experience of managing social and community projects, and with an ethical integrity which allows them to confront circles of corruption and the temptation of gaining personal power. Evangelical churches can manage their own social projects in favour of their neighbours, or work beside churches which already have a structured programme of social action. They can cooperate with people's efforts from within their own resources, or with the help of others fight against poverty or injustice, or cooperate with the actions of non-governmental organisations be they evangelical or non-evangelical. In other words, the missionary insertion into the city demands widening the borders of our social relations.

These two previous issues lead to a more political theme, but one which is no less important, necessary and key in terms of transformational integral mission.

• *Transforming the historical reality.* Words and discussions can convince and mobilise a social body or a particular community; however they do not always change power relationships or situations of institutionalised violence. A necessary political step will be then to put oneself into those spaces where public policies which affect all citizens are decided. In other words, evangelical church leaders or leadership teams need to start to promote new models of social and political leadership from the ground up, social and political directors who actively participate in social movements and in local governments such as mayors or councillors. Once in these spaces of power, they need to be exemplary models of transparent public management, with periodic accountability, allowing all citizens and neighbours free access to information, continually being open to inquiry.

Evangelical church leaders or leadership teams need to start to promote new models of social and political leadership from the ground up.

Is this an unrealisable dream? No. I know a growing number of social directors and social activists who are evangelicals—men and women who are exemplary models of public management and who by their example show us that it is possible to be a good social director and a good politician without losing one's way, one's evangelical identity, and the evangelical requirement of preaching the good news of the Kingdom of God and His justice.

To clarify then, especially in Latin America, Christian mission has to be integral. When the mission of the church limits itself almost exclusively to the verbal proclamation of the gospel, disconnected from a commitment to good works and social justice, it will have as visible fruit good people, good neighbours or good parents, with an outstanding private ethic, but a poor public ethic, deficient and of little use for social transformation. A mutilated gospel, dedicated to the salvation of bodiless souls, disconnected from the historical reality, will never produce exemplary citizens who are preoccupied by the search for the common good and committed to the concrete actions of fighting against poverty and extreme poverty, the defence of human rights, the responsible care of our common home, the protection of helpless social sectors and the battle for a democracy in which all citizens have equal opportunities and where social justice is a palpable every-day reality, especially for the poor and the oppressed.

Translated from the Spanish by Sylvia Hathaway

Dr **Dario López Rodriguez** *was born and raised in Lima, Peru, and grew up in abject poverty. Since 1992, Dr. López has been the pastor of the Mt. Sinai Church of God, located in the marginal district of Villa María del Triunfo, in Lima, Peru. His pastorate has been characterized as one of Pentecostal passion for wholistic ministry, including personal, social and spiritual transformation. Throughout his ministry, Dr. López has kept the biblical concern for needy children and marginalized women at the center of his pastoral and prophetic work. Presently, the Mt. Sinai church, with approximately 200 members, serves over 350 poor children each day with elementary education and meals. The ministry has also included a new church plant in an area of even greater poverty. Several of the women who have been discipled under Dr. López' ministry have become actively engaged as leaders in grassroots community organizations for social change and have marched on the Palace of Government, demanding the passage of laws favouring poor children and families. Dr. López has served as General Director of the Association of Evangelical University Groups in Peru, as President of the National Evangelical Council of Peru, and has taught at a number of Latin American seminaries and universities. He has recently served on several governmental commissions dealing with issues of children's rights and religious equality. Holding a Ph.D. from the Oxford Centre for Mission Studies/Open University of England, where he completed a thesis on the topic of Evangelicals and Human Rights in Peru, he is the author of twelve books and numerous journal articles. His hard-hitting book,* La Misión Liberadora de Jesús *(The Liberating Mission of Jesus, translated by Rick Waldrop), serves as a textbook.*

Notes

1.   We are speaking of the materially poor, living below the poverty line, with limited access to public health services and a quality education, who live in areas which do not have basic services of water, drainage and electric light, and who are underemployed or casually

employed. However there are also those who are segregated or discriminated against for social, political, cultural, religious or economic reasons and excluded. While the material poor belong to the world of the excluded, they are not the only ones who form part of this multifaceted world. Immigrants from the South are excluded in the Northern hemisphere, immigrants from rural areas are excluded in the cities, as are members of Amazonian villages and inhabitants of the Andean villages. Those who are suffering a terminal illness may also be excluded, so may members of religious minorities, prostitutes, drug addicts, homosexuals and the physically disabled.

2.   López, D., *The Liberating Mission of Jesus: The Message of the Gospel of Luke*, Eugene-Oregon: Pickwick Publications, 2012. The term 'preferential' does not mean exclusivity or a complete appropriation of the love of God. The God of life, if indeed He is impartial in His love, opts for the poor and the excluded who do not have anyone to defend them. He identifies himself with the dispossessed, with the defenceless, with the victims of legalised injustice, with the underprivileged of the world condemned to live in situations of death and violence. That does not signify that all the poor and all the excluded, owing to their being poor or excluded are necessarily believers, or that they are saved because of their lack of material possessions or because of their being excluded. The poor and excluded, like any other human being, need to respond to the demands of the gospel to form part of the community of the kingdom; in other words, they need to repent of their sins, accept Jesus Christ as Lord and Saviour, and obey the principles of the Kingdom of God in their private and public life.

3.   Míguez Bonino, J., *Rostros del Protestantismo Latinoamericano*, Buenos Aires-Grand Rapids: Nueva Creación-William B. Eerdmans Publishing Company, 1995, pp.16-18. Míguez Bonino identifies four aspects which, from his point of view, shape Latin American Protestantism: the liberal aspect, the evangelical aspect, the Pentecostal aspect and the "ethnic aspect". He specifies, moreover, that 'in Latin America "protestant" and "evangelical" (or "evangelistic") have been synonymous.' (p. 6). In my case I prefer the term 'evangelical'. Samuel Escobar clarifies that: "The majority of these 'protestants' in Latin America prefer to call themselves evangelicals... The preference for the term 'evangelical' indicates a historical reality which is important to remember. The majority of the missionaries who came to preach from a Protestant tradition belonged, due to their convictions and vocations, to a particular wing or sector of European or North American Protestantism. It is this sector which in English is called 'Evangelical' which is further defined as conservative in the fundamentals of doctrine and which is strongly evangelizing and missional in practice."' (Quoting Escobar, S., "Qué significa ser evangélico hoy?" *Revista Misión*, Marzo-Junio de 1982, pp.14-18, 35-39.)

4.   The following are, according to Samuel Escobar, the distinctive points of the evangelical identity in Latin America: the theological inheritance of the Reformation, the evangelising passion, personal piety, Anabaptist attitudes, the puritan ethic and the social dimension of the gospel. (Escobar, S., "Qué significa ser evangélico hoy?", pp.16-18)

5.   Escobar, S., *La Fe Evangélica y las Teologías de la Liberación,* El Paso (Texas): Casa Bautista de Publicaciones, 1987, p.45.

6.   Escobar, S., *Tiempo de Misión: América Latina y la misión cristiana hoy*, Santafé de Bogotá-Ciudad de Guatemala: Ediciones Clara-Semilla, 1999, p. 79.

7.   Escobar, 1999, p.90.

8.   Escobar, 1999, p.35.

9.   Costas, O., "La vida en el Espíritu". *Boletín Teológico*, June 1986, p.17.

10.   In the last two decades in social and political situations of terrorist violence and indiscriminate repression of the forces of order, sectors of the Peruvian evangelical com-

munity have been discovering that defending human dignity is part of the integral mission of the church and constitutes a legitimate way of living in the Spirit. They have been discovering also that historically during the dismantling of democratic legality, as occurred during the dictatorship of Alberto Fujimori (1992-2000), the defence of the rule of law represented a way of giving testimony to its love for life. The same can be said with respect to the ever increasingly visible presence of evangelical women who, inserted into social movements organised during the last two decades in the Peruvian context, fought from day to day together with women from other religious persuasions against poverty and the lack of opportunities in a class society which had condemned the poor to the midden of history. (Lopez 1998; Lopez 2008a)

11.   Escobar, 1999, p.10.

12.   López, D., Los evangélicos y los derechos humanos: la experiencia social del Concilio Nacional Evangélico del Perú 1980-1992. (Lima: CEMAA, 1998); "Construyendo un Nuevo rostro público: Evangélicos y violencia política 1980-1995". In Fernando Armas, Carlos Aburto, Juan Fonseca, José Ragas, eds. *Políticas divinas: Religión, diversidad y política en el Perú Contemporáneo*. Lima: Instituto Riva Agüero-Pontificia Universidad Católica del Perú, 2008, pp.347-373.

13.   Comisión de la Verdad y Reconciliación, *Informe Final, Tomo III. Primera parte: El proceso, los hechos, las víctimas*. Lima: Comisión de la Verdad y Reconciliación, 2003, pp.379-477.

14.   Comisión de la Verdad y Reconciliación, *Informe Final, Tomo I. Primera Parte: El proceso, los hechos, las víctimas*. Lima: Comisión de la Verdad y Reconciliación, 2003, p.31.

15.   Paz y Esperanza, *"Evangélicos asesinados: Cuadros estadísticos al 31 de diciembre de 1992"*. unpublished paper, 1993, p.1.

16.   López, *Los evangélicos y los derechos humanos*.

17.   López, D., "Just Wealth: How Is the Poverty of the Poor in the Global South a Matter of Justice for the Rich in the Global North". In Brian McLaren, Elisa Padilla and Ashley Bunting, eds. *The Justice Project*, Grand Rapid: Baker Books, 2009, p.151.

18.   López, *The Liberating Mission of Jesus*, p.28

19.   López, D., "Evangelicals and Politics in Fujimori´s Peru". In Paul Freston, ed. *Evangelical Christianity and Democracy in Latin America*, Oxford: Oxford University Press, 2008, pp.131-161.

Peace and Violence

The minority Christian experience in India

How do minorities get justice? Judging from this study of minority rights (or the lack of them) in contemporary India, the answer seems to be–with great difficulty! Here Dr John Dayal details the way that justice for minorities, originally skilfully written into the Indian constitution, has become increasingly problematic.

The Asian Centre for Human Rights called it 'India's Christianophobia'. 'That secular India suffers from entrenched Christianophobia is well-established but not publicly acknowledged by the State and the society at large. Nothing reflects it more than the denial of reservations to the Dalits who converted into "Christianity" solely because of their religion', ACHR director Suhas Chakma said in a special report in January 2012. 'Dalits' is what the former untouchable Indian castes now call themselves in a militant rejection of the system crafted three centuries ago, and codified by Manu, the Hindu law giver.

Chakma noted that though the British ruled for 190 years from 1757 to 1947, they did not impose their religion as the previous rulers had done. No major group which had formal religions converted to Christianity. In North East India, which now has a large concentration of Christian populations, those who were practicing formal religions did not convert into Christianity. The tribal peoples like the Chakmas and Mogs who practiced Buddhism did not convert into Christianity, nor did the Tripuris and Manipuris who had been converted to the Vaishnavaite sect. Only the ethnic groups who had their local religions, usually referred to as 'animistic', converted into Christianity. This was also true of the Dalits across the country, and in large numbers especially in Andhra Pradesh and Tamil Nadu.

More than six decades after the people of India gave themselves a Constitution guaranteeing a 'secular' nation, with government equidistant from all established religions, Muslims and Christians and even Sikhs have arguably come face to face with a harsh reality—that India, despite its protestations of keeping equidistant from all religions, does after all have a state religion, even if by "default", and that that is Hinduism, the faith of the majority.

India, despite its protestations of keeping equidistant from all religions, does after all have a state religion.

According to the 2001 census India had at that time a population of 1.15 billion of which Hindus—including the former untouchable castes or Dalits—constitute 80.5 percent of the population, Muslims 13.4 percent, Christians 2.3 percent, and Sikhs 1.9 percent. Groups that constitute less than 1.1 percent of the population include Buddhists, Jains, Parsis (Zoroastrians), Jews, and Baha'is.

Despite the presence of approximately 150 million Muslims and 25 million Christians, the Hindu ethos and its political compulsions permeate every facet of life—governance, the justice-dispensation machinery, public institutions and economic and development processions. This is aggravated by an aggressive assertion of identities in the complex caste matrix, confined not just to Hinduism, but aggressively percolating to Christianity and Islam. The impact of a fast globalised economy on the lives of Tribals living in poverty in a land flush with mineral wealth, and an acceleration of large migrations to the six megalapolises of Delhi, Mumbai, Bengaluru, Hyderabad, Kolkata and Chennai, collectively become a short fuse to the powder keg of this nation of 1.2 billion people on the cusp of the second decade of the twenty-first century who see, but do not share in, the oil, land, and digital booms. The emergence of a powerful Maoist movement in a third of the Union's 35 States and central territories is the violent response to exploitation of resources by multinationals and the mass displacement of people by government acquisition of their homelands. Hate campaigns and mass violence against Muslims and Christians is the response of militant Hinduism against religious minorities seen variously as polluting 'Indic' purity or poaching on the margins of the majority faith.

The starkness of the poverty statistics and inequity is counterpoised tragically with the comparative figures of death and devastation of Muslims and Christians butchered in two major pogroms in the last ten years—in 2002 in Gujarat and more recently in 2008 in the Kandhamal district of Orissa—in a manifestation of cultural nationalism and xenophobia not seen since the bloodletting of the partition of India in 1947. The third set of statistics is the abysmal representation of the religious minorities in Parliament and legislative assemblies, in the higher echelons of the bureaucracy and the police, and most tellingly, on the benches of the

Supreme Court, the High Courts and the District and Sessions Courts, where criminal justice is dispensed.

The Indian government is always shy of revealing the extent of inter-religious violence, and it takes much goading to come anywhere near the truth. Official figures are typically half or a third of those spoken of by the victims' communities or human rights organisations such as the United States Commission for International Religious Freedom, Christian Solidarity Worldwide, the UN Special Rapporteur and Amnesty International. In a rare answer in the Upper House of Parliament, the Rajya Sabha, India's junior minister for home affairs, Ajay Maken noted that there were at least 3,800 communal clashes reported in India between 2004 and 2008, marking a steady rise over the years. The highest incidence of such violence in 2008 was reported from the eastern state of Orissa with 180 incidents, all against Christians, followed by the north-central state of Madhya Pradesh with 131, Uttar Pradesh state in the north with 114, western Maharashtra with 109 and Karnataka in the south with 108, half of them against Christians and the rest against Muslims. The Ministry of Home Affairs, whose reports are contested by minority communities for blatant under-recording, has been quoted by USCIRF in its Annual Report for 2009-10 as admitting to 826 communal incidents in India in 2009, in which 125 persons died and 2,424 were injured. compared to 943 incidents in 2008 in which 167 persons died across the country. The government recorded 76 incidents of Hindu-Christian violence in 2009, which resulted in two deaths and 44 injuries, compared to 44 deaths and 82 injuries in 2008. The Ministry of Minority Affairs informed the parliament that the National Commission for Minorities received 2,250 complaints in 2008-09. The Muslim community submitted the most complaints.

Gujarat's anti-Muslim violence in February-March 2002 shocked the nation and the world. The President and the prime minister called it a blot on the cultural traditions of India. The government took more than three years to reveal its figures, sanitised figures as most activists said immediately. The federal or Union government told Parliament that 790 Muslims and 254 Hindus were killed, 223 more people reported missing and another 2,500 injured. More than 100,000 people fled their homes. Human rights groups feared the toll to be as high as 2,000 Muslims killed. The National Human Rights Commission (NHRC), an official body, found evidence of premeditation in the killings by members of extremist groups espousing Hindu nationalism, commonly recognised

> *Gujarat's anti-Muslim violence in February-March 2002 shocked the nation and the world.*

as the Rashtriya Swayamsewak Sangh and its spawn, going by the names of Vanvasi Kalyan Ashram, Vishwa Hindu Parishad and Bajrang Dal with a large dose of complicity by the State political and administrative apparatus, headed by chief minister Narendra Modi. Many police officers were named in subsequent enquiry commissions for their role in the violence sparked by a fire on a train at the Godhra railway in Gujarat on 27 February 2002 in which 59 Hindu pilgrims perished. Recently, a police officer said the Gujarat government had authorised the killing of Muslims after the riots, a charge the state government denies. This violence was marked by extraordinary barbarity, especially violence against women. The Supreme Court and special investigative teams are still investigating allegations of mass rape of women, including genital mutilation, the tearing out of foetuses from pregnant women's bellies, and the burning alive of entire families in their homes. Among the victims was a former Member of Parliament, a Muslim, who was burned alive. Another feature of the violence was the deliberate attempt to economically disempower the Muslim community. Their businesses, big and small, were meticulously targeted for arson, as were 523 places of worship, 298 dargahs, 205 mosques, and 3 churches where Muslims had sought to take shelter. Preventive arrests of 17,947 Hindus and 3,616 Muslims were made. It is interesting to note that barring the occasional incident of retaliation, the Muslims were the overwhelming target of the riots, and yet in the arrests, while 27,901 Hindus were arrested, so were as many as 7,651 Muslims. In firing by the police, again, Muslims were the apparent target–93 Muslims were killed as well as about 75 Hindus.

Human Rights Watch criticized the Indian government for its failure to address the resulting humanitarian condition of the people, the 'overwhelming majority of them Muslim', who fled their homes for relief camps in the aftermath of the events; as well as the Gujarat state administration for engaging in a cover-up of the state's role in the massacres. The violence spread to 151 towns and 993 villages in fifteen of the state's 25 districts as it raged unchecked between February 28 and March 3, and after a drop, restarted on March 15, continuing sporadically till mid June.

The violence in Orissa between 23 August and 1 October 2008 was comparatively on a much smaller scale, but was historically unique in being targeted against Christians. It differed from earlier anti-Christian violence in its intensity and stark severity, sharing with Gujarat aspects of government complicity and an apparent free hand to the Sangh Parivar (the family of organisations of Hindu nationalists) consisting of the Bajrang Dal and the Vishwa Hindu Parishad. For almost a month and a half, the district of Kandhamal, on a plateau in the midst of the state of Orissa, was out of bounds, even to the government's troops, while the killer gangs roamed the countryside, killing perhaps as many as a hundred people—the government acknowledges 37 deaths—burning down 5,500 houses in 300 villages, destroying 296 big and small churches, and forcing as many as 55,000 people to flee their houses. The National People's Tribunal on Kandhamal, chaired by retired Delhi high court chief justice A.P. Shah in its 2010 report noted that two years later, thousands of people had still not come back to their homes. They had been barred from their villages by the Hindutva gangs which openly declared that they would allow the Christians to return only on the condition they gave up their faith and converted to Hinduism. Vishwa Hindu Parishad leader Dr Praveen Togadia, held by Christians to be the mastermind behind the pogrom, openly declared that people (Christian missionaries and clergy) who were responsible for proselytising the Tribals in the first place ought to be beheaded.

The government has continued to look on rather helplessly, as is evident to human rights activists and the international media. The two fast track courts have meted out a senseless justice in which the killers have been let off in most of the cases because the killers have successfully forced all eyewitnesses to their crimes to renege in court. In over 30 murder cases tried in the fast track courts up to the end of 2012, not one person has been convicted for murder. Orissa chief minister Naveen Patnaik, who was in a coalition with the Bharatiya Janata party during the violence, and returned to power after severing relations with that party, told the state legislature that the attacks were mainly led by right-wing outfits such as the Vishwa Hindu Parishad and its youth wing Bajrang Dal. The chief minister's indictment of the organisations connected with his former political allies is the first such confirmation of the involvement of these hyper-nationalistic groups in violence against religious minorities.

Hinduism has changed, and with it civil society too

India's main religious minorities, the Muslims, Christians and Sikhs, have noted changes in Hinduism since Partition 1947, both in an evolving theological sense, and in terms of popular religious culture. With it has changed, in a more subtle manner, the mind-set of the 200 million middle class. Many civil and democratic structures, along with the courts' interpretation of laws, reflect this change in a subtle but visible manner, as do the bureaucracy and police, now heavily penetrated by the Sangh Parivar, as jurist, something noted by A.G. Noorani in his perceptive book *The BJP and The RSS—A Division of Labour*. This has surprised no one. It was inevitable. The aftermath of the Emergency of 1975-79 imposed by Prime Minister Indira Gandhi, who suspended the Constitution and civil rights, gave a certain legitimacy to the Sangh Parivar whose leaders were jailed together with the leadership of the socialist and Marxist parties. The SITE [Satellite Instruction Television Experiment] in 1976 triggered and made possible a Hindu mass cultural and evangelistic mobilisation fifteen years later. The image of Indira Gandhi's dead body for example–she was assassinated by two Sikhs from among her bodyguards–is widely held to have goaded mobs who indulged in the mass violence against Sikhs for three days after her death on 31 October 1984. This violence once and for all shattered the long propagated Hindu myth that Sikhs were not a separate religion but a 'sword arm of Hinduism' meant to protect the Brahmin and the Holy Cow from Islamic aggressors. The last major Hindu aggressive evangelisation was BJP leader and RSS acolyte Lal Krishan Advani's infamous Rath Yatra which culminated in the demolition of the Babri Masjid on 6 December 1992. A string of bomb blasts followed in Mumbai–carried out by local Muslim youth, according to police, at the behest of West Asian based Indian Islamic mafia.

This has led to the classic contradiction of the average Hindu: villager, urban lumpenproletariat, middle class, even the billionaires of Indian Inc., feeling vulnerable and cornered. They are also becoming increasingly suspicious of religious minorities, particularly Muslims and Christians which are now branded even in academic circles as 'non-Indic' faith groups, a term unheard of before 1992. They are reluctant therefore to concede any further rights or favours to them. Cross-border terrorism, the rise of Al Qaeda, the unrelenting vicious circle of military and police atrocities, disobedience and mass secessionist violence in the Kashmir valley, all tend to reinforce the contemporary Hindu middle class and civil society stance against Islam and Muslims. And by extension it is carried over against Christians, whose tenuous linkages with the British Raj are periodically paraded under the sun in a name-and-shame exercise whenever there is a demand for more rights by that micro-minority. The Dalit assertion, and since the 1980s, the Other Backward Communities' rise to political power, has added further to the sense of deprivation and emasculation of the upper castes who, powerless before the more numerical OBC-Dalit combination in popular rhetoric and political mobilisation, have taken out their ire on Muslims and Christians. There is no surprise at a continuous assertion of majoritarianism, with any concessions given specially to Muslims being classified as minority 'appeasement' in a 'vote bank politics by the Congress'.

It is also clear that concepts of secularism have changed.

It is also clear that concepts of secularism have changed. The Supreme Court of India under Chief Justice

J.S. Verma said Hindutva (the movement commending Hindu nationalism) was a 'way of life' and could not be equated with 'narrow fundamentalist Hindu religious bigotry'. The Supreme Court's failing to, or refusing to, define religions, especially Hinduism and its differentiation from the ideological aspects of Hindutva has had deep implications. Structured institutions such as the subordinate courts and the National Commission for Minorities thereafter have not been able to reach conclusions on critical issues such as conversions, especially forced conversions to Hinduism of Adivasi-Tribals and marginalised Christians under the use of the ideology of *ghar wapsi*, or 'homecoming'. It is interesting to note that at the turn of 2009, one of the two major judicial issues before the nation were writs in the Supreme Court demanding that Dalit Christians and Muslims be restored the rights given to all scheduled castes irrespective of religion in the 1950 Constitution. This had been taken away by a Presidential order in 1950 which confined reservations and other affirmative action just to Hindus because of the unspoken fear that there would be large scale conversions to Christianity if Dalit Christians were given reservations in government jobs and educational institutions. High level commissions set up by the government, the last under former Chief Justice Rangnath Misra, have recommended that the Presidential order be rescinded, as it contravened the secular spirit of the Constitution by giving preferential treatment on the basis of religion just to Hindus, and later also to Sikhs and Buddhists.

The other of the two legal issues is the Decennial national census automatically classifying Tribals as Hindus even if they are professing other faiths such as nature worship. This had been objected to on the grounds that it denied Tribals their right to a religious identity, and that it inflated the census data in favour of Hinduism. Not surprisingly again, pro-Hindutva political groups are vehemently fighting against the demands of the Christians and the Muslims.

The million-death bloodletting of Partition had done two things. First, in the killing of Hindus and Sikhs in West Punjab and other provinces, it reinforced the popular image of a ruthless militant Islam at perpetual war with Hindu India. But of course it also fully exploded the carefully nurtured myth of a pacific Hinduism. It was quite clear in the killing fields of Bihar, Uttar Pradesh, Delhi and the then PEPSU-Punjab that when the religious madness took over, Hindus could kill with the best in the world. A dozen judicial enquiry commissions into communal riots since 1947, including the Sri Krishna Report on the Bombay riots and the several reports on the Guajarati carnage, have documented the nature of this violence in morbid narrative and macabre detail. It is a moot question if recent violence by Hindutva groups would have been possible if it were not that societal hesitations had been submerged in the violence and memories of 1947. It is not for nothing that even India, much less Pakistan, has been unable to dare set up a truth and reconciliation commission to go back and exorcise the ghosts of partition and its displacements and massacres. There is an argument that the RSS and its daughter groups would not been able to rise after 1977 in the manner in which they did if there had been a proper understanding between the communities on 1947 realities, the shared tragedy of the two communities, and therefore the possibility of co-existence in the short term and reconciliation in the long term. This failure of understanding means that Hindu-Muslim inter-community violence today is not only tolerated, it is expected.

This failure of understanding means that Hindu-Muslim inter-community violence today is not only tolerated, it is expected.

At the institutional level, this has been condoned, if not actually encouraged, by the absence of the Muslim community in particular in the police and judicial processes. Police officer V.N. Rai, now vice chancellor of a university, in his widely quoted thesis, documented the impact of such lop-sided community representation in the uniformed services. He has spoken of how Muslims are targeted even if they are not aggressors and how crime and punishment are grossly exaggerated in the case of minority communities. The current rash of custodial deaths and fake encounters is part of the same process, deserving a separate treatment of its own. Governments, irrespective of the political party in power, have deliberately not taken action, and when pressed by reports such as the Justice Sri Krishna Report on the 1992-93 violence in Mumbai, have chosen to put the document into cold storage, rather than evoke majority ire by punishing guilty policemen and politicians. The Supreme Court had to intervene aggressively to try to undo the gross miscarriage of justice in the criminal cases arising out of the massacre of Muslims in Gujarat in 2002, taking the trial of several celebrated cases out of the territorial jurisdiction of Gujarat. In other cases, they set up Special Investigating Teams under retired officers of the Central Bureau of Investigations to dig out the truth that had been carefully buried in a conspiracy involving the state government, the police, the political parties and even the subordinate courts.

Political aberrations, on their own, can perhaps be corrected through general elections, which have been almost always on schedule in India and reasonably without taint. But they cannot succeed on their own. There is a lack of public pressure from the massive middle class and more frighteningly, from those institutions called civil society. These include the Media, which while it helps by publicising transgressions, unfortunately is also guilty of demonising minorities. Also less helpful than they might be are the NGOs, which have increasingly been seen as mercenary and highly bureaucratic groups focussed on development issues rather than on human rights–barring such honourable exceptions as the People's Union for Civil Liberties, ANHAD, SAHMAT and some other human rights groups supported by Muslim and Christian religious entities.

The crisis in the middle class and civil society has been brilliantly articulated by political psychologist Ashish Nandy in his famous essay 'Obituary of a Culture', and by academics such as Shamsul Islam, Rononjen Roy, and others who have written extensively on militant Hinduism, even the militarisation of Hinduisation under such organisations as the RSS, the Bajrang Dal, the Shiv Sena and their regional equivalents. Nandy noted that the most venomous, brutal killings and atrocities take place when the two communities involved are not distant strangers, but close to each other culturally and socially, and when their lives intersect at many points. 'When nearness sours or explodes it releases strange, fearsome demons.'

> *The most venomous, brutal killings and atrocities take place when the two communities involved are not distant strangers, but close to each other.*

Gujarat had been leading up to such an exorcism for a very long time. It is a state that has seen thirty-three years of continuous rioting interrupted with periods of tense, uncomfortable peace. During these years, a sizeable section of Gujarat's urban underclass has begun to see communalism and rioting as means of livelihood, quick profit, choice entertainment, and as a way of life. The urban middle class in Gujarat is now the most communalised in the country; it has become an active abetter and motivator of communal violence. Sections of it participate in the looting enthusiastically, as we have seen in the course of the recent riots; those that do not, often participate in the violence vicariously. Nandy notes that a situation of civil war has arisen, because minorities now know that they cannot hope to have any protection from the state government. Lower-level functionaries of the state government have been complicit with rioters many times and in many states. But Gujarat 2002 was probably the first time after the anti-Sikh riots of 1984 that the entire state machinery, except for some courageous dissenters among the administrators and in the law-and-order machinery, has turned against the minorities. This, in more recent times, has been seen in such unlikely places as West Bengal and Kerala, both until recently ruled by the non-communalistic Left Front. Whereas in

Bengal, the land-based violent protests led to police atrocities against Muslim peasantry, in Kerala the talk of 'Love jihad', the so called luring of Hindu girls by Muslim youth and their subsequent conversion to Islam, was seen as a conspiracy not just by civil society but by mass-circulation media and the courts too.

Nandy and others raise the fear that minorities will now have to, 'for good or worse', prepare to protect themselves. His worst case scenario is that this is creating a new breeding ground for terrorism with, inevitably, the state crackdown and violence that follows. Most of us, however, join Nandy in noting that 'almost nothing reveals the decline and degeneration of Gujarati middle class culture more than its present Chief Minister, Narendra Modi. Not only has he shamelessly presided over the riots and acted as the chief patron of rioting gangs, the vulgarities of his utterances have been a slur on civilised public life'. It is, incidentally, a matter of record that the titans of Indian industry have lauded Modi as the best administrator they have ever seen, and his Gujarat the best place for economic growth.

Solutions and Structures

Sometime in 2000, this writer earned the dubious distinction of becoming the first Christian, or perhaps the first Indian, to give testimony on the welfare situation of Indian religious communities before the United States Commission on International Religious Freedom, an organisation under the US Department of State, and several other international Human Rights fora. This had become necessary in the wake of a spurt in anti-Christian violence between 1997-1999, culminating in the burning alive of Australian leprosy worker Graham Stuart Staines and his two sons, Timothy and Philip, in Orissa by a Bajrang Dal activist, Dara Singh. The testimony evoked a hostile reaction, not just from the government, but from right wing political parties. The first reaction was from the Bharatiya Janata party and the Media. The BJP and its chief office bearer of the time, Mr Venkkaiyya Naidu, held an official press conference at the party headquarters in New Delhi to demand official action against the writer whom he described as a traitor to Mother India and as a person who was spreading mischievous lies about the country. India Today, the leading newsmagazine of the time, and several daily newspapers took up the issue, and the BJP line. They interviewed prominent Congress Catholic leaders as well as the Church hierarchy. Mrs Margaret Alva, now governor of a state in North India and then a leading light of the Congress, went on record to denounce me and defend the Indian record on freedom of faith.

The Church felt itself cornered and took the easy way out, disowning the writer entirely.

Clearly, the Church and the so-called political leadership of the community had felt afraid even to admit to the violence against it. The only explanation of their behaviour is that they did not want to rock the boat. It had nothing to do with peace building, or even with the theology of forgiveness, made famous by the statement of Staines's widow who told television cameramen that she forgave Dara Singh, the killer of her husband and two sons. The established Church finds itself cornered, partly because of its need to protect the large number of educational and medical institutions it runs, which can be put under pressure either by the majority community or by the state apparatus, as Bishops have found in the past sixty years. This also is the reason why the Church has not been able to successfully articulate the development needs of the Christian community, and explains the many ways its progress has been hindered in the past years. In fact, there is no collective statement made by the Church impressing on the government the need to focus attention on the economic development of a micro-minority which has given to the nation so much in the important fields of education and medicare. The Church has had no success in articulating the crisis in tribal areas where the implementation of the Forest Act in an arbitrary manner and several other administrative actions, have led to large scale deprivation, alienation of land, and mass migrations. It has been most reluctantly that some of the Church groups (but not all) have found the courage to support the cause of the Dalit Christians seeking government reservations and other benefits given to Dalits of the Hindu, Sikh and Buddhist faiths. This creates a major crisis—the Christian legislators are silent because they have not been elected by a Christian constituency, and the disunited Church finds itself powerless and therefore unwilling to take up issues and rake up controversies. The collective structural silence is deafening.

> *The Church has not been able to successfully articulate the development needs of the Christian community.*

The development crisis in the Muslim population has been now tabulated by government agencies, including the Justice Rajender Sachhar Committee set up by the Prime Minister, Dr Manmohan Singh, and the National Commission for Religious and Linguistic Minorities headed by Justice Rangnath Misra. Their reports were made public towards the end of 2009. They have comprehensively shown the developmental stress upon the Muslim community and the problems they have as citizens of India to get their rights in such critical areas as education, employment and professions. Slowly, but certainly, the Muslim leadership and intelligentsia, showing a much more united face than has been shown by their counterparts in the Christian community, have been trying to mobilise public opinion by organising massive rallies under the patronage of organisations such as the Jamiat-e-ulema Hind and the Jamat-e-Islami.

A small group of Christians has been trying to rouse the Planning Commission of India and the national government on these issues, with very mixed results. The Planning Commission allocates funds and sets yardsticks for the allocation of government resources to various segments of society in the states, and the Christian community fears it has not been given a fair hearing. Some issues are singular to them, because of demographic dispersal and disempowerment in some spheres, especially those concerning Dalit Christians. Some issues concern them more than others, because of their historic commitment and presence in the areas of Education, Medicare and social work among the marginalised and the poor. Other issues have been generated because of the fact that even among minorities, governmental action and proactive developmental activity has been uneven. Compared to other minorities—the Muslims are five times as many, and the Sikhs, for instance, are concentrated in Punjab and therefore exercise considerable political power at the national level—Christians have been on the margins of political consciousness of the governments in power over the decades, and especially in recent years.

Test surveys by the All India Catholic Union and the All India Christian Council show that the Christian community in reality lacks an upper middle class (except in Goa, Mumbai and Kerala), does not have an entrepreneurial class, and displays little self-employment amongst the youth, particularly among the Dalits and rural communities. There is vast under-employment amongst educated youth in urban areas. The National Minorities Development Finance Corporation has failed singularly in reversing poverty and unemployment. The Christian community has done no formal survey to gauge the social and economic infirmity of the people, and particularly of the youth, in the hinterland. Christians have allowed the growth of myths about their economic status based on the images of a few well off people from Goa, Bombay, Kerala or the metropolitan areas of Delhi and Calcutta. The vast majority of Christians amongst the Dalits in Tamil Nadu and Andhra, the tribals in Central and East India, and the Dalits and others in the Punjab and Uttar Pradesh are amongst the most economically deprived.

So many decades after Independence in 1947 the security of religious minorities remains a dominant issue.

The twenty-first century is no longer new, but so many decades after Independence in 1947, and the promulgation of the Constitution in 1950, the security of religious minorities remains a dominant issue. The Christian community had felt itself very safe in India in the formative years of the democracy under Jawaharlal Nehru, and then under the premierships of Lal Bahadur Shashtri, Indira Gandhi and Rajiv Gandhi. But after a spurt of violence in 1998-1999, hate crimes against the Church and the Christian community have been increasing alarmingly since 1997, averaging about 250 incidents a year. But 2007 and 2008 have seen such violence reach an unprecedented level. The violence has not been confined to Orissa. Fourteen other States were affected, seven seriously. Karnataka is now second only to Orissa in crimes against Christians. Battalions of Central forces are needed to maintain peace, and yet a sense of deep insecurity still permeates the community. The situation in Chhattisgarh is also getting out of hand, very rapidly. The Catholic Union and the Christian Council, which are the two vocal community groups active in human rights, have called on the Union Government that it must carry out a full investigation into the nationwide activities of extremist groups accused of the incitement and perpetration of violence against minority groups. This investigation must include Hindutva groups, their foreign finances, and their penetration into the administrative and police apparatus. The situation in Orissa particularly brings urgency to the demand for the enforcement of the rule of law, the ending of the way that state, the police and the criminal justice dispensation system disregard the need to assure freedom of faith. In state after state, the community has watched in utter helplessness as uniformed policemen accompany assailants attacking institutions, churches and house churches. In States such as Manipur, whole villages have even dared to pass laws against Christians, banning conversions and excommunicating people. Pastors and priests have been arrested on false charges, denied bail, and harassed. Often, the police have stood by while priests, pastors and lay persons were beaten up, often in the glare of television cameras. The subordinate magistracy and judiciary have often been partisan in their conduct. This situation must end.

The government did try to bring in a Prevention of Communal Violence Bill in 2005. The Bill was shot down by the Muslim intelligentsia who correctly maintained that it empowered not the victim but the state, and could lead to an absolute miscarriage of justice. The Christian community was entirely ignored in the draft bill, and it is now insisting that government take cognisance of its concerns and apprehensions. Rehabilitation of victims of religious-based violence seems to have been left to the Church whereas it should be for the governments to reconstruct damaged and destroyed homes, institutions and Churches, and provide adequate and commensurate compensation to the victims. These would be a deterrent, in fact, to violence against the community. The national Advisory Committee of the government, under the chairmanship of Mrs Sonia Gandhi, helped draft an improved Bill against communal and targeted violence with rehabilitation and reparations measures. But this Bill has been shot down by the BJP as being anti-Hindu. It remains to be seen if the government will have the courage to introduce it in Parliament.

It is only now that the Christian community, again through the AICC and the AICU, has started seeking redress for the economic deprivation and to make possible reversal of unemployment and under-employment amongst Christian youth, stressing the need for a National Commission on the lines of the Justice Rajender Sachhar Commission set up for Muslims. This would survey and assess the quantum of deprivation, marginalisation and lack of devolution of developmental initiatives suffered by the Christian community. There is over eight per cent joblessness among Christian youth, the highest among minorities. Tribal Christian girls are amongst the most deprived in terms of education and nourishment. Rural employment generation schemes and central special components for marginalised groups do not reach their Christian counterparts in Tribal and rural India. There is no real assessment as to what extent institutions such as the National Minorities Financial Development Corporation, or sundry scholarship schemes have benefitted the Christian community even if they may have benefited some other minorities. Government is at last under some pressure to ensure fair spending on a pro rata basis on the Christian community from schemes meant to benefit the minority communities. However, Dalits, Tribals, landless labour and marginal farmers, coastal and fishery workers and urban youth remain major victims.

The legal and academic fraternity have focussed little on the erosion of minority rights under Article 30 (the right of minorities to run their own educational institutions). Various state governments and political parties have tried to infringe upon Article 30, and have made persistent efforts to erode the rights of minorities to run and administer educational institutions. Christian educational institutions have frequently had to approach the Supreme Court of India to try to protect these fundamental rights. The ironically titled Freedom of Religion Bills actually erode the constitutional right to freedom to profess, practice and propagate faith. They have become instruments of persecution, and in fact, provide an excuse for criminal and communal elements to target the Church and Christian workers in particular when they exercise their right to propagate their faith. The community is now demanding that Government must assure there will be no effort in the future to infringe upon, erode, or nibble at minority educational and other constitutional rights under any pretext. Activists are also pointing to the shrinking of what they describe as the 'Secular-Spiritual Space'. State and city administrations are auctioning land for schools and hospitals in the open market at commercial rates. The result is that the church and voluntary sector can no longer get legal possession of low-cost land for providing educational and health facilities to the marginalised groups at affordable prices. In addition, new townships and urban spaces, most of them now in the private sector, do not provide for simple and basic secular spaces, including plots of land for churches and cemeteries. In many new urban conglomerates in the emerging landscape, there is, in fact, no provision for cemeteries at all. In the light of past experience, the community response to the government's proposal to bring forward a bill for an Equal Opportunity commission has been met by some anxiety. The existing institutions such as the national Human Rights commission and the National Commission for Minorities have been seen as not really helping the people, and yet another central body created without community participation can hardly be expected to invoke confidence.

In an overview, it is quite clear that an environment of suspicion marks the relationship between the federal and provincial governments and their institutions and agencies on the one hand, and the two major religious minorities, the Muslims and the Christians. It is not surprising that they see a conspiracy in every new move.

But the union and state governments show no political will to withdraw controversial legislations that seriously warp the freedom of faith guarantees in the Constitution. These include the Foreign Contribution Regulation Act (FCRA) which strangulates international financial support to the non-governmental sector, including Christian institutions, and the many so called 'freedom of religion' bills in Gujarat, Orissa, Chhattisgarh, Arunachal Pradesh, Madhya Pradesh, and Himachal Pradesh. In August 2009 the regulations for enforcing the Arunachal Pradesh laws were adopted. Gujarat has a Freedom of Religion Act (2003) and Rules (2008) which proscribes religious conversions by means of allurement, force, or fraud, a clause which effectively bans conversions to Christianity while allowing conversions to Hinduism. Other laws that militate against the spirit of freedom of faith include the Andhra Pradesh anti-propagation law, the 1967 Unlawful Activities Prevention Act, the 1988 Religious Institutions (Prevention of Misuse) Act, the 1946 Foreigners Act, and the 1869 Indian Divorce Act.

The 2007 Andhra Pradesh law, called the 'Propagation of Other Religions in the Places of Worship or Prayer (Prohibition) Law' is intriguing as it effectively bans Christian or Islamic religious activity in a range of hills where a major Hindu temple is situated. Punishment for violations of the act can include imprisonment up to three years and fines up to 5,312 Rupees. Madhya Pradesh, Rajasthan, Uttar Pradesh, and West Bengal have laws regulating the construction of public religious buildings and the use of public places for religious purposes.

The Supreme Court of India has become the court of last appeal for Muslims and Christians to challenge the union and state governments on many of these laws as the legislative process and civic forums are almost entirely monopolised by the majority community, which also has an absolute access to the police and subordinate judicial apparatus. The numbers of Muslims in the Police and civil cadres, and in state legislatures, is abysmally small. And as the communities have discovered to their shock after years of advocacy, the future seems to be also without redemption.

Dr John Dayal is one of India's foremost voices on human rights, and particularly the situation of religious minorities, having been a writer and activist for the past four decades. He is a member of several governmental bodies, including the National Integration Council, and holds senior roles in numerous non-governmental organisations and networks, including as co-founder and Secretary General of the All India Christian Council, and a member of the Justice and Peace Commission of the Catholic Bishops' Conference. He has had a long and distinguished career in the media and in academia. He has authored and contributed to several books, and regularly writes articles on human rights issues in India. He has a long record of investigating and producing substantive and influential documentation on communal violence in India, including Hindu-Muslim rioting and violence against Sikhs, Muslims and Christians. He is one of India's leading experts on the situation in Orissa state, following the communal violence in 2008.

Migrants, Justice and Border Lives

*Migrants suffer not only the trauma of physical displacement, but often the unseen effects of psychological and emotional pain, particularly when forced from homes and communities because of acute poverty and conflict. A growing trend, and a significant issue for the coming decades, will be forced migration resulting from the negative effects of environmental degradation arising from human-induced climactic change. **Andy Kingston-Smith** invites us to consider compassionate and just responses through the mission of the Christian community, both locally and globally.*

The shifting sands of time

People are on the move; they always have been and they always will be. Historical studies testify to this reality, to a greater or lesser extent. If migration is nothing new, is there anything significant we can deduce from contemporary patterns of people-movement, and, indeed, from future projections for the remainder of this century? An important question is to consider the implications of such people movement, both on the migrant, and his/her family and on society, local and global. In an increasingly overcrowded and urbanised world the sheer physical movement of people directly impinges on and affects global society in new and in, perhaps, more intense ways than

> *In an increasingly overcrowded and urbanised world the sheer physical movement of people affects global society in new and more intense ways.*

ever before. Thanks to globalisation and phenomena such as the 'butterfly effect', the repercussions of such movement resound in deeper and wider ways. So an occurrence at a local level ripples out like waves, and has unforeseeable consequences elsewhere. Such waves are often invisible until they are manifest on a distant shore. An absolutely vital aspect of these shifts is to consider how the Christian community, and the church at large, should respond and offer understanding, empathy and solidarity. This then should lead to advocating on behalf of those who have no voice, and challenging the injustices that often accompany this dynamic.

Whilst humans have always moved in search of shelter and food to sustain the lives of immediate family, recent history, not least in the West, has been marked by increasing settledness; settledness that derives from the comfort and security that post-Enlightenment living has increasingly provided us. Our lives are more protected from and less affected (at least directly) by the forces of nature than ever before. Our engineering, farming practices, sophisticated economic and financial structures and governing arrangements provided greater order during the passage of the 18th and 19th centuries. However, economic depressions, two major (and countless other) world wars, increased resource depletion, human population growth and inequality patterns have cast a shadow on Enlightenment optimism.

By the 20th Century nature, no longer needed to be conquered. At last we were 'masters of our own destiny'; at least that is how we often thought. Manuel Castells, the Spanish sociologist, in his outstanding work *The Network Society*,[1] distinguishes between two great historical ages and the movement into a third one. Castells argues that the 'first model of relationship between [nature and culture] was characterised for millennia by the domination of nature over culture', so that human existence was characterised by 'the struggle for survival under the uncontrolled harshness of nature'. The shift in the modern era since the beginnings of the Enlightenment period in the 17th Century and the triumph of reason, subsequently more concretely evidenced in the Industrial Revolution 'saw the domination of nature by culture, making society out of the process of work by which humankind found both its liberation from natural forces and its submission to its own abysses of oppression and exploitation'.

This exploitation was often marked by people movement, be it transatlantic slaves from the West coast of Africa to the banana plantations of the Caribbean, or the numerically lesser but hugely powerful movement of imperialists and colonisers establishing Western political domination over much of the 'uncivilised world'. Castells, however, concludes by asserting that humanity has moved into a third age, the Information Age, 'marked by autonomy of culture *vis-à-vis* the material bases of our existence'. We can quite clearly see the explosion of the technological age all around us now. However, in our scramble for the latest iPad incarnation or smartphone handset, are we merely repeating the insatiable appetite for consumption of the early imperialists? Again, our feasting on rare and precious minerals that make up the complex components in such devices is driven by slave labour within the heart of Africa. Castells is right to say that arriving at the Information Age 'is not necessar-

In our scramble for the latest iPad incarnation or smartphone handset, are we merely repeating the insatiable appetite for consumption of the early imperialists?

ily an exhilarating moment'. Rather poignantly he muses that, 'alone at last in our human world, we shall have to look at ourselves in the mirror of historical reality'. If the Information Age teaches us one thing, it is that it is increasingly difficult to hide behind the veil of ignorance. Our actions and inactions hold us to account, not only to those around us but to the rest of humanity in starkly visible ways. The global village has truly arrived, and as Castells chillingly warns, having stared into that mirror of historical reality 'we may not like the vision.'

Social and environmental 'tectonic-plates' are shifting; increasing environmental disturbance suggests that nature is fighting back, but this time there are billions more humans on the receiving end. The next decades will surely be marked by increasing vulnerability and insecurity for humanity and this will have profound effects not only on the comforts we have been used to, but will inevitably lead to sharper polarisations in many aspects of economic, social and environmental justice. Increased elitism at the sharp end of the wealth/poverty inequality gap and, more radically still, studies predicting increasing divisions in the human race, point to some of the major human challenges that lie ahead.

This chapter will consider a few implications that flow from the questions raised above, noting too the increasingly powerful effects that climate change and forced migration will have on human dignity and consciousness, and the thriving or otherwise of inter-personal relationships. I would like to pose the following: what kind of Christian community do we need to be, not only now, but in 50 years from now? How will this community respond to the rapid changes (many of which will have serious implications for a major part of the wider global community) anticipated in our economic, social and cultural relations?

It is time to re-consider that age-old question, 'who is my neighbour?', as we seek to be salt and light in the days ahead. In particular, what lessons can we deduce from re-appraising kingdom values in the light of such issues and how might we encourage fresh carnivalesque approaches to human existence; ones that affirm life and 'life in all its fullness'?

Migrant realities

Much recent migration has been increasingly forced by shifts in economic and labour patterns. The decades after WWII saw hundreds of thousands of immigrants arrive in the UK. Colonial ties provided ready access for Caribbean immigrants offering their services to help reconstruct the physical devastation resulting from war, and this initial wave was followed by a further significant influx of immigrants from India and Pakistan.

Jehu Hanciles in his fascinating article, *Migration and Mission: Some Implications*[2] plots the historical movements of people and posits a number of challenges for the Christian Church in its mission. He cites an article from *The Economist* in 2002, *The Longest Journey: A Survey of Migration* [3] which estimated the number of migrants (defined as people who have spent one or more years outside their homeland) at 150 million worldwide. That number has, undoubtedly, increased significantly in recent years, bolstered by the growing tide of environmental refugees.

Moving from one location to another is deeply dislocating, and not just in practical terms. Salman Rushdie recounts how such dislocation plays tricks on the mind, both positive and negative. In his essay, *Imaginary Homelands*, Rushdie explores the disjunction between his early childhood in Bombay and his youth at Rugby school and Cambridge University, together with later adult years living in London. One of his motivations for writing the novel *Midnight's Children* was an attempt to reconcile these very different worlds; not an unusual exercise for others with similar experiences. However, his attempt to 'return home' to the childhood of Bombay depicted in the old black and white photo in his study, proved impossible, as this 'disjunction between past and present, between here and there, made 'home' seem far-removed in time and space, available for return only through an act of imagination'.[4] It was not always possible to simply go back to that life, for 'home becomes an especially unstable and unpredictable mental construct built from the incomplete odds and ends of memory that survive from the past.'[5] Rushdie's remarks that memories of his Bombay childhood could only be recalled as 'fragmentary, partial memories, often of small mundane occurrences' remind us that life and our 'truths' are, not only highly subjective, but partial, incomplete and often confusing. 1 Corinthians 13:12 tells us (at the risk of misapplying the original context) that, 'now we see only a reflection as in a mirror; then we shall see face to face. Now I know in part; then I shall know fully, even as I am fully known.' No view of life is complete.

This is similar to the Kingdom portrayal of the 'now' but 'not yet' tension that we live in today. Maybe the migrant experience of seeing life in such fragmentary forms actually reveals a dimension that more static experiences have missed. If so, the 'truths' discovered by such boundary-crossers ought to be taken more seriously and in turn become not only a tool of empowerment for the migrant but educational wisdom for the rest of us. Whilst Rushdie's reflections were made 'in broken mirrors, some of whose fragments have been irretrievably lost', nevertheless such acknowledgement is in itself profound and enlightening, and adds a few more colors to the kaleidoscope of human experience. In learning to 'reflect reality in "broken mirrors", the migrant comes to treasure a partial, plural view of the world [precisely] because it reveals all representations of the world as incomplete.'[6]

> *In learning to 'reflect reality in "broken mirrors", the migrant comes to treasure a partial, plural view of the world.*

One of the deepest repercussions for the migrant is the vulnerability that results from foraging away from the 'comforts' and 'security' of home. Of course, many come from situations that may hardly be described as comfortable or secure. The story of the Israelites coming out of Egypt cautions us that sometimes the vulnerable prefer to go back to situations of injustice and oppression[7] because at least they know what it is; 'better the devil you know...', as we might say. It seems amazing that they should hanker after an oppressed past, in favour of an unknowable, yet potentially freeing future. In reality, the migrant's sojourn may often possess features of a desert experience; the milk and honey land of 'plenty' may conversely become a place of 'drought'. Spiritual and emotional decay and even death may result from the dislocation resulting from an unfamiliar experience. Hope is a strong driver, and rightly so, yet how often do we hear of tragic stories where such hope is ill-conceived and leads to disaster.

I was deeply struck by the recent story of the migrant who fell to his death from the landing gear of an airplane coming into land at Heathrow airport in London.[8] His story is not unusual but what was shocking was the almost certain death he had been willing to trade in for the extremely slim chance (only 24% survival rate according to 96 recorded cases) of a better life. There are justice issues in both the 'push' and 'pull' factors at play in such cases and these are strong enough to lead to extreme risk-taking. Deborah Harris, chief operating officer at the Refugee Council remarked that, 'in conflict situations, people often have to leave their homes at very short notice, and may have no access to money or belongings so are forced to take desperate measures to escape.' Jon Kelly added in his BBC article that 'it's hard to imagine [that] even the most afflicted migrant would undertake a journey that was almost certain to lead to their death. It's easy to assume that ignorance of the sheer level of risk is what leads the stowaways to press ahead.' The reality of life is so grim for many that the opportunity to seek refuge or asylum proves irresistible. This is very much the dark side of the migration phenomenon. Whilst thousands of people daily complete 'safe' passage into a new chapter of their lives, for many this is not the case, for the journey remains highly risky. We regularly hear of drownings from capsized boats and stowaways suffocating in freight lorries. Leaving aside the physical dangers, the psychological and emotional damage of crossing borders is often not understood by the migrant. Such ignorance is compounded by the lack of compassion and understanding afforded by locals 'welcoming' the stranger in.

This 'us' and 'them' concept remains prominent in human consciousness despite claims to the contrary in the name of 'integration' and 'multiculturalism'. It is the suspicion of 'the other', such a powerful tool in the propaganda wars of dominant ideologies, that discourses from the margins seek to address and critique. The dislocation resulting from a person moving away from their home often brings powerlessness, ignorance and confusion, and yet aren't these some of the very concepts that Jesus sought to address in his rebuke of the Pharisees' treatment of ordinary Jews? Such a state of vulnerability seems to 'invite' callousness and abuse and reveals the evil which continues to grip the human heart. Modern-day trafficking is rife with the preying on the vulnerable by the powerful; it is a power-imbalance fuelled by lust and the love of money. It is clear that Jesus' teaching 2,000 years ago remains as apt and relevant today as it did then.

Migrant issues: the power of connectivity and the network

Issues of identity, purpose, meaning and, ultimately, 'reality' are never far from postcolonial discourse and subaltern studies. There exists a dichotomy between the pain of present-day experience and the virtual nature of the sanitised computer-generated 'dream-world' of the future; an ideological smorgasbord of notions flowing across boundaries and subject to the flows of the 'switch-holders'. Castells describes these 'switch-holders' as power-brokers; those with powerful financial and political interests, often voices in the media world, or in dominant and relatively unaccountable corporations.[9] They are seemingly able to dictate to government agents, and their decision-making powers and influence are usually way outside the control of the personal experience of the disempowered migrant; yet the domain of the migrant may be deeply affected by them. The migrant thus becomes a pawn in the machinations of such 'switch-holders' even to the point of being outside the direct protection of state legislation. Migrant workers often fall into this in-between state, where employment rights, for example, barely exist, if at all.

Power is 'diffused in global networks of wealth... information, and images, which circulate and transmute in a system of variable geometry and dematerialised geography'[10] and yet migrants are often not afforded equal access to the network. Castells summarises this new social order, which he calls the Network Society, in his concluding chapter, as 'an automated, random sequence of events, derived from the uncontrollable logic of markets, technology [and] geopolitical order...'[11] It is those on the margins of such society who experience those moments when the elastic of their identity eventually snaps, or the liquidity of their worth finally drains away.

This concept of connectivity is important. Our networked world requires us to be evermore connected if we are to climb the ladder of success. Such connectivity undoubtedly brings benefits, but what about those who simply cannot connect? The irony is that social media such as Twitter and Facebook have assumed great significance for the disempowered. They are not only able to find a voice but have also found innovative ways of joining their resources in resisting injustice through collective enterprise. The Arab Spring was unquestionably aided in its spread and achieved some modicum of success through the connectivity of ordinary people seeking just redress from oppressive regimes. Nevertheless, this tool also assumes significance for migrants seeking solidarity and support from each other when living in the midst of hostile environments. Olu Oguibe's brilliant article remains as true today as when he wrote it at the inception of the digital era. He argues that where influence increasingly resides in those who are not only connected, but have the power and means to control such connectivity, then those who remain outside such channels of influence and connection are marginalised further.[12] Even today we must remember that large swathes of humanity still remain unconnected to the World Wide Web.

The issue of migrant labour and the subjection of that to powerful 'switch-holders' may be illustrated by the experience of Indian and other migrants in the construction of the city of Dubai. One dimension worthy of discussion is the extent to which the liminal space (this will be considered further below) occupied by the many immigrant workers, acts as a catalyst in the search for spiritual answers to their predicaments. Was slavery in Egypt really better than the aimless wanderings in the Sinai desert where the promise of new beginnings tantalisingly remained just a mirage for a generation of Israelites? What is true freedom and how is it measured? There is a tangible conundrum facing those thousands of migrants lured by false promises and subjected to the harsh temperatures of the burning Gulf sun, whilst labouring to build towers befitting of Mammon's increasingly ambitious aspirations.[13] To encounter stories of spiritual quests and treasures uncovered, as documented in the Bible Society's summer 2009 publication, *Unburdening migrant hearts*, gives one hope to believe that God's plan remains at work during 'Egyptian captivity', as we know from the biblical accounts of the distant past.

Migrant issues: a lost past, a confusing present and a fearful future

Let's return to the theme considered earlier; the disjunction between past and present experience taken up by Rushdie (*Imaginary Homelands*) when speaking of Indian migrants. Rushdie considers that the 'physical alienation from India almost inevitably means that we will not be capable of reclaiming precisely the thing that was lost; we will...create fictions, not actual cities or villages, but invisible ones, imaginary homelands, Indias of the mind'.[14] Still there remain further concepts to explore, ones that help to illustrate the predicament of the migrant state, vulnerable to perpetrations of injustice.

This theme of 'imaginings' connects with the issue of 'borders'. Whilst migrants pass through the physical and political borders of the world, these borders will not be the last ones they face. The psychological and cultural borders of the nation-state will present migrants with challenges just as taxing. It is here that the culture of the 'new home' may forever be used to exclude migrants from being accommodated inside the borders of the nation. Paul Gilroy in his book, *The Black Atlantic*, articulates the theme of restless sojourning with the concept of 'roots' and 'routes'. The migrant does 'not have secure roots which fix him into place, in a nation or an ethnic group', but rather is orientated by 'itinerant cultural routes which take him, imaginatively as well as physically, to many places and into contact with many different peoples'.[15] This nomadic restlessness and cultural interaction through routes heightens the rootlessness of the migrants' physical and psychological state.

Homi Bhabha and Hanif Kureishi are two penetrating writers who have contributed to the discourse of the shadowy existence of the 'in-between' state. Kureishi's tale of confused relationships straddling his British and Pakistani identities in *My Beautiful Launderette*, demonstrates that the 'in-between' world of the migrant becomes the reality also for subsequent generations of migrants. The differentness of skin color runs more than skin-deep. It may be an indelible mark that can never be erased, a permanent reminder of not belonging to either world, but somewhere in between. Whilst there is the advantage of being able to relate to either or both (to some degree), the discrimination of the imaginative borders may preclude the migrant and his/her descendants from establishing roots. It places the migrants' sense of belonging into the 'hybrid community of the in-betweens' and this is what partly makes up the migrant identity.[16]

Bhabha, himself an Indian migrant from Bombay, who now resides in the US, having also spent time residing in the UK, expounds on this theme of 'borders' in his book, *The Location of Culture*. He critiques the broad sweep of time within which those who live 'border lives' find themselves as mere dots on the long line of history, "our existence today is marked by a tenebrous sense of survival, living on the 'border line' of the 'present', for which there seems to be no proper name other than the current and controversial shiftiness of the prefix 'post': postmodernism, postcolonialism, postfeminism..."[17] Bhabha's book is not an easy read, but patient consideration of his writing brings rich reward. What we might draw from this is that the 'in-betweenness' of the liminal space provides interesting and creative possibilities, whilst not forgetting that it also provides a shadowy space where the migrant's vulnerability is at risk from a myriad of injustices being perpetrated, as has been noted

The liminal space provides interesting and creative possibilities. It also provides a shadowy space where the migrant's vulnerability is at risk from a myriad of injustices.

previously. For example, the human trafficking industry thrives on just this vulnerability in its victimisation of millions worldwide.

This raises a significant premise. Do present times suggest that we all might identify with this sense of insecurity, of not quite knowing what is next? We have moved, Bhabha seems to suggest, from a 'post-' era into something 'beyond', perhaps a new 'pre-' or 'neo-' era. Have migratory mindsets now become universal and not merely owned by the more obviously displaced? Internal displacement characteristic of the post-modern suspicion of the grand meta-narrative leads us to deconstruct what we had previously built up, the unchanging fixed 'truths' of modernist and traditionalist agendas. Have we now entered a time of abandoning external reference points and taken on a more illusory undefined notion, that which lies on the new horizon of the 'beyond'? If this is the case, at least to some extent, then we have much to learn from the migrant's experience and consequent state of mind.

Furthermore, if Bhabha is correct in interpreting the present predicament, does this not provide a platform from which the upside-down values of the Kingdom may get not only a fresh hearing, but serious re-consideration as a narrative to be re-evaluated with the many other pseudo-ideological and religious narratives competing for the attention of the discerning reader? In essence, do we have enough confidence that the good news of the Christian narrative is sufficiently captivating by itself?

Bhabha's 'border' is the place of transitory crossing, the interstitial or liminal state, where polarity and binary opposites give way to 'shifting complex forms of representation that deny binary patterning', where past and present co-mingle and conflict, so that 'imaginative border-crossings are as much a consequence of migration as the physical crossing of borders'.[18] If we are to continue our premise that the postmodern hermeneutic is a present-day reality, might we surmise that an inherent internal displacement is also a symptom of an increasingly globalised existence? What we may say with some certainty is that the migrants' identity, resulting from paradoxical global experiences, is concretely uncertain, and therefore ours is unwittingly too. This revelation might help to act as a deterrent from becoming too full of ourselves and, one hopes, such humility might lead to the migrant being treated more sympathetically and compassionately. If we are able to stand in solidarity with the migrant, since our identities may have more in common than we might think, then we may more ably stand together in true friendship. The 'protection' this affords the migrant then becomes invaluable and allows for the dignity and rights of the migrant to be advocated for and upheld.

Climate-induced migration (CIM)

Having considered the psychological condition of the migrant, this might be a good time to earth our discussion. One area that has received little consideration within the Christian community is CIM. The relationship between economic and political factors in being drivers creating people-movement is well understood. However, the increasing media interest in global warming and climate change in general, coupled with the repercussions of intense disasters and other environmental fall-out resulting in increased suffering and forced migration, is becoming critical and needy of urgent attention. We shall now turn to consider issues of CIM before we consider how the Church needs to respond both now and in the coming decades, as CIM becomes an increasing global problem, and, significantly, no respecter of national boundaries. We will briefly dip into two recent examples from different corners of the globe.

Hurricane Katrina: shaking the American consciousness

It may be fair to say that the fallout of hurricane Katrina which struck New Orleans in late August 2005 was a pivotal moment in raising North American consciousness to the increasing intensity of the storms affecting the south coast of the US. It raised queries as to whether these were random occurrences or part of a trend deserving of deeper responsiveness. Of course, such storms were not new nor infrequent, but the sheer scale of the intensity and destruction of Katrina and the significant forced migration of the city's residents (some of whom eventually returned, but many of whom never did) left deep scars on the city's identity. The portrayal of Alvin in the film *Age of Stupid*[19] is profound. It was not simply a matter of the stark images of a deserted New Orleans, but the revelation and impact of Katrina's devastation on Alvin's understanding of how climactic events seem to be increasingly linked to pollution (CO_2 emissions) emanating from increased human activity. Alvin had been an oil driller with Shell (the BP disaster in the Gulf of Mexico struck shortly after the film was shot) and his candid admission of the exploitation and lack of environmental respect of his work carried the marks of tortured self-realisation.

A year after the hurricane struck, 100,000 citizens had relocated permanently to Houston bringing attendant financial and social strains to that city. However, the result for New Orleans was devastating. Not only a huge clean-up cost ensued, but social repercussions too; 'crime is resurgent, and New Orleans is now the deadliest city in the United States', wrote Donatien Garnier.[20] Scientific evidence demonstrates that Katrina is not likely to be a one-off, as she added, 'this incident convinced [Evangela and her family] that Katrina would most likely not be an isolated occurrence...and that it would now be impossible to return to a city as fragile as New Orleans.' 'Our confidence is gone' Evangela concluded, 'New Orleans has lost the confidence of its citizens.'

It is imperative to note that the above example took place in the US. This is especially so, as many experts warn us that it will be the poorer parts of the globe that will experience the toughest task of dealing with the future effects of climate change. The profundity of the disaster might not have had the global impact of the events of and following 9/11, but the potential paradigm-shift in American consciousness, certainly at a local level, if not nationally, cannot be underestimated. It makes us realise that no country on earth is, or ever will be, immune from having to deal with the increased displacement of humans resulting from the increasingly negative effects of climate change. This raises important justice issues, such as the allocation and distribution of economic resources, the social and psychological scars of forced displacement, and the likelihood of increased deprivation and resulting crime, to name but a few.

The melting of the snows: repercussions for the city of La Paz, Bolivia

Common phenomena being experienced around the world is that of melting glaciers and the accelerating melt of the Arctic, the Antarctic and Greenland's ice-sheet. Numerous scientific reports have publically revealed growing alarm within the scientific community. One of the obvious repercussions of ice-melt is rising sea-levels but there are also complicating factors that increased fresh-water chunks of ice create to long-established ocean currents with consequent repercussions for weather patterns. These events will clearly impact human existence and the settledness of living on coast lines and areas vulnerable to increasingly unpredictable weather. Warming of the seas releasing huge methane deposits and the realignment of the Gulf Stream are just two further examples of how Greenland's shrinking ice-sheet is already beginning to affect long-established eco-systems in the North Atlantic. The total melting of the Arctic in the summer months, now predicted in just a few short years, also raises the threat of international conflict over virgin resources and the opening of new trade routes.

However, there is a more immediate justice issue, one directly linked to the melting of mountain snows. The people of La Paz, Bolivia, have relied to a limited extent on the melting of the snows from the mountains that half-surround the city. This melt has helped to supply water to the three million inhabitants of La Paz and its neighbouring urban sprawl, El Alto. El Alto, now approaching two million inhabitants itself, is considered to be one of Latin America's fastest growing cities aided principally by the internal migration of local *Aymara* families looking for work and shelter to replace their previous subsistence way of life on their traditional lands, lands which are becoming increasingly barren and difficult to farm in a globalised economy. During the three years that we lived in La Paz, the shrinkage of the snow-line on Mount Illimani, despite an elevation of over 21,000 feet, was clearly visible to the naked eye. This was more graphically illustrated by the warming effects for the continuing viability of skiing at Chacaltaya, the world's highest ski resort at over 17,000 feet above sea level. I can distinctly remember standing on the only remaining patch of snow, a 200-metre run just a foot or two thick at best. The ski resort had ceased to function, of course, and all that was left was the Italian-made ski-lift, transported from the Alps decades earlier, and the collection of black and white photos of a by-gone era adorning the lodge. These photos depicted a time when the mountain truly resembled the Alps in the full-flush of the winter ski season. There is more than a passing resemblance with the nostalgic musings of Rushdie's historical Bombay.

El Alto's water problems were to become a battleground. Like the 'water wars' that hit Cochabamba, in central Bolivia in 2000-2002, the Government's plans to encourage the privatisation of the local water supply by engaging private French contractors met with huge resistance by local inhabitants. When local poor families are effectively forced to pay an average year's wage for the privilege of connecting to the mains water supply, then it is not surprising that issues of economic justice are inflamed. The question over whether free (or at least affordable) access to water is a fundamental right that such a community might demand from its Government remains open to debate. Such issues demonstrate the fragility of securing long-term water access. The threat of a dwindling supply from the mountains may have played a part in the implementation of ill-conceived 'quick-fix' solutions.

These brief examples illustrate the increasing competition for access to dwindling resources, and the pressures to migrate in search of a better life. Such searching is almost exclusively in the direction of the city where increased overcrowding leads to a plethora of tensions and strains. Jørgen Randers, in his enlightening book *2052—A Global Forecast for the next forty years* considers the migration to the city as an inevitable one-way flow, both now, and in the future, in a time of runaway climate change.[21] The city, in his view, will provide shelter from progressively hostile rural contexts where nature's 'revenge' will become ever more evident. He casts a vision of increased social challenge for huge numbers of humans living in tight communities, but his generally positive outlook nevertheless acknowledges the foreseeable problems that this particular scenario creates. A contributing article within Randers' work by Per Arild Garnasjordet and Lars Helm refers to the global scenario of 2052 as being one containing 'cities of gold' on a 'planet of slums'.[22] These economic inequalities of the future will fuel, amongst other challenges, increased inter-generational conflict. Our generation, and the ones before us, are leaving a planet with an ecological and economic burden that many of our children and grandchildren

> *O*ur generation, and the ones before us, are leaving a planet with an ecological and economic burden that...our children and grandchildren will find hard to accept.

will find hard to accept, and their anger is not likely to be left silent. We shall turn now to consider some responses from the Christian community.

Theological interpretations from the underside

The Catholic theologian Daniel Groody has articulated a response to the plight of migrants in his article, *Crossing the divide; foundations of a theology of migrants and refugees*.[23] The title, given the previous discussion, is illuminating in itself. He uses four concepts to re-conceptualise the difficult and contentious issue of migration in today's globalised world. In particular he considers migration to offer

> a rich hermeneutic for some of the most foundational dimensions of human existence and...a different vantage point for making moral choices; it illuminates the gift and demand of Christian faith in light of the pressing social problems of the modern world, and it opens up a space to bring out what is most human in a debate that often diminishes and dehumanizes those forcibly displaced.

The *imago Dei*, *verbum Dei*, *missio Dei*, and *visio Dei* are foundations of a larger theology of migration that form the basis of Groody's thesis. In articulating these theological constructs and seeking to interrelate the same to contemporary issues, he affirms the wider interdisciplinary task with which theology must engage not least in the area of the social sciences. No longer are issues of creation, incarnation, mission, God's justice and the reconciliation of all things (as culmination of the salvific vision and purposes of the Kingdom of God) merely to be debated, or to be construed and preserved within the narrow confines of the churches' theology and experience, but they need to re-assume great significance for the experience of those on the underside of life. Groody is clear what some of the goals of such a theology lead to:

> Migrants and refugees bring to the forefront of theological reflection the cry of the poor, and they challenge more sedentary forms of church in social locations of affluence and influence. The migrant reveals the paradoxical truth that the poor are not just passive recipients of charitable giving but bearers of the gospel that cannot be encountered except by moving out into places of risk and vulnerability (Matthew 25:31-46).

We can see that the reality of the world of the migrant is one where issues of (in)justice are never far away. Their condition might have been the result of a multiplicity of injustices committed at personal and/or structural levels, or if not, they are most likely to lead to that state, especially in the case of refugees and those forcibly displaced. Groody concludes by articulating his theology of migration in the context of mission being carried out within a disordered political economy: 'it seeks to foster human dignity in the poor and vulnerable, to challenge any structures and systems of society that divide and dehumanize, and to uplift all efforts to build a more just and humane world.' Such a theology of migration 'seeks to understand what it means to take on the mind and heart of Christ in light of the plight of today's migrants and refugees'. A key point is that the Christian community by virtue of its non-partisan identity is ideally placed to reduce the dividing space of 'no-man's land' and instead actively move into that liminal space that Bhabha invites us to, in order to meet the migrant there; a neutral space where there are no power-games, but rather a standing together. Not only that, but, as Bhabha argues, this is a creative space of possibility: in theological terms, this is a place where we might move away from rigid dogma, and re-encounter the crucified, resurrected, and ascended Christ in truly personal ways. This incarnational concept has been most powerfully provided by Christ himself. As true believers and disciples it provides us with the example to follow likewise.

Diasporic hermeneutics

Groody works closely with the Latino culture, and much of his study is embedded in the particular tensions of US/Mexico border-life. The lives of Latino immigrants have spawned numerous theological studies both from outside and, more critically, from within migrant and diasporic communities. Traditionally, the term 'diaspora' has referred to the Jewish exile, although Khalid Koser notes the increased assimilation of the word in African communities in London, for, *inter alia*, reasons of identification and solidarity with the victimisation of the dispersed Jews and African slaves.[24] There appears to be a close relationship between the concepts of migration and displacement, although in diaspora situations there may be a stronger sense of 'settledness' in the new home, whilst retaining significant connections with previous homelands.

It is in this context that certain shifts in Global Christianity may be readily understood. Global Christianity has exploded exponentially in the last century or two evidenced more recently in the growth of African churches in London, as Segovia notes when analysing Andrew Walls' historical treatise.[25] Having acknowledged these tremendous demographic shifts, Segovia poses the question; what does this mean for Biblical criticism, for the 'angle of vision afforded by such a web of diasporic experiences will be increasingly applied, to both modernist and postmodernist readings of the original Biblical texts'? His own experience growing up in Cuba and emigrating to the US, of both belonging and 'otherness', has led him to construct a diasporic hermeneutic from his position of 'disaggregated' identity. A point of connection with Bhabha's 'beyond' is the concept that this discourse on displacement, assimilated in Liberation theology, finds a home in the 'identity of instability and geographical conflict'. Through the reality of 'struggle' the biblical text acquires fresh meaning and is a point of reference for those whose lives are defined by such struggle and for whom the realities of stability, and absence of threat, remain elusive.

Segovia considers anti-hierarchical and anti-competitive hermeneutical constructs as an important part of a postmodern theologian's role.[26] It is this 'reading-across' approach which characterises the new diasporic hermeneutic in addition to anti-empiricist and anti-objectivist readings. Liberationist theologians have often developed the authenticity of their theology by forming and re-forming it in the arena of displaced existence. It is for these reasons that theological voices from the margins, including diasporic communities, must be welcomed, heard and considered thoughtfully and seriously. On a more practical note, it helps the displaced to identify more closely with the desert sojourn of the Old Testament Hebrew people, the earlier stories of Abraham and Joseph, and the later exilic discourse of the Babylonian experience. When one consciously applies this perspective to Scripture, we see the obvious parallels with the experience of God's people through both the Old Testament and the diasporic communities in the early church that the Apostle Paul interacted with. Such a comparison brings comfort to the displaced. It is the comfort of having a God intimately acquainted with the struggles of rootlessness, identity, struggle and persecution, so characteristic of the migrant experience.

Refreshing our theology in the light of the biblical narrative

Since migration is a significant element in the biblical narrative, theological reflection here is not new. People have had to move, either through their own fault, the fault of others, or as a result of events and circumstances beyond their own control. A scan through the Old Testament is replete with such examples.

The banishment from Eden (Genesis 3:23) and Cain's exile (Genesis 4:10-16) were migratory events resulting from the exercise of human choice; extremely poor ones in both cases, with historically-defining consequences. One of the implications of these events has been the restless wandering of a never satisfied spirit. Rather than tending the 'roots' of the original and beautiful garden, the wandering toil of endless 'routes' has brought humans into increasing competition for land and resources, the strivings for 'choice-options' (see the story of Lot in Genesis 13) and the displacement of the fruitfulness and rootedness of others. Lot's choice, initially attractive, was the plain of the Jordan, well-watered and green, although this, subsequently, led him to live in the urban setting of Sodom, a place described as festering with men, 'wicked and...sinning greatly' (Genesis 13:13).

Genesis is full of other examples of migration. The commencement of the Hebrew occupation of Egypt can be traced back to an ecological disaster that necessitated migration in the name of survival. Genesis 42: 48-56 tells the story of famine that afflicted not only Egypt, but all the lands around it. The need to buy food led to Joseph's brothers departing the land of Canaan and ultimately being reconciled with their long-lost brother in the land of Egypt. That joyous event and the subsequent settling of the Hebrews in Egypt becomes the forerunner of the great injustices the Hebrew people were to suffer at the hands of their Egyptian hosts. Slavery, that great tool of Empire, became their harsh and increasingly desperate everyday experience until God was moved to act by the heart cry of His people. This led to their wonderful liberation in the exodus out of Egypt. This massive migration became a defining historical and theologically-important event for the Jews, whose own Messiah would, millennia later, bring freedom and liberation not only to the responsive Jews of his time, but also to Gentiles. This latter group would be reached through the on-going mission of the Church acting in obedience to the Great Commission of Matthew 28:19-20. This mission, the *missio Dei*, was only possible after the Messiah underwent his own earthly and life-saving journey to Egypt and back, later followed by the greatest spiritual migration of all, the resurrection from the dead.

> *The Messiah underwent his own earthly and life-saving journey to Egypt and back...followed by the greatest spiritual migration of all, the resurrection from the dead*

What is evident from the biblical narrative is that ecologically-driven migration is nothing new. It has become synonymous with suffering and joy, captivity and liberation. It seems that human experience then, as now, is significantly played out in the field of movement, and displacement. Our migratory heritage is a fact and it has shaped our DNA. We are curious beings by nature, often tempted by the greener grass on the other side of the fence, and so there must be an element of our psyche that can, and should, empathise with displaced peoples. That human connection is an important starting point in any ministry, where solidarity and standing alongside the vulnerable can almost be a solution in itself.

Jesus' words that 'foxes have holes and birds of the air have nests, but the Son of Man has no place to lay his head' (Luke 9:58), may easily form a central tenet of our discourse, for the landless are also displaced and vulnerable to migratory forces. The Brazilian *Movimento Sem Terra* (Movement of Landless Rural Workers, 'MST') is a political response to the huge inequalities existent in contemporary Brazil.[27] Where 60% of the land lies idle and, conversely, where millions live in the squalid conditions of the *favela*, the Church has an issue to address, and rightly so. The legacy of Portuguese colonial policy is now a nation of extremes, where two-thirds of the cultivated land is owned by just 3% of the population. These statistics are comparable with many other regions of Latin America, which have been the subject of past colonial rule, both Portuguese and more widely, Spanish. In Brazil, vast estates have been held by a tiny minority of wealthy landowners. The MST, one of the largest grassroots organisations in the world, has assisted 250,000 families in winning land titles to over 15 million acres of land. There is no doubt that the numerous indigenous Amazonian tribes have a valid contribution to make in these disputes; the 'protected', but geographically limited reserves are cruel compensation for traditionally nomadic ways of life; inequitable gestures towards these original dwellers of the land. We experienced similar situations during our time in Bolivia, where the tension between community and individual rights was often played out. My protest that our neighbour had trespassed on our land, having broken down the dividing fence in order to access the water stream adjacent to our land, fell on deaf ears. The community right to water trumped any Western notion of private property and individual rights.

A theology of migration re-tells us that a separation of politics and Christianity is artificial.

A theology of migration re-tells us that a separation of politics and Christianity is artificial, and that theology from the 'underside' is formed and sharpened by this reality. The words of American Catholic nun Dorothy Stang, 'the Angel of the trans-Amazon', murdered whilst defending the land-rights of disenfranchised indigenous peoples in the Brazilian Amazon continue to echo: 'It is not my safety but that of the people that really matters, all of the Sisters of Notre Dame working in Brazil work very closely with our people and want to be a sign of hope. It is wonderful to be a part of this struggle and this is the contribution of Notre Dame.'[28]

Implications for the Church and mission

Randers strongly argues that an increasingly evident trend is urbanisation, and not simply the flight to the city for social and employment reasons. He presents a scenario of rurality becoming increasing hostile, a place where the elements are not controlled to the degree possible in the city. It is ironic that having moved out of the Age of the domination of Nature, we may well move back to that, at least in part, after 250 years of human 'progress'. Global warming through massively increased CO_2 and methane emissions is an example of how industrialisation and our rapacity for consumption are now reaping very unfortunate results. Overwhelming scientific evidence has proven this reality, beyond reasonable doubt. We no longer need prophetic imagination to see this actuality unfolding before our eyes. The connection between human activity and climate change might have been partly obscured in the face of the historical ebb and flow of CO_2 levels, but now that the scales have fallen from our eyes, these huge challenges stare back at us like never before.

The flight to the city will exacerbate land issues, bringing overcrowding and social deprivation; the 'cattle-herding' of migrants into smaller and smaller 'sheds'. The migration process from the rural countryside of the *Altiplano* to the city of La Paz has created unforeseen complications for the *Aymara* people. As traditional rural subsistence farmers with strong local community bonds and clear rules for the administration of community justice (not too dissimilar to Old Testament Hebrew social life) life in the city comes as a big shock. What confronts these migrants in the urban context is a whole raft of new struggles against urban poverty and decay, crime, addiction, and the 21st Century's equivalent of the slave trade: the trafficking industry in its various evil forms. An important question for us then is how do we meaningfully demonstrate a gospel of hope and reconciliation in such situations of conflict, and point to the eschatological Kingdom to come?

A vexing question has been the relationship between power and sacrifice. The Christian faith is essentially a generous one. It is a faith expressed through giving out and through preferring the needs of others; a faith where generosity, release, and sacrificial love are principal hallmarks. Christ's life, death and resurrection point to a hope which is extended out of our own trivial consciousness and provides a vision of 'the good' for others. Perhaps the Christian is most effective when living in that liminal space between two, or more, worlds without unnecessarily getting into binary-only constructs of 'top-down' and/or 'bottom-up'. After all, our life is a sojourn between this world and the next, not that we should demean the very real materialism of our current existence. Bhabha's articulation of this liminal space, as a place of possibility and creativity, opens up fresh meaning to the migratory journey. In leaving the 'old' behind and confronting the 'new', this physical and mental journey of possibility provides opportunity to develop a hybrid approach to life. Hybridity offers the possibility of connecting (at least in some way) with a world beyond one's previous (and limiting) experience.

So our sojourn through this life may also prevent us from rooting too deeply into familiarity and security. Instead we are called to humbly incarnate the presence and love of Christ in whatever culture we find ourselves, and to communicate that love across great divides, where our differentness becomes just that little less tangible. This is a key point, since we are called to live in community and not as islands. This living in community means mixing with those who may be radically different to us; racially, socially and economically. This 'hybrid' identity, whilst manifesting clear external features must more seriously result from circumcision of the heart. We are to avoid being 'individuals seeking individual satisfaction and individual escape from individually suffered discomforts'.[29] In ministering to the displaced we are to live out Matthew's instruction (Matthew 25:35-36) as summarised by Jesus, 'whatever you did for one of the least of these brothers of mine, you did for me' (Matthew 25:40). Friendship demonstrated by a compassionate duty of hospitality to those who arrive in our midst encourages mutually-healthy integration and opportunity to share our faith in contextually-meaningful ways.

Such an approach should also subvert the temptation to react aggressively or passively in the heated cauldron of displacement, where a third approach is necessary. We might term this third approach 'Kingdom ethics'. Our resolve must be to reject any existing Kingdom theologies which have been readily seduced by the radical individualism of contemporary life, and embrace what living in community should be about, where we seek the welfare of others above our own. Jesus stirs us to this selfless vision of the 'self' (Matthew 16:25). Our priority must be the proper struggle of the universal body of Christ in this Age, placed above our own needs, wants, desires, ambitions and dreams. Living in the Kingdom means being obedient to the King; that is doing God's 'thing' together. As Leslie Newbigin perceived, 'it is the essence of that Kingdom that its joy is the joy of communion'[30] observed in the Trinity, expressed through the Body, and received by the marginalised.

We should also assert that mission when limited to the sphere of activity and influence of the Church is an incomplete praxis for mission. Equally, we might say that the activity of the Church needs to be expanded so as to encompass more of the mission of the Kingdom. As Ken Gnanakan contends, 'the church in its mission today must break out of its own small horizon and discover the implications of God's kingdom horizons. Only then will the reality of the kingdom of God become the dynamic of mission.'[31] Maybe it is in our weakness that we best minister to the global weak, especially those who remain disempowered by the clout and power of the globally-networked.

One final concept, worthy of brief discussion, is a further expression of this idea of community. Michael Frost outlines the appealing concept of *communitas* in his fascinating account of the emerging marginal church in his book *Exiles*.[32] He notes that the concept of *communitas* was developed from research carried out by British-American symbolic anthropologist Victor Turner into the ritualistic symbolism of the Ndembu tribe of Zambia. His own study of the book of Acts led him to postulate this concept as a critical component of the emerging marginal church body, especially when it engages in mission. 'I came to realise that Christian community results from the greater cause of Christian mission', he adds. The liminal experience of being an exilic community, neither existing within the comfort and knowledge of its own culture nor able to fully identify with the host culture, provides a unique context for the *communitas* spirit to flourish amongst displaced exiles. Frost draws on the text of the first chapter in Daniel as a tangible example of how Daniel and his companions, as Jewish exiles, dealt with the Babylonian culture around them with all the considerable pressures and culture-clashes this presented them, and specifically within the context of something as basic to the human body as food (Daniel 1:8-16). It was their *communitas* that bonded them together and helped them to not only cope with these pressures but to resist attempts by the Babylonians to inculturate them into their customs. Daniel's diplomatic manner and God's honour brought favour from king Nebuchadnezzar as a result (Daniel 1:18-19). In ministering to the displaced exile we are likewise to express Matthew's instruction that 'whatever you did for one of the least of these brothers of mine, you did for me.' Thus we might conclude that friendship experienced through *communitas* and hospitality are two very practical ways in which we can identify with and reach out to the displaced.

Concluding reflections

The above discussion is an attempt to share a few reflections on how migrant dynamics can provide unique opportunities for Christians to model not only Christlikeness to those in need, but also to identify more closely in spirit with the marginalised and disenfranchised. Empathy borne out of genuine connection stands a greater chance of being translated into loving acts of kindness and works of justice.

In the shift from the rural to the urban lurk many dangers. Global cities are highly impersonal places, where one can disappear into an endless flow of information overload and profit-making enterprise, leading to crises of identity; a place where human beings 'in the multiple space of places, made of locales increasingly segregated and disconnected from each other',[33] become progressively dehumanised, psychologically vulnerable and socially marginalised. The shock that awaits the migrant on arrival in the 'promised land' provides the Christian community with an opportunity to minister grace, mercy and love into situations of often extreme volatility. A sensitive positioning towards the 'alien' helps to demolish the pedagogically-dominant colonialist approach of which we have been guilty in the past, and which we often replicate still today.

Growing tensions resulting from this rural to urban migration allied with a rising population on a finite planet will increase pressure on food supplies, the use of natural resources and will, most likely, result in runaway climate change. These issues will be felt ever more acutely in the coming decades and they raise important questions that need careful consideration. The role of the Church, now and in the future, in reaching out to those suffering on the margins of life, both locally and globally, is without question. However, it is how the Church needs to 'be' that will continue to exercise our imagination and our resolve.

We know how God's story ends. The new heavens and new earth will one day be revealed in their full glory. This is the time and place where suffering will be no more, and the nations will receive their healing from the leaves of the tree of life (Revelation 22:1-2). Eden will be restored, displaced no more, and 'home' will have found its ultimate meaning and resting-place. However, for many this remains an illusory image. Until then the struggle for justice must go on.

*A*ndy *Kingston-Smith* *grew up in Santiago, Chile, the son of missionary parents and later practised as a commercial property lawyer for 10 years. He and his wife Carol served with Latin Link in Bolivia for a few years before joining Redcliffe College faculty in 2008. He teaches on a number of modules concerning missiological engagements with justice-related issues in socio-political, economic and environmental contexts. In the church context, Andy has served in a variety of mission-related, pastoral, teaching/preaching and leadership roles. Until recently he combined his role at Redcliffe with a role in Latin Partners (http://www.latinlink.org), supporting Latin American missionaries living and working in the UK and Europe and also served on the committee of the Back to Europe initiative which is helping to mobilise, support and train the mission movement coming into Europe from the Global South. Andy and Carol jointly founded the jusTice initiative in 2010, a justice, advocacy and reconciliation in mission initiative, housed at Redcliffe College, (http://www.redcliffe.org/SpecialistCentres/ JusticeAdvocacyandReconilicationinMission) and this year has seen the commencement of the recently-validated MA course in Justice, Advocacy and Reconciliation in Intercultural Contexts (http://www.redcliffe.org/Study/PostgraduateCourses/ JusticeandMission), for which he is course leader. Andy also regularly edits editions of*

*Redcliffe's online journal Encounters (*http://www.redcliffe.org/SpecialistCentres/ EncountersMissionJournal*) and is involved in hosting public lectures and conferences at Redcliffe on justice-related issues in mission.*

Notes

1.   Castells, M., *The Rise of The Network Society*, 2nd ed., Oxford: Blackwell, 2000. His concluding chapter, pp.500-509, outlines these historical shifts and explains his understanding of the Information Age that we have moved into.

2.   Hanciles, J., 'Migration and Mission: Some Implications', *International Bulletin of Missionary Research*, 27:4, October 2003, p.146.

3.   Article in the Economist, dated 2nd November 2002, cited in Hanciles, 2003, p.146.

4.   McLeod, J., *Beginning Postcolonialism*, 2nd ed., Manchester: Manchester University Press, 2010, pp. 242-244.

5.   McLeod, 2010, p.243.

6.   McLeod, 2010, p.248.

7.   For references of Israelites grumbling in the desert, see, for example, Exodus 16:3, and 17:3.

8.   See a BBC article published online earlier this year; *How often do plane stowaways fall from the sky?* viewable at http://www.bbc.co.uk/news/magazine-19562101

9.   A thoughtful and penetrating account of the switch-holders and the implications for those outside 'the network' is found on p.501-508 of Castells, 2000.

10.   Castells, M., *The Power of Identity*, 2nd ed., Oxford: Blackwell, 2004.

11.   Castells, 2000, p.508.

12.   See Oguibe's essay, 'Connectivity and the Fate of the Unconnected', in Goldberg & Quayson, eds., *Relocating Postcolonialism*, Oxford: Blackwell, 2002.

13.   'At the peak of construction [of the Burj Khalifa, the world's tallest man-made structure at over 2,700 feet tall], over 12,000 workers and contractors were on site every day, representing more than 100 nationalities' – article viewable at http://www.burjkhalifa. ae/language/en-us/the-tower/construction.aspx

14.   McLeod, 2010, p.243.

15.   McLeod, 2010, p.249.

16.   McLeod, 2010, p.251.

17.   Bhabha, H., *The Location of Culture*, London: Routledge, 1994, p.1.

18.   McLeod, 2010, pp.251-252.

19.   *The Age of Stupid* produced by Spanner Films, 2009, depicts a man living alone in 2055 looking at old footage of seven real people from now and asking 'why didn't we stop climate change when we had the chance?'

20.   Garnier, D., *Climate Refugees*, Massachusetts Institute of Technology, 2010. This book provides a collection of nine real case studies of climate refugees, from around the world.

21.   Randers, J., *2052 – A Global forecast for the next forty years*, White River Junction: Chelsea Green Publishing, 2012.

22.   pp.171-174. Their conclusion is a mixed one, somewhat akin to the ambivalence of Bhabha's liminal space, 'the megacity will be the social and physical environment of the lives of a majority of people in 2052. This will be an environment that is diverse and fluid, without clear borders between locations and without stable structures and ideologies to give guidance as to how one's life is supposed to be.' In the author's view, our constant connection to the Internet (remember Oguibe's warning regarding connectivity) '[will mean that such future human] mentality will be different from ours in profound ways.'

23.   Groody, D., 'Crossing the divide; foundations of a theology of migration and refugees', *Theological Studies*, 70, 2009, viewable at http://www.nd.edu/~dgroody/Published%20 Works/Journal%20Articles/files/TSSeptember09Groody.pdf

24.   Koser, K., *International Migration: A Very Short Introduction*, Oxford: Oxford University Press, 2007, p.26.

25.   Segovia, F., (ed.), *Interpreting beyond borders*, Sheffield: Sheffield Academic Press, 2000, pp.20-22.

26.   Segovia, 2000, p.65.

27.   Young, R.J.C., *Postcolonialism: A Very Short Introduction*, Oxford: Oxford University Press, 2003, p.45.

28.   Environmental News Service (2005), viewable at http://www.ens-newswire.com/ens/ feb2005/2005-02-14-03.asp, Brasilia

29.   Bauman, Z., *Liquid Times—Living in an Age of Uncertainty*, Cambridge: Polity Press, 2007, p.103.

30.   Newbigin, L., *Signs amid the Rubble—The purposes of God in Human History*, Grand Rapids: Wm. B. Eerdmans Publishing Co., 2003, p.23.

31.   Gnanakan, K., *Kingdom Concerns—A Theology of Mission Today*, Leicester: Inter-Varsity Press, 1993, p.131.

32.   Frost, M., *Exiles—Living Missionally in a Post-Christian Culture,* Peabody: Hendrickson Publishers, Inc.,2006 p.108.

33.   Castells, 2000, p.507.

Climate Justice

Contemporary developments in science, policy, action and theology

Martin & Margot Hodson provide an update on the science and policy of climate change. This is one of the key issues facing humanity this century and the most negative impacts will be on the poorest in the world. They investigate climate justice through advocacy and mitigation. Finally their theological reflection offers a clear biblical foundation for caring for creation though ethical living, practical action and advocacy..

If there is one single issue that could define this century it is climate change. Although there are still those who would wish to say that it is not happening or that it is not human-induced, such positions are becoming increasingly untenable. In this chapter we will assess where we stand on climate change in 2012. We will begin by looking at the science of climate change, concentrating particularly on the most recent data and observations. We will then consider the policy situation leading up to and following on from the Rio+20 conference earlier this year. We will also look briefly at what is being done about the situation we find ourselves in, by way of action. Our final section will concern what Christians can and should do, and we will reflect theologically on where we stand. A key question being asked is quite simply; is there any hope?

Climate Science

In this section we will not spend our time going over the basics of climate change science. For those who wish to find out more about this we would recommend Maslin[1] for a brief overview and Houghton[2] for a more in depth treatment. Instead, we will just concentrate on what has happened in about the last twelve months. The whole area of climate science is changing quickly, but we will soon find that the climate itself is also changing very rapidly.

Global carbon dioxide (CO_2) emissions have been increasing since the beginning of the Industrial Revolution due to the burning of fossil fuels, but the increase has been particularly marked since about 1950. At the end of 2011 the data was assembled to assess CO_2 emissions from the two decades from 1990 (the reference year for the Kyoto protocol) to 2010.[3] It was reported that emissions had increased by 49% in those two decades and by a worrying 5.9% in 2010 alone. Although global emissions have been steadily increasing, the United States is now reporting decreased emissions.[4] It appears, however, that this decrease has more to do with switching from coal to cheaper gas, than to measures restricting CO_2 emissions. It should be noted that on a *per capita* basis CO_2 emissions are between 10 and 50 times higher in high income countries than in developing countries.[5]

Over the last year there has been a considerable battle in the United States over the Keystone XL pipeline that would bring oil from the tar sands in Alberta, Canada to Texas. The extraction process is very damaging to the local environment in Alberta, and poses some threat to important aquifers should the pipeline ever break. The amount of carbon locked up in the tar sands is huge and would contribute a massive amount of CO_2 to the atmosphere should it ever get burnt. Many have argued that the best policy is to leave the tar sands underground and to concentrate on developing renewable energy sources. James Hansen, the top NASA climate scientist, stressed the dangers of exploiting the tar sands stating that it would be "game over for the climate" if the carbon was used.[6]

If CO_2 emissions have then continued to increase, we would expect that the concentration of CO_2 in the atmosphere would also increase, unless significant amounts are absorbed and sequestered by plants or the oceans. The atmospheric concentration of CO_2 was about 280 ppm at the beginning of the Industrial Revolution, reached 315 ppm in 1950 and it has climbed to 394.49 ppm as of July 2012.[7] We are increasing by about 2-3 ppm in the atmosphere every year. During the last year the first reports came in of readings surpassing 400 ppm in isolated areas away from industrial activity in the Arctic.[8] It is estimated that the global average CO_2 concentration will reach this figure in about 2016. So it is safe to conclude that our CO_2 emissions have led to an increase in the concentration of the gas in the atmosphere.

As CO_2 is a greenhouse gas, we would expect that the temperature of the atmosphere would begin to rise as the concentration rises. In 2007 the

Intergovernmental Panel on Climate Change (IPCC) reported that over the period 1906-2005 there had been a 0.74 [0.56 to 0.92]°C increase in global temperature.[9] Others have been less certain. In the Climategate episode in 2009, hacked emails from the Climate Research Unit in Norwich were used to cast doubt on the idea that there had been a rapid temperature increase in the 20th Century. A group of more sceptical scientists, The Berkeley Earth project based at Berkeley, California in the United States, decided to re-investigate the phenomenon. After three years work they have begun to publish their findings on-line.[10] They considered more than a billion temperature records and showed that the mean global land temperature had risen by about 1°C since the mid-1950s. In July 2012, the leader of the project, Richard Muller, wrote a remarkable article in the New York Times in which he stated, "Last year, following an intensive research effort involving a dozen scientists, I concluded that global warming was real and that the prior estimates of the rate of warming were correct. I'm now going a step further: humans are almost entirely the cause."[11] It is too early to say whether the work of The Berkeley Earth project will dampen the controversy over the science of climate change.

> *'Last year...I concluded that global warming was real and that the prior estimates of the rate of warming were correct. I'm now going a step further: humans are almost entirely the cause.'*

What are the future predictions with regard to temperature change? The most recent modelling of future temperature scenarios has suggested increases of between 1.4 and 3.0°C by 2050 assuming medium emissions, which is in a similar range to that suggested by the IPCC in 2007.[12] Scientists and policymakers have often suggested a target of limiting global temperature rise to 2°C above the average temperature before the Industrial Revolution. Although even a 2°C rise will cause considerable problems, it is nowhere near as bad as the scenarios that might arise with greater rises.[13] There is little doubt that increases in global average temperature will have serious impacts, but in many respects temperature extremes are even more important.

A recent analysis by James Hansen and his team compared global temperatures for two 30-year periods; 1951–1980 and 1981–2010.[14] Daily maximum temperatures shifted towards higher values in the last 30 years. One very important change has been the appearance of extremely hot events in the summertime, very much warmer than during the earlier period. These extreme events covered much less than 1% of Earth's surface during 1951–1980, but now cover around 10%. The authors concluded that extreme heat waves, including those in Moscow in 2010 and in parts of the United States in 2011, were a consequence of global warming as the chance of their happening without global warming would be extremely small. As we write this chapter in the summer of 2012 the United States is again in the grip of an extreme heat wave (July 2012 was their hottest ever month), accompanied by drought and wild fires. Hansen considers that once the data analysis is complete the present heat wave will also be attributed to climate change.

If the temperature rises then one of the effects we would expect to see is ice caps and glaciers beginning to melt. The northern polar ice cap has been shrinking at an alarming rate for some time. Earlier predictions that it might completely disappear by the 2080s now seem very optimistic, and it is possible that this might happen, at least in the summer, within the next few decades.[15] Ironically, oil companies are already lining up to explore the Arctic Ocean once it is free of ice. In August 2012 the Arctic sea ice extent was below the 2007 record low. In August 2012 reports came in that the huge ice cap over Greenland had undergone unprecedented summer melting.[16] The problem with the Arctic sea ice melting is not confined to effects on animals such as polar bears. Because the ice is white it reflects a lot of incoming energy from the sun. Without the ice, global warming will speed up even faster. Sea ice, as it is floating, does not contribute much to sea level rise, but the ice over the Greenland land mass will do as it melts. The speed of sea level rise this century is one of the most difficult parameters to predict, but it now seems possible that we might see in excess of one metre by 2100, more than enough to cause major problems for low lying islands and coastal communities.

> *I*t now seems possible that we might see a rise in sea level in excess of one metre by 2100.

Higher temperatures mean that there is more energy in the atmospheric system, and this tends to lead to more droughts, more floods and more extreme weather events. We mentioned above the 2012 drought in the United States. Drought has also been experienced this year in Brazil, Spain, Morocco, Russia, and the Ukraine. Flooding events this year have also happened in Argentina, Brazil, China, Honduras, Ethiopia, the United Kingdom, Bangladesh, Madagascar, the Philippines, Cambodia, Spain and Florida. Some of these events would have occurred without any influence from global warming, but anecdotally they do seem to be happening more often and have worse effects. In fact, the weather system seems to be less stable than it was, and shows less reliable patterns. This has been termed "global weirding" by some climate scientists, including Katharine Hayhoe, a Christian, and an atmospheric scientist at Texas Tech University.[17] It has become clearer that events such as the extreme heat waves we are now seeing can be directly attributed to climate change. The statistical work by Hansen and others has established this beyond reasonable doubt. It is, however, much harder to assess this for events such as droughts, floods, hurricanes and tornados, although we would expect such events to show an overall increase at a time of warming.

In November 2011 a group of scientists gathered at the Royal Society in London for the conference "Climate Change: Biodiversity and People on the Front Line", which was organised by RSPB, WWF and Natural England. The report on the meeting came out in 2012, and is freely available.[18] The meeting mostly concentrated on the climate change / biodiversity interaction. Climate change is already having major effects on animals and plants. In the spring in temperate zones, plant buds are bursting earlier and flowers are coming out earlier. Birds are laying eggs earlier and insects are active earlier. In general, organisms that are able to move are moving towards the poles or up mountains. The changes are happening in all environments investigated, and are particularly fast in the oceans. The longer term worry is that the changes will be too fast, this century, for many organisms to adapt, and many will become extinct.

Thus far we have had little directly to say about the impacts of climate change on people, but this will change for the rest of this paper. As we write this in August 2012, there are already warnings of a coming food crisis due to the impacts of the drought in North America.[19] Food prices are likely to rise on a global scale from an already high level[20], and this will have its greatest impacts on the poor. Pest species change their distributions as the climate warms, tending to move northwards in the northern hemisphere. Because of the exceptionally hot weather in Texas in the summer of 2012 the mosquitoes carrying the West Nile Virus Fever have been more active than normal leading to at least ten deaths. This has caused the authorities in Dallas to resort to aerial spraying.[21]

The poor are affected worst wherever they happen to be. We immediately think of the poor in the developing world who are taking the brunt of the effects of climate change, but we should also remember events like Hurricane Katrina in 2005, discussed briefly in another chapter by Andy Kingston-Smith, which devastated New Orleans in the richest country in the world, the United States. The well off were able to escape the worst effects of the hurricane whilst many of the poor were left behind to cope with the devastation. Although the developed West is responsible for the vast majority of the emissions, it will be the poor who suffer most. Christian Aid stated in a 2006 report, "The potential ravages of climate change are so severe that they could nullify efforts to secure meaningful and sustainable development in poor countries. At worst, they could send the real progress that has already been achieved spinning into reverse. No other single issue presents such a clear and present danger to the future welfare of the world's poor. Climate change, then, is a pressing poverty issue."[22]

So far we have painted a pretty bleak picture of the science of climate change as it stands in 2012. But what is humanity doing about this problem? We will now turn to assess the policy situation.

Policy

Serious attempts to frame world policy on climate change can be dated from the United Nations Conference on Environment and Development (UNCED), commonly known as the Earth Summit, in Rio de Janeiro, Brazil in 1992. Scientists were already concerned at the rise in atmospheric CO_2 concentrations, as documented by the first report of the IPCC in 1990, and governments appeared to be ready to act. The Framework Convention on Climate Change (FCCC) was approved by 162 countries in Rio and it was agreed that these countries should take, "precautionary measures to anticipate, prevent or minimise the causes of climate change and mitigate its adverse effects. Where there are threats of irreversible damage, lack of full scientific certainty should not be used as a reason for postponing such measures."[23] The FCCC set in train a process to look at emissions reductions under the Conference of Parties (COP) meetings. In 1997 COP 3 met in Kyoto, Japan and agreed to reduce greenhouse gas emissions by 5%, relative to a 1990 benchmark, by 2012 (the Kyoto Protocol). This then required ratification by each government. The process took until November 2004 when Russia eventually signed and the Protocol entered force on 16th February 2005. The United States is the one country that never ratified the Protocol, and Canada withdrew from it in 2011. President George W. Bush strongly opposed the Kyoto Protocol on the grounds of the potential damage that it might cause to the US economy, and that large nations including China and India were not involved. By the middle of the first decade of the 21st Century it was clear that work needed to begin on an extension of, or replacement for, the Kyoto Protocol that would include all nations.

In 2007 the IPCC released its fourth report, which was even clearer on the potential dangers of human-induced climate change than the previous three reports. A whole series of meetings led up to the crucial COP 15 in Copenhagen, Denmark in December 2009. The expectations before the

Copenhagen meeting were high, and the activity beforehand, on all sides of the debate, was frantic. In many quarters the conference was billed as the "last chance" to save the planet. The sceptical lobby made much of the so-called Climategate episode that was outlined above, whilst the environmental and world development groups mobilised huge demonstrations around the world to persuade governments to act. COP 15 proved to be a big disappointment to all those hoping for a fair, binding agreement that would ensure that CO_2 concentrations, and thus global temperatures, did not rise beyond safe levels. The precise reason(s) for the failure of Copenhagen are still shrouded in mystery. Mark Lynas was in the room where world leaders hammered out the final, very weak, agreement in the early hours of the final day of COP 15.[24] His conclusion was that China was the nation most responsible for the debacle: "China was the big story: here was a new, emerging global superpower, going eyeball to eyeball with the United States—and winning." Lynas considered that China could not allow large cuts in emissions because of the likely impacts on its growing economy and the need to sustain growth in order to maintain internal stability. Although China was almost certainly a major reason for the poor outcome of Copenhagen, we cannot blame them for their attempts to bring their country up to the kinds of lifestyles enjoyed in the West. Copenhagen has proven to be a key moment in the fight against

> *We cannot blame the Chinese for their attempts to bring their country up to the kinds of lifestyles enjoyed in the West.*

climate change. Before Copenhagen there was much optimism that the problem could be tackled, but since then there has been considerable pessimism. The Copenhagen Accord made the 2°C global warming temperature increase limit international policy, but the most climate change vulnerable nations would have lobbied for a 1.5°C maximum, and this long term goal is open for review at some later date.

The FCCC process has continued since Copenhagen, with further COP meetings in Cancun, Mexico (COP 16) in 2010, and Durban, South Africa (COP 17) in 2011. The Durban conference agreed to the legally binding "Durban platform" involving all countries. The procedures for an emissions cutting deal will be in place by 2015, and this will take effect in 2020. As the Kyoto Protocol agreement ends on 31st December 2012 there will certainly be a gap between the commitment periods. Responses to the Durban Platform were predictably varied, with many politicians considering it a success, and others less certain.[25] For example Kumi Naidoo, of Greenpeace International, was quoted as saying, "Right now the global climate regime amounts to nothing more than a voluntary deal that's put off matters for a decade. This could take us over the 2°C threshold where we pass from danger to potential catastrophe."

One of the key areas that FCCC has been concentrating on is the funding of adaptation schemes for developing countries. At the Durban meeting some progress was made in creating a Green Climate Fund (GCF), and a management framework was adopted. The fund is to distribute US$100 billion per year by 2020 to help poor countries adapt to climate impacts. Tearfund and CAFOD have demanded that if the agreed 2020 target is to be met, the finance must be additional to existing aid budgets and be scaled up from 2013 onwards.[26]

The latest (June 2012) international meeting to address the climate change issue was the United Nations Conference on Sustainable Development (UNCSD), commonly known as Rio+20, meeting following 20 years after the original meeting in Rio de Janeiro. Rio+20 had a much bigger brief that just climate change[27], and expectations prior to the meeting were not high, partly because of the very large agenda. It is difficult to assess the effect of Rio+20 only a relatively short time after the meeting, but the main product was a 49 page document "The Future We Want", which had non-binding status. Twenty years after the first Rio meeting there was no doubt that the authors of the final report were very worried about the lack of progress on climate change: "We note with grave concern the significant gap between the aggregate effect of mitigation pledges by parties in terms of global annual emissions of greenhouse gases by 2020 and aggregate emission pathways consistent with having a likely chance of holding the increase in global average temperature below 2°C, or 1.5°C above pre-industrial levels."[28]

So where do we stand now on climate change in the global policy arena? Sir Bob Watson is a former chair of the IPCC and former chief scientist at the Department for Food and Rural Affairs, and frequently writes and speaks on climate change. Interviewed by the BBC in August 2012 he had this to say: "I have to look back on [the outcome of successive climate change summits] Copenhagen, Cancun and Durban and say that I can't be overly optimistic. To be quite candid the idea of a 2°C target is largely out of the window."[29] Some would suggest that we should entirely abandon the United Nations FCCC process, as it is too expensive and seems to be going nowhere. However, Evan Juska argues that this would be unwise and he considers that we need the FCCC for two reasons: climate change cannot be solved without international cooperation and the UN provides the most likely forum; and the effect that the international UN negotiations have had in catalysing progress on national climate change policies in the last 20 years.[30] The next FCCC meeting is due in Doha, Qatar (COP 18) at the end of 2012.[31]

We will give the last words in this section to Tearfund whose report "Dried up, Drowned out. Voices from poor communities on a changing climate,"[32] gathered the opinions of poor people living in the developing world concerning climate change. They are the people that are most affected by climate change, have done the least to cause it, and are those with the smallest voice on the international stage where decisions are made. This is a summary of the points made by poor communities to encourage rich nations and their governments to take action[33]:-

· Get serious about cutting emissions globally

· Respect the commitments made for the reduction of greenhouse gases and finance sustainable development

· Commit to investments on the necessary scale and in the long term. NGOs working on climate change have estimated that by 2020 at least US$200 billion per year will be needed for adaptation and mitigation

· Follow through on internationally binding agreements

· Face the truth: climate change is happening; it is not science fiction.

Action

It is quite evident from the above that climate change is a serious issue, and that it is a justice issue both for the human poor and for all other organisms resident on this planet. If the current scientific prognosis is anywhere near correct then this century could be a very difficult one, and even those who are currently well off may also suffer. What is on the table at the climate change negotiations appears to be woefully inadequate. In this section we will assess what can be done about the problem. There are a number of ways of categorising responses, and these could be broken down into mechanics, organisational level and type of action. Under mechanics we will include mitigation, adaptation and geo-engineering. Mitigation responses largely seek to reduce carbon emissions, whilst adaptation responses assume some level of climate change and attempt to prepare for it. One method, we will only briefly mention

> *Climate change is a serious issue... a justice issue both for the human poor and for all other organisms resident on this planet.*

here, is 'geo-engineering responses', which attempts to solve the problem by such means as artificially absorbing atmospheric CO_2, and putting giant reflectors into space. As yet geo-engineering is very much in the research stage, and has not been deployed, although many suggest we may need it in the future. It is also possible to consider the organisational level at which the response is made: individual; community; national; and international. The final classification involves the types of action that can be taken: education; advocacy; changing practices; and campaigning. Obviously these types of action could involve mitigation, adaptation or geo-engineering, and can often be taken at different levels. We will organise this section around the types of action that can be taken.

Education may not be seen by many as an "action" that can help deal with climate change. Unfortunately, however, there has been so much misinformation and so many confusing messages in the media that there still is a need for education. One of the major problems with education in this area is that it is easily possible to take a person from ignorance, or apathy, to a fatalistic "it's all too late" position without considering a realistic activist position. On the "Hope for Planet Earth"[34] tours of 2008 and 2009 we frequently found that teenagers were very familiar with climate change, but had adopted a highly fatalistic response, "we are all going to die". In the United States, sadly, climate scientists are suffering from a systematic persecution[35], and science itself is under suspicion by many from the Christian right. There is, undoubtedly, a need to re-think climate change education, and to work out what is appropriate for each age group and situation.

Advocacy is undertaken by individuals or organisations in order to affect the political process. It can occur at local levels, but is most well known at national and international levels. It is certainly an activity that many non-governmental organisations have been involved in with respect to climate change. Such activity has been very evident at the COP meetings and at Rio+20. Advocacy has had some effects on international policy, and the situation would have been worse without it. However, it has not delivered enough policy change at sufficient speed. There are those who feel that the endless rounds of international meetings are getting us nowhere, and would cite the well funded advocacy of the petrochemical and coal lobbies in the United States and elsewhere as a major reason. Some national governments are under major pressure from advocates who do not wish to cut carbon emissions, and so advocacy is a double-edged sword. When such countries arrive at international negotiations they often seem to be unable to make the needed policy decisions due to lobbying pressure back home.

Given the apparent lack of willingness of most governments and international bodies to make the necessary changes in policy, there are growing numbers of people who say we should essentially give up at that level and concentrate on what can be done locally. Much of this can be done by individuals changing aspects of their lifestyles, for example with transport, housing, and food.[36] Even more is possible at a community level, and so organisations like the Transition Network[37] have encouraged local activism as the solution to our problems. Transition groups will often look at energy, food and transport, and try to move communities along an "energy descent plan", aimed at decreasing dependence on fossil fuels. Very often such groups have been motivated more by concerns about peak oil than climate change. Whilst all this low carbon activity can only be good for decreasing emissions, the big question remains; will it be enough? Is this attempt at localism just blowing in the wind? Speaking at the "Sustainability in Crisis" meeting in Cambridge in 2011, Bill McKibben voiced serious concerns.[38] He cited the example of Vermont, his home state, and one of the greenest, most environmentally friendly areas in the United States. Vermont had highly developed organic agriculture, farmers' markets and a flourishing local green economy. Then on one day, 28th August 2011, the tail end of Hurricane Irene, which caused the closing of the subway in New York City, dumped huge amounts of rain on Vermont. This caused massive damage to crops, washed away soil, and destroyed many farms and bridges. McKibben argued that localism was fine, but these kinds of events suggest that it will not stop global climate change, and remains extremely vulnerable to it. He stated, "you can have the most beautifully designed local agricultural system in the world and if it rains 30% more than it ever rained before... then you are still not going to grow anything." He went on to say that we needed a "sprint" to beat global warming, and that in order to get the changes needed fast enough, work needs to be done at national and international levels.

The final category we need to consider is campaigning. This does overlap to some extent with advocacy, and many campaigners are involved in education, and also attempt to change their own lifestyles. Campaigning can take many forms, but here we will confine ourselves to the more obvious types of demonstrations. Many of these are symbolic, and not intended to have a direct effect on carbon emissions. So, for example, the Wave demonstration on 5th December 2009 mobilised thousands of people to march through London and Glasgow as a show of strength before the Copenhagen climate change meeting. Such events are entirely peaceful, and there is no intention to break any laws. However, there are now some, including the scientist James Hansen and the activist Bill McKibben, who feel that such campaigning is less effective than non-violent direct action. Such action, it is argued, is much more likely to gain the attention of the public and governments. In August 2011 over 1000 peaceful demonstrators were arrested outside the White House in Washington D.C. at a demonstration coordinated by Bill McKibben and 350.org. The demonstration concerned the building of the Keystone XL pipeline mentioned above. As we have already noted, the potential for carbon emissions from tar sands products is huge. Those arrested at the demonstration included Bill McKibben, James Hansen and the actress Daryl Hannah. On November 6, 2011, twelve thousand people formed a human chain around the White House to protest against the pipeline. Four days later President Obama announced a delay in the decision on the pipeline permit until at least 2013, while further environmental reviews were carried out. As we write there is still a battle going on over the pipeline with attempts to build sections of it being met by fierce resistance from 350.org and its allies. In many of these cases demonstrators are directly attempting to block the development of the pipeline, and their action is more than symbolic.

As yet, environmental demonstrations have been almost entirely non-violent; indeed the vast majority of the organisers of such demonstrations and those who take part would be horrified by any resort to violence. There is always the possibility that a radical violent wing might emerge, as in the animal rights movement, but fortunately this has not yet happened.

Engaging theology: how should the Church respond?

Having looked at possible responses to climate change, we will now examine the question, 'how should the Church respond?' There has been an increasing number of Christians who have become concerned by climate change, though this concern is not geographically uniform: it is stronger in the UK than in North America and is mixed in other areas. Plenty has been written to provide a biblical basis for creation care and the biblical imperative is now well-established.[39] Lifestyle responses have become embedded in many churches and the individual lives of Christians. Eco-Congregation in the UK has been especially good at facilitating churches to respond as communities to climate change and organisations such as A Rocha UK (with their Living Lightly project), Tearfund and Christian Ecology Link have all promoted lifestyle initiatives.[40] Some activists are scathing of these, seeing the only appropriate response to be prophetic advocacy and campaigning.[41] Other groups such as the John Ray Initiative (JRI)[42] believe it is important to respond at many different levels. Though concentrating on education and advocacy, JRI also encourages a lifestyle response. A few Christians have taken direct action and this section will consider whether this is an authentic Christian response.

An interesting biblical starting point is 2 Corinthians 5:17. This gives insight into the relationship between Christians and the world in the light of Christ's salvation. It can be translated: "So if indeed someone is in Christ the new creation has come, the old has passed and the new has arrived." New creation is revealed in and through each individual who has come to Christ. Conversion is therefore an eschatological event, as each person coming to Christ reveals something of the future hope when all will be made new. We can conclude that being "in Christ" means that a little bit of the new creation is exposed here and now amid our present suffering creation. For each Christian this means that we experience personal transformation in Christ. We carry the resurrection hope with us in the whole of our lives, whether we are doing something 'spiritual', or something very 'nuts-and-bolts'. The new creation is with us and we can see it worked out in our lives. But new creation is not just for individuals, it also impacts on us, and through us, as a community. As the church we are the body of Christ and so collectively we are new creation. We demonstrate that new creation in all that we do and in the way we are as people in society.

As the church we are the body of Christ and so collectively we are new creation.

As we look at the various ways in which we can respond to climate change, as Christians we should ask which response will reveal the new creation to those around us? In some situations it will be living in a new creation way by making the sort of lifestyle changes that are life-giving to the rest of nature on the planet. In other situations the response that will bring new creation will be one of advocacy, campaigning and direct action. The biblical description of the new creation has certain consistent features and three common strands emerge. The first is a restored harmony between God, humanity and the natural world. The second is a realisation of human welfare for the redeemed, the poor and the oppressed. The third is the establishment of a reign of justice and judgement on those who oppress. Each of these will now be addressed.

Isaiah anticipates a future where there will be harmony between human and animal; wild and domestic creatures (Isaiah 11:6-9, 65:25). Similarly, St. John foresees harmony between God, humanity and the whole of creation (Revelation 22:1-4). If Christians are to reveal the new creation, we will glorify God when we live out that harmony today. Given the damaging impacts of climate change, a key component has to be lifestyle choices that support this harmony. This will mean reducing carbon emissions through a myriad of different lifestyle choices. Joining a local Transition network or similar environmental group might help us develop lower carbon lifestyles. Whether we fly less, grow our own food to reduce food miles, cycle or put solar panels on our roofs, there are numerous ways in which we can live in a more climate-sustaining lifestyle. We must also be concerned at threatened biodiversity hotspots globally, and our care of nature, locally. So we might refuse to purchase items made from tropical hardwoods, or items grown on areas cleared of tropical forest. We might seek to demonstrate human and ecological harmony in our own local areas through positive recreation schemes, which strengthen local community and have a policy of encouraging ecological diversity.

Human welfare must also be a central concern to those who have found themselves belonging to the new creation community of faith. In Revelation 21:4, John's view of the future is one where: "he [God] will wipe every tear from their eyes. There will be no more death or mourning or crying or pain, for the old order of things has passed away." Suffering belongs to the old order and it is a Christian imperative to alleviate this as we represent and bring in the new order. Tearfund have worked for decades to demonstrate this new creation hope in

> *Suffering belongs to the old order and it is a Christian imperative to alleviate this…and bring in the new order.*

their relief and development work world wide, but they work against a backdrop of increasing suffering in many parts of the world. As noted above, Tearfund recently reported on their findings concerning the impact of climate change on local communities in the developing world.[43] They had interviewed their global partner organisations in 2005 and discovered that many parts of the world were already experiencing severe impacts from climate change, especially in the form of unusually severe droughts and floods. They concluded that urgent action was needed to mitigate these climate induced problems. In 2012, Tearfund again interviewed these global partners to assess what had changed. They found that the climate issues had become more severe: "A vicious cycle of floods and droughts has now become normal, reducing people's ability to meet their own needs and forcing many into poverty. Their animals and fish are dying. People are moving away from their homes to find work – sometimes never to return."[44] In 2005 the hope had been that international agreements would support poorer countries and enable communities to adapt to climate change. Sadly, their report concluded that despite many meetings between world leaders, they had not made effective agreements to make a difference to those suffering on the ground. A typical story comes from Bangladesh:

> Archona and Priambandhu have been married for 28 years. They live in Kaya Benia village in Bangladesh. They used to have 11 acres of land. Cyclones and floods have reduced that to two acres. They used to have a rice paddy that produced 2,000 kg of rice. That's all gone. Farming is no longer viable for them, so they've turned to fishing and growing a few vegetables for themselves. But salination means that the land is now poor, which means that the vegetables are poor quality too. For four months of the year, the whole of their land is flooded, meaning that they can't grow anything. 'We are suffering, losing our land and house,' says Archona. 'We don't know the future, but we can assume that we will lose it all.'[45]

Tearfund partners are responding to these situations to meet the humanitarian need. In Bangladesh they are building embankments to protect villages from flooding. They are also seeking to enable climate change victims to find new sources of income. These humanitarian responses are crucial but the message of this report is that these responses on their own will not address the suffering that is being caused by climate change.

In addition to ecological harmony and human wellbeing in the new creation, there is a strong thread of justice. Isaiah 11 begins by setting out the messianic task: "with righteousness he will judge the needy, with justice he will give decisions for the poor of the earth" (11:4). This thread is echoed in Revelation 19 and 20, where the new creation is ushered in with the restoration of justice. This aspect of demonstrating new creation undergirds those Christians who are actively involved in advocacy, campaigning and direct action. The advocacy route is taken by organisations such as Tearfund, JRI, CAFOD, A Rocha and Christian Aid. These organisations were represented at the Copenhagen climate change summit and most regularly encourage their supporters to write to their MPs and others to ask them to take action on climate change. In the United States, there have been a number of advocacy initiatives, which have tried to influence government, one being the Call to Action by the Evangelical Climate Initiative.[46] This is supported by over 300 senior Christian leaders and has had contact with political leaders.

Justice demands advocacy but for some it also requires direct action. Jesus turned over the tables in the Temple to restore it as a house of prayer for those who could only pray in the outer courts (Matthew 21:12-14). These were the Gentiles and also the blind and the lame that he went on to heal once he had cleared the Temple. Those Christians who take direct action see their activities as prophetic. Like Just War theory they would see the suffering of the innocent victims of climate change, both human and ecological, to be a justification for action. This is especially true in the face of inaction by most governments and the problem of dealing with a long-term threat through a democratic system that favours responses to short and medium term problems. Bill McKibben, mentioned previously in connection with the tar sands pipeline issue, is a committed Christian and his radical interpretation of his faith undergirds his environmental campaigning.[47] For McKibben, the radical life and teaching of Jesus justifies his actions on climate change issues. Bill takes some of his inspiration from the Sermon on the Mount and it is notable that his campaigning is always of a peaceful nature.

In 2011 and 2012, JRI and A Rocha UK jointly facilitated two gatherings on the theme of "hope". This sought to find a hope that would be realistic and sustaining in a world where we are experiencing the negative impacts of climate change. The hope that emerged was a robust hope that acknowledged the proximate hope of acting in the present and the eschatological hope of a restored future, and enables us to work that out in our present suffering world.[48] As "new-creation Christians" we are Christ's ambassadors, committed to the task of reconciliation (2 Corinthians 5:19-20). We are called to work towards that new creation for both ecology and humanity. We should work in practical ways, through advocacy and campaigning. There is also a place for direct action, provided that the action itself is consistent with the actions of Christ. In all this we should demonstrate the new creation and bring realistic hope to a suffering world.

Conclusion

The world faces a crisis with climate change this century. The climate is already changing and it seems to be happening faster than scientists had expected. The poor are those who are suffering the most from the effects of climate change. Global climate change policy is happening too slowly, with a replacement for the Kyoto Protocol now unlikely to happen until at least 2020. The target of restricting global warming to 2°C above pre-industrial times now seems unlikely to be met. There is, however, much that can still be done to limit the damage caused by climate change. Christians, both individually and collectively, have a huge role to play in this work, and, if nothing else, we can be bringers of hope to an otherwise hopeless world.

*D*r **Martin J Hodson** *is a plant scientist and environmental biologist, and is Operations Manager for the John Ray Initiative. He was the tour scientist for the Hope for Planet Earth tours, and writes and speaks widely on environmental issues. He has over 90 research publications. His recent publications include* Climate Change, Faith and Rural Communities *(with Margot Hodson, 2011) and* Functional Biology of Plants *(with John Bryant, 2012).*

*R*evd **Margot R Hodson** *is Vicar of Haddenham Benefice in Buckinghamshire and was previously Chaplain of Jesus College, Oxford. She has taught Environmental Ethics at Oxford Brookes University and is on the boards of The John Ray Initiative and A Rocha UK. Margot has published several books including* Cherishing the Earth, *(co-authored with Martin Hodson, 2008), and* Uncovering Isaiah's Environmental Ethics *(Grove Booklet E161, 2011).*

Notes

1. Maslin, M. *Global Warming: A Very Short Introduction* (2nd ed.), Oxford: OUP, 2008.

2. Houghton, J. *Global Warming: The Complete Briefing* (3rd ed.), Cambridge: Cambridge University Press, 2004.

3. University of East Anglia (2011, December 6). 'Global carbon emissions reach record 10 billion tons, threatening 2 degree target'. *ScienceDaily*. Accessed on August 17, 2012 at http://www.sciencedaily.com /releases/2011/12/111204144648.htm

4. Begos. K. 'U.S. Carbon emissions: 2012 levels at 20 year low'. *Huffington Post* (17th August 2012) accessed on August 17, 2012 at http://www.huffingtonpost.com/2012/08/16/us-carbon-dioxide-emissions-2012_n_1792167.html

5. EIA (Energy Information Administration) 2011. International Energy Statistics: CO_2 Emissions. US Energy Information Administration. Accessed on August 17, 2012 at http://www.eia.gov/cfapps/ipdbproject/IEDIndex3.cfm?tid=90&pid=44&aid=8

6. Hansen, J. 'Game over for the climate.' *The New York Times* (9th May 2012), accessed on August 17, 2012 at http://www.nytimes.com/2012/05/10/opinion/game-over-for-the-climate.html

7. Observed at Mauna Loa Observatory, Hawaii. The latest concentration can be found by consulting http://co2now.org/

8. NOAA (2012) *Carbon dioxide levels reach milestone at Arctic sites.* Accessed on August 17, 2012 at http://researchmatters.noaa.gov/news/Pages/arcticCO2.aspx

9. IPCC (2007) *IPCC Fourth Assessment Report: Climate Change 2007.* Accessed on August 17, 2012 at http://www.ipcc.ch/publications_and_data/ar4/syr/en/contents.html

10. The Berkeley Earth Project accessed on September 28, 2012 at http://berkeleyearth.org/

11. Muller, R.A. ' The conversion of a climate-change skeptic'. *The New York Times* (28th July 28, 2012) accessed on August 18, 2012 at http://www.nytimes.com/2012/07/30/opinion/the-conversion-of-a-climate-change-skeptic.html

12. Rowlands, D.J. et al. 'Broad range of 2050 warming from an observationally constrained large climate model ensemble', *Nature Geoscience* 5, 256-260, 2012

13. Lynas, M. *Six Degrees: Our Future on a Hotter Planet.* UK: Harper Perennial, 2008

14.   Hansen, J., Sato, M., Ruedy, R. 'Perception of climate change'. Proceedings of the National Academy of Sciences, USA accessed on August 18, 2012 at http://www.pnas.org/cgi/doi/10.1073/pnas.1205276109

15.   Freedman, A. 'Arctic sea ice melting on par with 2007 record'. *The Guardian* (1st August 2012) accessed on August 18, 2012 at http://www.guardian.co.uk/environment/2012/aug/01/arctic-sea-ice-melting-2007-records

16.   Morello, L. 'Greenland sets new summer melt record'. *Scientific American* (16th August, 2012) accessed on August 18, 2012 at http://www.scientificamerican.com/article.cfm?id=greenland-sets-new-summer-melt-record

17.   Hayhoe and other climate scientists appeared in the somewhat controversial BBC2 Horizon television programme "Global Weirding" shown on 16th May 2012. Some clips from the programme are available at http://www.bbc.co.uk/programmes/b01f893x

18.   Watts, O., Morecroft, M., Phillips, J. and Taylor, J. eds. *Climate Change: Biodiversity and People on the Front Line*. RSPB, Natural England and WWF-UK. Accessed on August 18, 2012 at http://www.rspb.org.uk/Images/climatechangeconferencereport_tcm9-317417.pdf

19.   Walker, R. 'The perfect drought'. *Huffington Post* (10th August 2012) accessed on August 18, 2012 at http://www.huffingtonpost.com/robert-walker/midwest-drought_b_1764896.html

20.   *FAO Food Price Index*. Accessed on September 30, 2012 at http://www.fao.org/worldfoodsituation/wfs-home/foodpricesindex/en/

21.   Kuta, S. 'West Nile Virus: Dallas, Texas attack plan includes aerial insecticide spray assault'. (17th August 2012) accessed on August 18, 2012 at http://www.huffingtonpost.com/2012/08/17/dallas-west-nile-virus_n_1791551.html

22.   Christian Aid, 'The climate of poverty: facts, fears and hope'. Report: May 2006

23.   Houghton, J. 'Global warming, climate change and sustainability: Challenge to scientists, policy makers and Christians', *JRI Briefing Paper 14*, 2009, Third edition accessed on August 18, 2012 at http://www.jri.org.uk/wordpress/wp-content/uploads/JRI_19_Copenhagen.pdf

24.   Lynas, M. *The God Species: How the Planet can Survive the Age of Humans*. London: Fourth Estate, 2011, pp. 229-234

25.   BBC *Reaction to UN climate deal*. BBC web site (11th December 2011) accessed on September 29, 2012 at http://www.bbc.co.uk/news/science-environment-16129762

26.   Tearfund and CAFOD 'Quick off the blocks? UK adaptation finance and integrated planning'. Ed. S. Boyd accessed on September 28, 2012 at http://tilz.tearfund.org/webdocs/Tilz/Research/Quick_off_the_blocks_D5.pdf

27.   Heather, H. and Hulme, S. 'Whose Earth?' Rio +20. *JRI Briefing Paper 22* accessed on September 28, 2012 at http://www.jri.org.uk/wordpress/wp-content/uploads/JRI_22_Rio_20.pdf

28.   UNCSD 'The future we want'. *Report of the United Nations Conference on Sustainable Development. Rio de Janeiro, Brazil (20–22 June 2012)* United Nations, New York, 2012 accessed on September 28, 2012 at http://www.uncsd2012.org/content/documents/814UNCSD%20REPORT%20final%20revs.pdf

29.   Ghosh, P. 'Science adviser warns climate target "out the window"' (23rd August 2012) accessed on September 28, 2012 at http://www.bbc.co.uk/news/science-environment-19348194

30. Juska, E. ' Why the UN still matters on climate change'. Huffington Post (27th September 2012) accessed on September 28, 2012 at http://www.huffingtonpost.com/evan-juska/united-nations-climate-change_b_1920300.html

31. *Doha Climate Change Conference - November 2012* accessed on September 29, 2012 at http://unfccc.int/meetings/doha_nov_2012/meeting/6815.php

32. Southam, H. ed. *Dried up, Drowned out. Voices from poor communities on a changing climate.* Teddington: Tearfund, 2012 accessed on September 28, 2012 at http://www.tearfund.org/driedupdrownedout/

33. Southam, H. ed. p 18

34. Morrice E. and Moffat F. eds. (2009). *Hope for Planet Earth. A Christian Response to Climate Change. A multimedia DVD resource for churches.* SJI: London

35. Bagley, K. 'America is only nation where climate scientists face organized harassment.' *Inside Climate News* (10th Sept 2012). Accessed on September 12, 2012 at http://insideclimatenews.org/news/20120910/america-only-nation-where-climate-scientists-face-organized-harassment

36. Valerio R. *'L' is for Lifestyle. Christian living that doesn't cost the earth*, IVP; Revised edition, 2008

37. The Transition Network accessed on September 13, 2012 at http://www.transition-network.org/

38. McKibben, W. 'Sustainable Consumption'. Lecture given by Bill McKibben as part of the Sustainability in Crisis Conference, Faraday Institute, Cambridge, UK (27th September 2011) accessed on September 13, 2012 at http://www.sms.cam.ac.uk/media/1180044;jsessionid=4DEF76E6FF232DBAA941D8838148E351

39. See for example, Hodson, M.J. and Hodson, M.R. *Cherishing the Earth, how to care for God's creation*, Oxford: Monarch, 2008; Bookless, D. *Planetwise*, Nottingham: IVP. 2008 or Spencer, N. and White, R. *Christianity, Climate Change and Sustainable Living*, London: SPCK, 2007

40. The web sites for these organisations are: Eco-Congregation, http://www.eco-congregation.org/ ; A Rocha UK, http://www.arocha.org/gb-en/index.html ; Living Lightly, http://arochalivinglightly.org.uk/ ; Tearfund, http://www.tearfund.org/ ; and Christian Ecology Link, http://www.christian-ecology.org.uk/ (all accessed on September 29, 2012).

41. Clifford, P. *Angels with Trumpets: The Church in a Time of Global Warming*, London: Darton, Longman & Todd, 2009

42. *The John Ray Initiative* accessed on September 29, 2012 at http://www.jri.org.uk

43. Southam, H. ed. (2012) ibid

44. Southam, H. ed. p 6

45. Southam, H. ed. p 11

46. *Climate Change: An Evangelical Call to Action*, accessed on September 29, 2012 at http://christiansandclimate.org/

47. McKibben, W. (2005) 'The Christian paradox: How a faithful nation gets Jesus wrong', *Harpers Magazine*, August, accessed on 28th September 2012 at http://www.harpers.org/archive/2005/08/008069

48. Bauckham, R. 'Ecological Hope in Crisis?' *JRI Briefing Paper 23*, 2012 accessed on September 28, 2012 at http://www.jri.org.uk/wordpress/wp-content/uploads/JRI_23_Hope_Bauckham.pdf, See also *Anvil*, 29:1, http://www.anviljournal.org (available from March 2013)

Human Dignity, Equality, and Liberty in Classic Protestant Perspective

*This chapter[1] offers a historical angle on the concept of human dignity as a precursor to contemporary notions of human rights. Luther is not generally known for theologising on such issues, so **John Witte Jr.** helpfully examines some of Luther's 16th Century writings to argue that freedom and rights not only have a long-standing tradition in Protestant thought, but find their culmination in God's perfect law in the new heavens and new earth. Until then, egalitarian notions of equality and liberty still require significant development for a just societal order.*

Human Dignity as Modern "Ur-Principle"

"A sense of the dignity of the human person has been impressing itself more and more deeply on the consciousness of contemporary man," Pope Paul VI declared in his preface to *Dignitatis Humanae* (1965). "And the demand is increasingly made that men should act on their own judgment, enjoying and making use of a responsible freedom, not driven by coercion but motivated by a sense of duty."[2]

This was an historic statement about human dignity, signaling a momentous swing in the pendulum of world opinion. Only two decades before, the world had stared in horror into Hitler's death camps and Stalin's gulags where all sense of humanity and dignity had been brutally sacrificed. In response, the world had seized anew on the ancient concept of human dignity, claiming this as the "ur-principle" of a new world order.[3] The Universal Declaration of Human Rights of 1948 opened its preamble with classic words: "recognition of the inherent dignity and of the equal and inalienable rights of all members of the human family is the foundation of freedom, justice, and peace in the world."[4]

By the mid-1960s, church and state alike had translated this general principle of human dignity into specific human rights precepts. In *Dignitatis Humanae* and several other documents produced during and after the Second Vatican Council (1962-1965), the Roman Catholic Church took some of the first decisive steps. Every person, the Church now taught, is created by God with "dignity, intelligence and free will... and has rights flowing directly and simultaneously from his very nature."[5] Such rights include the right to life and adequate standards of living, to moral and cultural values, to religious activities, to assembly and association, to marriage and family life, and to various social, political, and economic benefits and opportunities. The Church emphasized the religious rights of conscience, worship, assembly, and education, calling them the "first rights" of any civic order. The Church also stressed the need to balance individual and associational rights, particularly those involving the church, family, and school. It urged the abolition of discrimination on grounds of sex, race, colour, social distinction, language, or religion.[6] Within a decade, various Ecumenical groups, some Protestants, and a few Orthodox Christian groups crafted comparable comprehensive declarations on human rights, albeit with varying emphases on the concept of human dignity.[7]

Not only the world's churches, but also the United Nations and several nation-states issued a number of landmark documents on human dignity and human rights in the 1960s. Foremost among these were the two great international covenants promulgated by the United Nations in 1966, each of which confirmed the belief in the "inherent dignity" and "the equal and inalienable rights of all members of the human family," and the belief that all such "rights derive from the inherent dignity of the human person."[8] The International Covenant on Economic, Social, and Cultural Rights (1966) posed as essential to human dignity the rights to self-determination, subsistence, work, welfare, security, education, and cultural participation. The International Covenant on Civil and Political Rights (1966) set out a long catalogue of rights to life and to security of person and property, freedom from slavery and cruelty, basic civil and criminal procedural protections, rights to travel and pilgrimage, freedoms of religion, expression, and assembly, rights to marriage and family life, and freedom from discrimination on grounds of race, colour, sex, language, and national origin. Other international and domestic instruments issued in the later 1960s took close aim at racial, religious, and gender discrimination in education, employment, social welfare programmes, and other forms and forums of public life, viewing such discrimination as a fundamental betrayal of the "dignity and equality inherent in all human beings."[9]

So matters stood half a century ago. Today, the concept of human dignity has become ubiquitous to the point of cliché; a moral trump frayed by heavy use, a general principle harried by constant invocation. In the past thirty years, there have been more than 1,000 books and more than 10,000 scholarly articles on dignity published in English alone. We now read regularly of the dignity of animals, plants, and nature; the dignity of luxury, pleasure, and leisure; the dignity of identity, belonging, and difference; the dignity of ethnic, cultural, and linguistic purity; the dignity of sex, gender, and sexual preference; the dignity of aging, dying, and death. At the same time, the corpus of human rights has become swollen to the point of eruption, with many recent rights claims no longer built on universal norms of human dignity or other ontological foundations but aired as special aspirations of an individual or a group.

> *Today, the concept of human dignity has become ubiquitous to the point of cliché; a moral trump frayed by heavy use, a general principle harried by constant invocation.*

On the one hand, the current ubiquity of the principle of human dignity testifies to its universality. And the constant proliferation of new human rights speaks to their power to inspire new hope for many desperate persons and peoples around the world. Moreover, the increased pervasiveness of these norms is partly a function of emerging globalisation. Since the first international documents on human dignity and human rights were issued, many new voices and values have joined the global dialogue, especially those from Africa, Asia, and Latin America, and from various Buddhist, Confucian, Hindu, Islamic, and Traditional communities.

> *The constant proliferation of new human rights speaks to their power to inspire new hope for many desperate... peoples around the world.*

On the other hand, the very ubiquity of the principle of human dignity today threatens its claims to universality. And the very proliferation of new human rights threatens their long-term effectiveness for doing good. Human dignity needs to be assigned some limits if it is to remain a sturdy foundation for the edifice of human rights. Human rights need to be founded firmly on moral principles like human dignity, lest they devolve into a gaggle of wishes and wants. Fairness commands as broad a definition of human dignity as possible, so that no legitimate human good is excluded and no legitimate human rights claim is foreclosed. But prudence counsels a narrower definition of human dignity, so that not every good becomes part of human dignity, and not every aspiration becomes subject to human rights vindication.

The task of defining the appropriate ambit of human dignity and human rights today must be a multi-disciplinary, multi-religious, and multi-cultural exercise.

The task of defining the appropriate ambit of human dignity and human rights today must be a multi-disciplinary, multi-religious, and multi-cultural exercise. Many disciplines, religions, and cultures around the globe have unique sources and resources, texts and traditions that speak to human dignity and human rights. Some endorse dignity and rights with alacrity and urge their expansion into new arenas. Others demur, and urge their reform and restriction. It is essential that each community be allowed to speak with its own unique accent, to work with its own distinct methods on human dignity and human rights. It is also essential, however, that each of these disciplines, religions, and cultures develops a capacity for

It is essential that each community be allowed to speak with its own unique accent, to work with its own distinct methods on human dignity and human rights.

conceptual bilingualism; an ability to speak with insiders and outsiders alike about their unique understanding of the origin, nature and purpose of human dignity and human rights.

My task in this chapter is to test the meaning and take the measure of human dignity and human rights in the classic Protestant tradition. I start with Martin Luther's famous little tract, *Freedom of a Christian* (1520), one of the anchor texts for his emerging "two kingdoms" theology. This tract, I argue, was something of a Protestant *Dignitatis Humanae* in its day, a grand theory of human dignity, liberty, equality, and responsibility, ultimately grounded in the sovereignty of God. Luther's early theory provided an alternative both to earlier Christian teachings that based human dignity on a person's reason, class, and vocation, and to later Enlightenment teachings that based human dignity on inalienable rights and popular sovereignty. The Conclusion draws out some of the enduring insights of these early Protestant writings, and their pertinence for contemporary discussions of human dignity, equality, and rights.

Saint and Sinner, Priest and King

Martin Luther's *Freedom of a Christian* (1520) was one of the defining documents of the Protestant Reformation, and it remains one of the classic tracts of the Protestant tradition still today.[10] Written on the eve of his excommunication from the Church, this was Luther's last ecumenical gesture toward Rome before making his incendiary exit. Much of the tract was written with a quiet gentility and piety that belied the heated polemics of the day and Luther's own ample perils of body and soul. Luther dedicated the tract to Pope Leo X, adorning it with a robust preface addressed to the "blessed father." He vowed that he had to date "spoken only good and honourable words" concerning Leo, and offered to retract anything that might have betrayed "indiscretion and impiety." "I am the kind of person," he wrote in seeming earnest, "who would wish you all good things eternally."[11]

Luther was concerned, however, that the papal office had saddled Leo with a false sense of dignity. "You are a servant of servants" (*servus servorum*) within the Church, Luther wrote to Leo, citing the classic title of the Bishop of Rome.[12] And as a "servant of God for others, and over others, and for the sake of others," you properly enjoy a "sublime dignity" of office.[13] But the "obsequious flatterers" and "pestilential fellows" of your papal court do not regard you as a humble servant. Instead, they treat you as "a vicar of Christ," as "a demigod [who] may command and require whatever you wish." They "pretend that you are lord of the world, allow no one to be considered a Christian unless he accepts your authority, and prate that you have power over heaven, hell and purgatory." Surely, you do not believe any of this, Luther wrote to Leo, tongue near cheek. Surely, you can see that "they err who ascribe to you alone the right of interpreting Scripture" and "who exalt you above a council and the church universal." "Perhaps I am being presumptuous" to address you so, Luther allowed at the end of his preface. But when a fellow Christian, even a pope, is exposed to such "dangerous" teachings and trappings, God commands that a fellow brother offer him biblical counsel, without regard for his "dignity or lack of dignity."[14]

In later pages of the *Freedom of a Christian* and in several other writings in that same crucial year of 1520, Luther took aim at other persons who were "puffed up because of their dignity."[15] He inveighed at greatest length against the lower clergy, who, in his view, used the "false power of fabricated sacraments" to "tyrannize the Christian conscience" and to "fleece the sheep" of Christendom.[16] He criticized jurists for spinning the thick tangle of special benefits, privileges, exemptions, and immunities that elevated the clergy above the laity, and inoculated them from legal accountability to local magistrates.[17] He was not much kinder to princes, nobles, and merchants, those "harpies," as he later called them, "blinded by their arrogance," and trading on their office, pedigree, and wealth to lord it over the languishing commoner.[18] What all these pretentious folks fail to see, Luther wrote, is that "there is no basic difference in status... between laymen and priests, princes and bishops, religious and secular."[19] Before God all are equal.

Luther's *Freedom of a Christian* thus became, in effect, his *Dignitatis Humanae*; his bold new declaration on human nature and human freedom that described all Christians in his world regardless of their "dignity or lack of dignity," as conventionally defined. Pope and prince, noble and pauper, man and woman, slave and free, all persons in Christendom, Luther declared, share equally in a doubly paradoxical nature. First, each person is at once a saint and a sinner, righteous and reprobate, saved and lost, *simul iustus et peccator*, in Luther's signature phrase.[20] Second, each person is at once a free lord who is subject to no one, and a dutiful servant who is subject to everyone. Only through these twin paradoxes, Luther wrote, can we "comprehend the lofty dignity of the Christian."[21]

Every Christian "has a two fold nature," Luther argued in expounding his doctrine of *simul iustus et peccator*. We are at once body and soul, flesh and spirit, sinner and saint, "outer man and inner man." These "two men in the same man contradict each other" and remain perennially at war.[22] On the one hand, as bodily creatures, we are born in sin and bound by sin. By our carnal natures, we are prone to lust and lasciviousness, evil and egoism, perversion and pathos of untold dimensions.[23] Even the best of persons, even the titans of virtue in the Bible, Abraham, David, Peter, and Paul, sin all the time.[24] In and of ourselves, we are all totally depraved and deserving of eternal death. On the other hand, as spiritual creatures, we are reborn in faith, and freed from sin. By our spiritual natures, we are prone to love and charity, goodness and sacrifice, virtue and peacefulness. Even the worst of persons, even the reprobate thief nailed on the next cross to Christ's, can be saved from sin. In spite of ourselves, we are all totally redeemed and assured of eternal life.[25]

It is through faith and hope in the Word of God, Luther argued, that a person moves from sinner to saint, from bondage to freedom. This was the essence of Luther's doctrine of justification by faith alone. No human work of any sort, even worship, contemplation, meditation, charity, and other supposed meritorious conduct, can make a person just and righteous before God. For sin holds the person fast, and perverts his or her every work. "One thing, and only one thing, is necessary for Christian life, righteousness, and freedom," Luther declared. "That one thing is the most holy Word of God, the gospel of Christ."[26] To put one's faith in this Word, to accept its gracious promise of eternal salvation, is to claim one's freedom from sin and from its attendant threat of eternal damnation. And it is to join the communion of saints that begins imperfectly in this life and continues perfectly in the life to come.

A saint by faith remains a sinner by nature, Luther insisted, and the paradox of good and evil within the same person remains until death. But there is "a difference between sinners and sinners," Luther wrote. "There are some sinners who confess that they have sinned but do not long to be justified; instead, they give up hope and go on sinning so that when they die they despair, and while they live, they are enslaved to the world. There are other sinners who confess that they sin and have sinned, but they are sorry for this, hate themselves for it, long to be justified, and under groaning constantly pray to God for righteousness. This is the people of God," the saints who are saved, despite their sin.[27]

This brought Luther to a related paradox of human nature; that each Christian is at once a lord who is subject to no one, and a priest who is servant to everyone. On the one hand, Luther argued, "every Christian is by faith so exalted above all things that, by virtue of a spiritual power, he is [a] lord."[28] As a redeemed saint, as an "inner man," a Christian is utterly free in his conscience, utterly free in his innermost being. He is like the greatest king on earth, who is above and beyond the power of everyone. No earthly authority, whether pope, prince, or parent, can impose "a single syllable of the law" upon him.[29] No earthly authority can intrude upon the sanctuary of his conscience; can endanger his assurance and comfort of eternal life. This is "the splendid privilege," the "inestimable power and liberty" that every Christian enjoys.[30]

On the other hand, Luther wrote, every Christian is a priest, who freely performs good works in service of his or her neighbour and in glorification of God.[31] "Christ has made it possible for us, provided we believe in him, to be not only his brethren, co-heirs, and fellow-kings, but also his fellow-priests," Luther wrote. And thus, in imitation of Christ, we freely serve our neighbours, offering instruction, charity, prayer, admonition, and sacrifice even to the point of death.[32] We abide by the law of God so far as we are able so that others may see our good work and be similarly impelled to seek God's grace. We freely discipline and drive ourselves to do as much good as we are able, not so that we may be saved but so that others may be served. "A man does not live for himself alone," Luther wrote, "he lives only for others."[33] The precise nature of our priestly service to others depends upon our gifts and upon the vocation in which God calls us to use them.[34] But we are all to serve freely and fully as God's priests.

"Who can then comprehend the lofty dignity of the Christian?" Luther wrote. "By virtue of his royal power he rules over all things, death, life, and sin." The person is entirely free from the necessity of doing good works and fully immune from the authority of any one. But by virtue of "his priestly glory, he is omnipotent with God because he does the things which God asks and requires."[35] He devotes himself entirely to doing good works for his neighbor, he submits himself completely to the needs of others.

Such are the paradoxes of the Christian life in Luther's view. We are at once sinners and saints; we are at once lords and servants. We can do nothing good; we can do nothing but good. We are utterly free; we are everywhere bound. The more a person thinks himself a saint, the more sinful in fact he becomes. The more a person thinks herself a sinner, the more saintly she in fact becomes. The more a person acts like a lord, the more he is called to be a servant. The more a person acts as a servant, the more in fact she has become a lord. This is the paradoxical nature of human life. And this is the essence of human dignity.

Luther intended his *Freedom of a Christian* to be a universal statement for his world of Christendom; a summary of "the whole of the Christian life in a brief form," as he put it in his preface to Leo.[36] He grounded his views in the Bible, liberally peppering his tract with all manner of biblical citations and quotations. He wove into his narrative several strong threads of argument pulled selectively from a number of Church Fathers and late medieval Christian mystics. He published his tract both in Latin and in simple German, seeking to reach both the scholar and the commoner alike. He wrote with a pastoral directness and emotional empathy, convinced that if he could point out the Jekyll and Hyde in everyone, his readers would find both ample humility and ample comfort. So convinced was Luther of the veracity and cogency of his views that he believed even the Jews, the one perennial sojourner in his world of Christendom, would convert *en masse* to the Gospel once they heard it in this simple form.[37] Though this latter aspiration proved fanciful, Luther's views on human dignity did command an impressive readership among Christians. *Freedom of a Christian* was a best seller in its day, going through twelve printings in its first two years, and five editions by 1524. It remained a perennial favourite of commentaries and sermons long after Luther's passing, and well beyond the world of Lutheranism.[38] It is no small commentary on the enduring ecumenical efficacy of Luther's views of human nature, dignity, and freedom that they lie at the heart of the "Joint Declaration on the Doctrine of Justification," signed by Catholic and Evangelical leaders on October 31, 1999.

What all this elegant dialectic theology meant for the nature of freedom of the Christian in this world, Luther's little tract did not so clearly say. Luther did make clear that all Christians have the freedom and duty to follow the Bible conscientiously and to speak out against human ideas and institutions that conflict with the Bible. The Bible was for Luther the great equaliser of Christians, to the remarkable point of allowing Luther, a lowly Augustinian monk from an obscure German town, to address His Holiness Leo X as if he were the pope's equal. Luther also made clear that clergy and laity are fundamentally equal in dignity and responsibility before God. The traditional assumption that the clergy were superior to the laity and entitled to all manner of special privileges, immunities, and exemptions was anathema to Luther. Luther at once laicized the clergy and clericized the laity, treating the office of preaching and teaching as just one other vocation alongside many others that a conscientious Christian could properly and freely pursue.[39]

> *The traditional assumption that the clergy were superior to the laity was anathema to Luther.*

Luther's *Freedom of a Christian*, however, was no political manifesto on freedom. Spiritual freedom may well coexist with political bondage, Luther insisted. The spiritual equality of persons and vocations before God does not necessarily entail a social equality with all others.[40] Luther became doubly convinced of this discordance after witnessing the bloody Peasants' Revolt in Germany in 1525, and the growing numbers of radical egalitarian and antinomian experiments engineered out of his favorite theological doctrines of the priesthood of all believers and justification by faith alone. In the course of the next two decades, Luther defended with increasing stridency traditional social, economic, political, and ecclesiastical hierarchies as a necessary feature of this earthly life.

Luther came to defend this disparity between the spiritual and temporal dimensions of human freedom, dignity, and status with his doctrine of the two kingdoms. God has ordained two kingdoms or realms in which humanity is destined to live, Luther argued, the earthly or political kingdom and the heavenly or spiritual kingdom. The earthly kingdom is the realm of creation, of natural and civic life, where a person operates primarily by reason, law, and passion. The heavenly kingdom is the realm of redemption, of spiritual and eternal life, where a person operates primarily by faith, hope, and charity. These two kingdoms embrace parallel forms of righteousness and justice, truth and knowledge, but they remain separate and distinct. The earthly kingdom is distorted by sin, and governed by the law. The heavenly kingdom is renewed by grace and guided by the Gospel. A Christian is a citizen of both kingdoms at once, and invariably comes under the distinctive jurisdiction of each kingdom. As a heavenly citizen, the Christian remains free in his conscience, called to live fully by the light of the Word of God. But as an earthly citizen, the Christian is bound by law, and called to obey the structures and strictures of ecclesiastical, political, and parental authority, even if they are sometimes hard and abusive.

Protestant Instincts about Human Dignity and Freedom Today

Nearly half a millennium after its publication, *Luther's Freedom of a Christian* still shapes many Protestants' instincts about human dignity, liberty, equality, and rights.

First, Luther's doctrine of *simul iustus et peccator* renders many Protestants instinctively skeptical about too optimistic a view of human nature, and too easy a conflation of human dignity and human sanctity. Such views take too little account of the radicality of human sin and the necessity of divine grace. They give too little credibility to the inherent human need for discipline and order, accountability and judgment. They give too little credence to the perennial interplay of the civil, theological, and pedagogical uses of law, to the perpetual demand to balance deterrence, retribution, and reformation in discharging authority within the home, church, state, and other associations. They give too little insight into the necessity for safeguarding every office of authority from abuse and misuse. A theory of human dignity that fails to take into account the combined depravity and sanctity of the human person is theologically and politically deficient, if not dangerous.

This cardinal insight into the two-fold nature of humanity was hardly unique to Martin Luther, and is readily amenable to many other formulations. Luther's formula of *simul iustus et peccator* was a crisp Christian distillation of a universal insight about human nature that can be traced to the earliest Greek and Hebrew sources of the West. The gripping epics of Homer and Hesiod are nothing if not chronicles of the perennial dialectic of good and evil, virtue and vice, hero and villain in the ancient Greek world. The very first chapters of the Hebrew Bible paint pictures of these same two human natures, now with Yahweh's imprint on them. The more familiar picture is that of Adam and Eve who were created equally in the image of God, and vested with a natural right and duty to perpetuate life, to cultivate property, to dress and keep the creation (Gen 1:26-30; 2:7, 15-23). The less familiar picture is that of their first child Cain, who murdered his brother Abel and was called into judgment by God and condemned for his sin. Yet "God put a mark on Cain," Genesis reads, both to protect him in his life, and to show that he remained a child of God despite the enormity of his sin (Gen 4:1-16).[41] One message of this ancient Hebrew text is that we are not only the beloved children of Adam and Eve, who bear the image of God, with all the divine perquisites and privileges of Paradise. We are also the sinful siblings of Cain, who bear the mark of God, with its ominous assurance both that we shall be called into divine judgment for what we have done, and that there is forgiveness even for the gravest of sins we have committed.

Luther believed that it is only through faith and hope in Christ that we can ultimately be assured of divine forgiveness and eternal salvation. He further believed that it was only through a life of biblical meditation, prayer, worship, charity, and sacramental living that a person could hold his or her depravity in check and aspire to greater sanctity. I believe that, too, as do many Christians today. But this is not to say that, in this life, Christians have the only insights into the two fold nature of humanity, and the only effective means of balancing the realities of human depravity and the aspirations for human sanctity. Any religious tradition that takes seriously the Jekyll and Hyde in all of us has its own understanding of ultimate reconciliation of these two natures, and its own methods of balancing them in this life. And who are we Christians to say how God will ultimately judge these?

Any religious tradition that takes seriously the Jekyll and Hyde in all of us has its own understanding of ultimate reconciliation of these two natures.

Luther also believed that the ominous assurance of the judgment of God is ultimately a source of comfort not of fear. The first sinners in the Bible, Adam, Eve, and Cain, were given divine due process. They were confronted with the evidence, asked to defend themselves, given a chance to repent, spared the ultimate sanction of death, and then assured of a second trial on the Day of Judgment, with appointed divine counsel; Christ himself, our self-appointed "advocate before the Father" (1 John 2:1). The only time that God deliberately withheld divine due process was in the capital trial of His Son, and that was the only time it was and has been necessary. The political implications of this are very simple: If

God gives due process in judging us we should give due process in judging others. If God's tribunals feature at least basic rules of procedure, evidence, representation, and advocacy, human tribunals should feature at least the same. The demand for due process is a deep human instinct, and it has driven Protestants over the centuries, along with many others before and with them, to be strident advocates for procedural rights.

Second, Luther's doctrine of the lordship and priesthood of all believers renders many Protestants instinctively jealous about liberty and equality, but on their own quite distinct theological terms. In the modern liberal tradition liberty and equality are generally defended on grounds of popular sovereignty and inalienable rights. The American Declaration of Independence (1776) proclaimed it a "self-evident truth" "that all men are created equal [and] ... are endowed with certain unalienable rights." The Universal Declaration of Human Rights (1948) proclaimed "[t]hat all men are born free and equal in rights and dignity." Protestants can resonate more with the norms of liberty and equality in these documents than with the theories of popular sovereignty and inalienable rights that generally undergird them.

The heart of the Protestant theory of liberty is that we are all lords on this earth. We are utterly free in the sanctuary of our conscience, entirely unencumbered in our relationship with God. We enjoy a sovereign immunity from any human structures and strictures, even those of the church when they seek to impose upon this divine freedom. Such talk of "sovereign immunity" sounds something like modern liberal notions of "popular sovereignty." And such talk of "lordship" sounds something like the democratic right to "self-rule." Protestants have thus long found ready allies in liberals and others who advocate liberty of conscience and democratic freedoms on these grounds. But, when theologically pressed, many Protestants will defend liberty of conscience not because of their own popular sovereignty, but because of the absolute sovereignty of God, whose relationship with his children cannot be trespassed. Many Protestants will defend certain unalienable rights not in the interest of preserving their personal privacy but in the interest of discharging their divine duties.

The heart of the Protestant theory of equality is that we are all priests before God. "You are a chosen race, a royal priesthood, a holy nation, God's own people" (1 Pet. 2:9; Rev 5:10, 20:6). Among you, "[t]here is neither Jew nor Greek, there is neither slave nor free, there is neither male nor female; for you are all one in Christ Jesus" (Gal 3:28; Col 3:10-11; Eph 2:14-15). These and many other biblical passages, among Luther's favorites, have long inspired a reflexive egalitarian impulse in Protestants. All are equal before God. All are priests that must serve their neighbours. All have vocations that count. All have gifts to be included. This common calling of all to be priests transcends differences of culture, economy, gender, and more.

Such teachings have led a few Protestant groups over the centuries to experiment with intensely communitarian states where life is gracious, lovely, and long. Most Protestant groups, however, view life in such states as "brutish, nasty, and short," for sin invariably perverts them. Structures and strictures of law and authority are necessary and useful, most Protestants believe. But such structures need to be as open, egalitarian, and democratic as possible. Hierarchy is a danger to be indulged only so far as necessary. To be sure, Protestants over the centuries have often defied these founding ideals, and have earnestly partaken of all manner of elitism, chauvinism, racism, antisemitism, tyranny, patriarchy, slavery, apartheid, and more. And they have sometimes engaged in outrageous hypocrisy and casuistry to defend such shameful practice. But an instinct for egalitarianism, for embracing all persons equally, for treating all vocations respectfully, for arranging all associations horizontally, for levelling the life of the earthly kingdom so none is obstructed in access to God, is a Lutheran gene in the theological genetic code of Protestantism.

> *An instinct for egalitarianism is a Lutheran gene in the theological genetic code of Protestantism.*

Finally, Luther's notion that a person is at once free and bound by the law has powerful implications for our modern understanding of human rights. For Luther, the Christian is free in order to follow the commandments of the faith; or, in more familiar and general modern parlance, a person has rights in order to discharge duties. Freedoms and commandments, rights and duties belong together in Luther's formulation. To speak of one without the other is ultimately destructive. Rights without duties to guide them quickly become claims of self-indulgence. Duties without rights to exercise them quickly become sources of deep guilt.

Protestants have thus long translated the moral duties set out in the Decalogue into reciprocal rights. The First Table of the Decalogue prescribes duties of love that each person owes to God; to honour God and God's name, to observe the Sabbath day and to worship, to avoid false gods and false swearing. The Second Table prescribes duties of love that each person owes to neighbours; to honour one's parents and other authorities, not to kill, not to commit adultery, not to steal, not to bear false witness, not to covet. Church, state, and family alike are responsible for the communication and enforcement of these cardinal moral duties, Protestants have long argued. But it is also the responsibility of each person to ensure that he and his neighbours discharge these moral duties.

This is one important impetus for Protestants to translate duties into rights. A person's duties toward God can be cast as the rights to religious exercise: the right to honour God and God's name, the right to rest and worship on one's Sabbath, the right to be free from false gods and false oaths. Each person's duties towards a neighbour, in turn, can be cast as a neighbour's right to have that duty discharged. One person's duties not to kill, to commit adultery, to steal, or to bear false witness thus gives rise to another person's rights to life, property, fidelity, and reputation. For a person to insist upon vindication of these latter rights is not necessarily to act out of self-love. It is also to act out of neighbourly love. To claim one's own right is in part a charitable act to induce one's neighbour to discharge his or her divinely-ordained duty.

The great American jurist Grant Gilmore once wrote: "The better the society the less law there will be. In Heaven, there will be no law, and the lion will lie down with the lamb. In Hell, there will be nothing but law, and due process will be meticulously observed."[42] This is a rather common Protestant sentiment, which Luther did much to propound in some of his early writings. But a Protestant, faithful to Luther's most enduring insights, might properly reach the exact opposite projection. In Heaven, there will be pure law, and thus the lamb will lie down with the lion. In Hell, there will be no law, and thus all will devour each other eternally. Heaven will exalt due process, and each will always receive what's due. Hell will exalt pure caprice, and no one will ever know what's coming.

John Witte, Jr., *B.A. Calvin College, J.D. Harvard, is Jonas Robitscher Professor of Law, Alonzo L. McDonald Distinguished Professor, and Director of the Center for the Study of Law and Religion Center at Emory University. A specialist in legal history, marriage law, and religious liberty, he has published 220 articles, 13 journal symposia, and 26 books. Recent book titles include: Sex, Marriage and Family Life in John Calvin's Geneva, 2 vols. (2005, 2013); Modern Christian Teachings on Law, Politics, and Human Nature, 3 vols. (2006); God's Joust, God's Justice: Law and Religion in the Western Tradition (2006); The Reformation of Rights: Law, Religion, and Human Rights in Early Modern Calvinism (2007); Christianity and Law: An Introduction (2008); The Sins of the Fathers: The Law and Theology of Illegitimacy Reconsidered (2009); Christianity and Human Rights: An Introduction (2010); Religion and the American Constitutional Experiment (3d ed. 2011); and Religion and Human Rights: An Introduction (2012). Professor Witte's writings have appeared in fifteen languages, and he has delivered more than 350 public lectures throughout the world. With major funding from the Pew, Ford, Lilly, Luce, and McDonald foundations, he has directed 12 major international projects on democracy, human rights, and religious liberty, and on marriage, family, and children. These projects have collectively yielded more than 160 new volumes and 250 public forums around the world. He edits two major book series, "Studies in Law and Religion," and "Religion, Marriage and Family."*

He has been selected eleven times by the Emory law students as the Most Outstanding Professor and has won dozens of other awards and prizes for his teaching and research.

Notes

1.   This article draws in part on my *Law and Protestantism: The Legal Teachings of the Lutheran Reformation*, Cambridge/New York: Cambridge University Press, 2002, esp. pp.87-117, 293-303. For further elaboration of these themes, see my *The Reformation of Rights: Law, Religion, and Human Rights in Early Modern Calvinism*, Cambridge: Cambridge University Press, 2007; and John Witte, Jr. and Frank S. Alexander, eds., *Christianity and Human Rights: An Introduction*, Cambridge: Cambridge University Press, 2011.

2.   Walter M. Abbott and J. Gallagher, eds., *The Documents of Vatican II*, New York: Herder & Herder, 1966, p.675.

3.   The term "ur-principle" is from Louis Henkin, et al., *Human Rights* (New York, Foundation Press, 1999, p.80.

4.   Ian Brownlie, ed., *Basic Documents on Human Rights*, 3d ed., Oxford: Oxford University Press, 1992, p.21.

5.   *Pacem in Terris* (1963), paragraph 9, in Joseph Gremillion, ed., *The Gospel of Peace and Justice: Catholic Social Teachings Since Pope John*, Maryknoll, NY: Orbis Books, 1976, p.203.

6.   Ibid.; *Documents of Vatican II*, p.675.

7.   Jürgen Moltmann, *On Human Dignity, Political Theology and Ethics*, trans. M. Douglas Meeks, Philadelphia: Fortress Press, 1984; Wolfgang Huber and Heinz Eduard Tödt, *Menschenrechte: Perspektiven einer menschlichen Welt*, Stuttgart: Kreuz Verlag, 1977; Wolfgang Vögele, *Menschenwürde zwischen Recht und Theologie: Begründungen von Menschenrechte in der Perspektive öffentlicher Theologie*, Gütersloh: Chr. Kaiser, 2001; Paul Middelton, ed., *The God of Love and Human Dignity*, London/New York: T & T Clark, 2007; George Newlands, *Christ and Human Rights: The Transformative Engagement*, Burlington, VT: Ashgate, 2006.

8.   *Basic Documents on Human Rights*, pp.114, 125.

9.   *International Convention on the Elimination of all Forms of Racial Discrimination* (1969), preface, in *Basic Documents on Human Rights*, p.148. See comparable language in *International Convention on Suppression and Punishment of the Crime of Apartheid* (1973), in ibid., p.162; *Convention on the Elimination of all Forms of Discrimination Against Women* (1979), in ibid., p.169.

10.   *De Libertate Christiana* (1520), in *D. Martin Luthers Werke: Kritische Gesamtausgabe* Weimar: H. Boehlaus Nachfolger, 1883-, 7:49-73 [hereafter WA], translated in Jaroslav Pelikan et al., eds., *Luther's Works*, Philadelphia: Muhlenberg Press, 1955-, 31:327-377 [hereafter LW]. A shorter German edition, *Die Freiheit eines Christenmenschen*, appears in WA 7:20-38.

11.   LW 31:334-336.

12.   LW 31:341.

13.   LW 31:341, 342. The quote is from *Luther: Lectures on Romans* [1515-1516], trans. Wilhelm Pauck, Philadelphia: Westminster Press, 1961, p. 8. Many of the teachings from these Lectures are repeated in Luther's *Freedom of a Christian*.

14.   LW 31:341-342. See similar sentiments in Luther's *Address to the Christian Nobility of the German Nation Concerning the Reform of the Christian Estate* (1520), LW 44:123-217, at 136.

15. Quotation is from Luther's *Lectures on Genesis 38-44* (1544), LW 7:182.

16. See esp. LW 44:126-155; *The Babylonian Captivity of the Church* (1520), LW 36:11-126; *Treatise on Good Works* (1520), LW 44:21-114, at 87-94, with expansion in *The Keys* (1530), LW 40:321-370. In LW 44:158, Luther recommended that a new imperial law be passed against papal appointments of clergy so that "no confirmation of any dignity whatsoever shall henceforth be secured from Rome." In LW 44:129 and LW 36:117, Luther attacked the notion that the clergy were special because of the "indelible mark" of their ordination, terming this "a laughingstock."

17. LW 44:157ff., 202ff.

18. LW 7:182ff.; LW 44:203ff. See also Luther's fuller statement in *Temporal Authority: To What Extent it Should be Obeyed* (1523), in LW 45:75-129.

19. LW 44:129.

20. LW 31:344-347, 358-361. The theme recurs repeatedly in Luther's later writings. See, e.g., LW 12:328, 27:230ff., 32:173; WA 39/1:21, 492, 552.

21. LW 31:355.

22. LW 31:344.

23. LW 31:344, 358-361; see also LW 25:120-130, 204-213.

24. See, e.g., LW 19:47-48, LW 23:146.

25. LW 31:344-354, 368-377.

26. LW 31:345.

27. Lectures on Romans, 120. See also LW 23:146; LW 12:328-330; LW 8:9-12.

28. LW 31:354.

29. LW 36:70, echoing LW 31:344-346.

30. LW 31:355-358.

31. LW 31:355-356; see also LW 36:112-116, 138-140, LW 40:21-23; LW 13:152, and esp. the long diatribe in LW 39:137-224.

32. LW 31:355; see also LW 36:241.

33. LW 31:364-5; see also LW 51:86-87.

34. LW 38:188; LW 28:171-172.

35. LW 31:355; see also LW 17:209ff.

36. LW 31:343.

37. *See That Jesus Christ was Born a Jew* (1523), in LW 45:129.

38. Mark U. Edwards, Jr., *Printing, Propaganda, and Martin Luther*, Berkeley, CA: University of California Press, 1981, pp.39, 64, 100-101.

39. See further Martin Luther, *Concerning the Ministry* (1523), in LW 40:21ff.

40. LW 31:354-356, 364-365.

41. See alternative exegeses in Ruth Mellinkoff, *The Mark of Cain*, Berkeley, CA: University of California Press, 1981; Claus Westermann, *Genesis 1-11: A Commentary*, repr. ed. Minneapolis: Augsburg Publishing House, 1990.

42. Grant Gilmore, *The Ages of American Law*, Chicago: University of Chicago Press, 1977, pp.110-111.

The Justice of Equality: A Biblical and Postcolonial Perspective

*Equality remains something to be aimed at, but Empire building, and its near-neighbour colonialism, are as old as history, and have been implicated in much injustice. The newly-born nation of Israel and the infant Christian church were alike delivered out of the womb of oppressive empires. That being the case, argues **Dr Jonathan Ingleby**, their histories can contribute to, and be interpreted by, postcolonial theory. So can ours.*

The French Revolution gave us the famous trio 'liberty, fraternity, equality'. We hear a good deal about freedom and something too about solidarity and community (fraternity) but the missing part of the equation in so much of our thinking today is equality. Also, I think it is reasonable to take it as read that injustice and inequality go together. There are, I know, those who claim that inequality is a good thing, that it reflects 'the way things are', that it allocates people to their proper station (as in the caste system!) that it promotes competition, which is also, apparently, a good thing. Recent studies, however, have suggested that inequality is bad for everyone, even the people at the top of the pile. I am thinking of books such as Richard Wilkinson and Kate Pickett's *The Spirit Level*, Daniel Dorling's *Injustice* and Tony Judt's *Ill Fares the Land*. Judt writes:

> It is the growing inequality in and between societies that generates so many social pathologies. Grotesquely unequal societies are also unstable societies. They generate internal division and, sooner or later, internal strife—usually with undemocratic outcomes.[1]

Also there is general agreement that equality before the law and equality of opportunity—with the real possibility of social mobility—are basic components of a just society. I would go further and say that good government has the responsibility of creating a more equal society and that that is its greatest contribution to justice, in a wide sense of the word (i.e. meaning more by the word than simply maintaining law and order). It can do this in a number of ways: by providing adequate educational and health services for everyone, by defending the weak and unfortunate against those who would exploit them, by progressive taxation (including death duties) and by ensuring decent working conditions and wages. These measures are eminently practical and doable, but they are not the main subject of this chapter.

What I want to look at here is the Biblical witness to an equal, and therefore a just society, and, at the same time, the way in which the post-colonial situation and postcolonial theory provide us with opportunities and incentives to put these Biblical principles into practice. What do I mean by these terms? I use 'post-colonial' with a hyphen to mean an historical period immediately after a prolonged period of imperialism or colonialism. 'Postcolonial' without the hyphen refers to the discourse, as produced by postcolonial studies.[2] Here is a description by Robert J. C. Young.

> Postcolonialism...is a general name for the insurgent knowledges that come from the subaltern, the dispossessed, and seek to change the terms and values under which we all live. You can learn it anywhere if you want to. The only qualification you need to start is to make sure that you are looking at the world not from above, but from below.[3]

Both Israel after the Exodus and the early Christian church were in a post-colonial situation.

As I shall try to explain, I consider that both Israel after the Exodus and the early Christian church were in a post-colonial situation, in that they had both come out of a recent experience of Empire. Their experience can therefore be described by means of postcolonial theory. Equally, Israel and church can contribute to a better understanding of that theory.

Old Testament Israel was a surprisingly equal society.[4] No doubt it often fell short of its own Yahwistic ideals, but the intention was clear. Reflecting on the history of the nation, the Old Testament authors, compilers and editors were convinced that the nation's birth was intimately tied up with the escape from imperial Egypt. It was not just that the people had been slaves there. They realised that there was something intrinsically dangerous to human well-being in a wealthy dynastic hierarchy (Deuteronomy 17:17-20), a standing army with the latest military technology (Deuteronomy 17:16), and an economic system based on the storage and therefore control of surpluses (contrast Exodus 1:11). Israel as originally constituted had none of these things. It had no ruling class: no king or nobles and its priestly caste was forbidden to own land. It had no standing army, and no big landed estates, and therefore no means of collecting large surpluses which could be hoarded. In due course Israel did decide to have a king, though it is clear that some of the later Biblical writers viewed this with great suspicion, and there were sharp warnings against turning the apparatus of government into a more imperial system (1 Samuel 8:10-18). The tribal pattern, which largely disappeared during the time of the monarchy, was perhaps more of a loss than is generally understood. Later, after the return from exile, Ezra and Nehemiah had to make strenuous efforts to restore Yahwistic practices in the community by challenging the behaviour of the elites which had formed during the exile and which had adopted foreign elitist patterns. Jesus in his day, thinking about Israel's future, re-tribalised the nation's leadership (Matthew 19:28) and was never fully accepting of the kingship titles that were ascribed to him (see e.g. John 6:15).

As mentioned above, equality extended to economic arrangements. The aim was a society of small farmers each with enough land to make a living ('every man under his own vine and under his own fig tree'). Attempts to create large estates were specifically condemned by the prophetic tradition (Isaiah 5:8). The small farmer, it was hoped, would be both politically and economically independent. Various equalising mechanisms, such as the Jubilee[5], were designed to perpetuate these arrangements. The general aim was *shalom,* meaning 'well-being' or 'health' in a general sense. The feeling of this is well captured by this quote from the *Movimento Sem Terra* in Brazil.

> Thus, health is how and where you live, what you eat, and how you make a living. It is feeling well physically, being mentally at peace, living in a family setting where there is respect, affection, and equality among all, respecting nature, and living in a society in which justice and equality go hand in hand.[6]

There was something else about early Israel. It was surprisingly inclusive. It is quite wrong to think of the Israel of the Exodus as a tight-knit group based on a carefully guarded ethnic particularity. The 'borders' of ethnic Israel were extremely porous[7] and where there was exclusion it was because there was an obvious threat to the *faith* of Israel. Except in matters of religious practice (you had to be circumcised to join in the Passover celebrations), aliens were treated in many ways just like Israelites. Indeed there was legislation (Deuteronomy 10:19, Jeremiah 7:6) in their favour, because, having no land of their own, they were presumed to be at a disadvantage.[8] Faith, not race, was the unifying principle for the time being. A true Israelite, a true descendant of Abraham, was somebody who had the faith of Abraham or, to put it another way, was somebody who lived according to the Covenant. This was an exclusive and an inclusive principle. Excluded were those who wished to introduce beliefs and practices which were not according to the Covenant faith of Israel. A foreign princess, for example, like Jezebel, was 'foreign' because she did not understand that in Israel even kings and queens were subject to the Covenant (see e.g. the story of Naboth's vineyard 1 Kings 21:1-16.) By contrast, people like Ruth the Moabite woman, was included because she was prepared to live wholeheartedly under the Covenant (Ruth 1:16) and its laws. She was so thoroughly included that she is listed as a famous ancestor of the even more famous King David (Ruth 4:17). The point is that under the Covenant all were equal. They were all 'children of Abraham' and had the rights and responsibilities of Covenant people. It is relevant that in the New Testament both John the Baptist and Jesus could see how important this idea of 'the children of Abraham' was. John the Baptist warned the crowds who attended his preaching that physical descent from Abraham was not what God reckoned with, but with repentance and the fruit of repentance (Luke 3:7-9). Jesus said of the tax-collector Zacchaeus that he was restored to his status as a 'son of Abraham' (Luke 19:9) because he had begun to act in a covenantal way (Luke 19:8 to be compared with Leviticus 6:4-5).

I think we underestimate the power of the idea that in the Kingdom of God there is an intended equality and that this is expressed initially by, so to speak, the rules of entry. People who claimed privilege—on whatever ground—found that they had to lay aside those privileges, if they were going to get in at all, while others who thought they were excluded, realised that this was not necessarily so, and that once included they were not second-class citizens. This was (and is) the 'justice' of the Kingdom. When Matthew uses the first Servant Song (Matthew 12:18-21 compare Isaiah 42:1-4) to describe the mission of Jesus he speaks of Jesus 'proclaiming justice' (verse 18) and 'leading justice to victory' (verse 20). How will Jesus do this? By very gentle methods it seems. There will be no shouting, no contention; rather, a patient restoration of the bruised and fragile (verses 19-20). All this adds to the sense that the Kingdom is a place where the weak and disadvantaged flourish, and because the naturally strong and advantaged can look after themselves, this is a recipe for a more equal society, and therefore a more just society.

Other New Testament evidence bears this out. The big struggle to welcome Jew and Gentile alike and to place them on an equal footing in the church is a hugely important New Testament theme. It is a central issue in the story of the expansion of the early church in Acts of the Apostles and also in the theology of the letters to the Galatians, Romans and Ephesians. It is not, however, the only issue to do with equality. Galatians 3:28 adds, rather surprisingly, to the equality of Jew and Greek in the church community, that of slave and free, and male and female. Paul clearly does not accept the related condition of master and slave, or the commonly practised patriarchy, as something which should obtain in the church.[9] His injunctions elsewhere to slaves to obey their masters and women to obey their husbands have to do with the acceptance of the 'household codes' which were then the societal norms, 'the way of the world' about which he and his fellow Christians had no choice. These codes could be purified and redeemed, that is to say given Christian meanings, but they could not for the time being be replaced. Paul was in a position to 'legislate' for the church; he could not do so for the Roman Empire! We see, nevertheless, how Paul began to invoke new patterns of behaviour even in society at large. In his letter to the slave-owner Philemon he suggested a hitherto unknown equality between master and slave on the grounds of Christian brotherhood. This should make a difference, argued Paul, when Philemon considered how to deal with his runaway slave (Philemon 15-16). In addition to slaves and masters and men and women, other status and ethnic discriminations were forbidden in Colossians 3:11—an injunction which comes just before one of the household codes mentioned above (3:22). We may feel that this is a long way from postcolonial justice, but Colossians 3:11 incudes the idea of discrimination against 'barbarians' (uncivilised people) a key term in the colonial lexicon.

One of the reasons why Israel in its earliest days was able to enshrine principles of equality and justice was that it stood in an in-between, provisional or liminal space. This was clearly true of the wilderness journey and we can perhaps trace certain elements of Israel's behaviour in the Promised Land to its sense that it had received foundational insights into Covenant and *Torah* while it was still a nomadic people. It is true that one Old Testament tradition records the wilderness experience as negative (see e.g. Psalm 95:8-11) but another views it as a honeymoon experience (Jeremiah 2:2-3, Hosea 2:14-15). Even the former considers the divine disapproval experienced by the wilderness generation to be a consequence of Israel's unwillingness to accept the new rules that Yahweh required them to live by now that they had left Egypt, rules to do with what Ched Myers has called 'Sabbath economics'.[10] Similarly, the New Testament church stood in a liminal position in a number of senses. The idea that Christians were 'strangers in the world' (1 Peter 1:1 NIV) was one. When Paul proclaimed that 'here, i.e. in the Christian community, there is no longer Greek or Jew, circumcised and uncircumcised, barbarian, Scythian, slave and free' (Colossians 3:11 again) it does raise the question: if there are none of these familiar identities, what has taken their place? As I shall go on to say, this does not mean that these identities have been totally erased, but it does mean that all of these believers have been cut loose in an important way from their cultural moorings, or to put it differently that they have come under an over-arching canopy—their identity in Christ—which makes their other identities contingent.

Postcolonialism as a discourse is rather happy with liminality, indeed it is one of its key ideas.

Postcolonialism as a discourse is rather happy with liminality, indeed it is one of its key ideas. It sees it as an in-between space where new formations can arise. It is linked, particularly in the thinking of Homi Bhabha, with hybridity. The two ideas—liminality and hybridity—are part of postcolonialism's counter-attack against binary thinking: 'us and them', 'black and white', 'civilised and barbarians', 'developed and under-developed', 'First World and Third World' and so on. It is an attack on 'essentialism', the idea that cultures have an essential core which makes them impenetrable by other cultures and which pushes other 'non-essential' elements to the margin with the intention of keeping them there. By contrast, as Homi Bhabha says, the 'interstitial passage between fixed identifications opens up the possibility of a cultural hybridity that entertains difference without an assumed or imposed hierarchy'.[11] The idea of 'difference without an assumed or imposed hierarchy' is a happy one. As we have said, we need not assume on the basis of Colossians 3:11 that the differences between Greek, Jew, circumcised and uncircumcised (Jew and gentile expressed religiously), barbarian, and Scythian have been completely erased. Community, after all, is not built on sameness but on difference. But we do need to know that those who 'have put on the new nature' (Colossians 3:10 REB) are equal in status in Christ. In this new equality all voices are to have their say. A hybrid community is designed to be multivocal: with no 'official' line. This also creates a less hierarchical and more just situation. In the equality and hybridity of 'the Carnival Kingdom' voices from the underside of society are given a hearing, perhaps for the first time. Here is an example:

> The idea of a polyphony of voices in society is implied in Bakhtin's idea of the carnivalesque, which emerged in the Middle Ages 'a boundless

world of humorous forms and manifestations opposed to the official and serious tone of medieval ecclesiastical and feudal culture.'[12]

The early church knew about 'a polyphony of voices' which went hand in hand with a non-hierarchical community (1 Corinthians 14:26-33, I Thessalonians 5:19-21). 'Conversation' in the early church was equal; it was, to use Rowan Williams' term 'a conversation of charity' because it did not need 'assurances of sameness, recognisability in respect of some external factor'.[13] When a gentile prophesied in the assembly he or she did not have to fear that all the Jews stopped listening! When a slave spoke up, even his or her master came under the authority of the message. Of course this was a very subversive process. In the Middle Ages, Carnival was not expected to last too long! There is within most societies a tendency towards order and authority that insists that there should be no alternatives. Every society has its authoritarians and it is they who usually come out on top.

Giles Fraser, writing in the *Guardian* recently came up with the comment: 'In the life of Jesus holiness is redefined as justice.'[14] The context of this remark was an article about the Occupy movement and in particular the contrast between the 'holiness' of the Occupiers' camp and the 'holiness' expressed by the majestic character of St Paul's Cathedral. Fraser suggested that you might find Jesus among the tents! My thought was[15] that Occupy's justice movement is, in fact, one of the liminal, hybrid, non-hierarchical communities that we have been thinking about. It is significant that it has been frequently condemned for lacking a programme, indeed a 'coherent narrative'. However, I would wish to contend that this apparent incoherence—in terms of advocating specific societal structures—was true for Jesus too. It is clear that Jesus knew on which side he was—he was on the side of the poor—and he knew what he did not want. For example, the oppressive behaviour of many of the Jewish leaders who used the purity and debt codes to keep themselves in power and to keep the people in subservience, was unequivocally condemned. But it would be difficult to distinguish anything akin to a programme in his teaching. He asked a lot of questions, challenged a lot of assumptions, told a lot of (rather enigmatic) stories and gath-

> *It would be difficult to distinguish anything akin to a programme in Jesus' teaching.*

ered disciples. His opponents knew somehow that he was a mortal threat to their hegemony, but they had great difficulty in accusing him of anything too specific. Perhaps that is how the rule of God, at least for the present, ought usually to proceed.

Let me restate my thesis in slightly different language. A culture of hierarchy inevitably means lack of freedom. Similarly aiming at uniformity means that the hybridity of a mixed situation has to be seen as a threat. But, as we have seen, hybridity, because of its mixed nature is the necessary condition for equality and justice, if only because in a truly hybrid situation nobody can stake a prior claim to superiority. Primordial communities, those based on age-old tradition and sentiment, tend towards hierarchy and uniformity. The antidote is the imagined community which is 'performed' rather than taught and which does not contain within its founding documents (real or imagined) an immutable text. Instead it describes itself in language that is descriptive rather than prescriptive. Truth is valued, but it is assessed critically not in a naïve way, and rationality is tempered by imagination and magic.

The above paragraph contains some of the key ideas of the postcolonial discourse. I hope by now it is becoming clear that I believe that early Israel and the early Christian church tried to live out many of these key ideas. They were 'imagined communities', hybrid and non-hierarchical, working things out as they went along, describing rather than prescribing, critically evaluating what they considered to be the truth. To prove this in any more detail would go beyond the scope of this chapter, but let me add one further example from each community, looking in particular at the question of leadership.

Moses, the charismatic leader, clearly found his leadership role 'too big a job for one man' and to his credit he was constantly looking around for help. He brought in the family (not very successfully) (Exodus 3:12-16); he delegated some of his authority over legal proceedings (Exodus 18:19-26); he appointed seventy elders who would 'bear the burden of the people' (Numbers 7:7) and so on. In fact he was simply inventing new leadership patterns as the situation developed. On the whole these patterns tended towards power-sharing, equality and justice.

In the early church, leadership patterns were equally confused—in a good sense. There was certainly nothing very hierarchical about them. They were always plural and always contextualised. The Jerusalem church adopted the Jewish synagogue pattern: elders with a *primus inter pares* (Acts 12:17, 15:13, 21:18), appropriate enough for a conservative Jewish group; the church at Antioch, predominantly gentile, was led by prophets and teachers (Acts 13:1); Paul's churches usually had elders and deacons (Philippians 1:1), but the church at Corinth did not have any formal leadership, they decided matters in the assembly (1 Corinthians 5:4-5), perhaps reflecting Greek democratic traditions. Those who are looking for a single pattern of New Testament church leadership will not find it. The charismatic freedom to invent and imagine led to an expression of the 'upside down king-dom' in practice—one of the earliest bishops of Rome was a slave.[16]

> *Those who are looking for a single pattern of New Testament church leadership will not find it.*

A friend of mine is fond of saying that we human beings should have 'roots down and walls down'. The communities I am trying to describe may sound as if they have their walls down, but have they adequate roots? It is instructive that Israel was given a land and even after the great exile of 587 BCE it never gave up the hope that it might return there. The Jewish diaspora before the time of Christ also kept in close touch with the mother-land. The land to some extent determined what sort of society Israel would be. For example the flatness of the terrain and the ease of irrigation in Egypt (the proximity of the Nile) made it possible for there to be big estates with abundant crops to be stored away, with the usual economic and political consequences. Palestine was very different. It was hill country and agriculture depended on uncertain rainfall. This kept the units of agriculture small, and made the farming more arduous and hand to mouth. The small independent farmer who could get the most out of the situation was the basic building block of the society.[17] Small farms and businesses were the basis not only of equality but also freedom and justice. (It is still true today.) It gave the Israelite family 'a place to stand', literally and figuratively, against big government and big business (big landowners).

I cannot resist at this point saying something about Israel and the land and the contemporary situation, because I can hear the objection that in recent times Israel's loyalty to the land has been the source of considerable *injustice*. I am not sure about this. The real source of injustice in the current situation is the excessive loyalty to a Zionist interpretation of the Jewish tradition, rather than loyalty to the land itself. If, for example, the land was considered to be the host of everybody living in Palestine—Jews and Palestinians alike and indeed anybody else—then you would come up with a very different picture. Politically, this would mean some sort of 'one state' solution, and the inhabitants of the land would have to treat each other as neighbours and not as enemies. Unfortunately this seems a distant possibility at present, largely because, as usual, if you despise others, you do not treat them justly. Any sort of real democracy within a single state would, from the Jewish point of view, give the Palestinians far too much power, and would not be acceptable to Zionists. But this proves my point. The primary concern for the Zionists is not the land, but their exclusive use of it. Of course, these exclusive attitudes are commonplace. All those right wing parties in the United States and Europe that resist the influx of migrants are working on the same principle, which is the opposite of the 'alien mandate' of the Old Testament.

It is also instructive that the first Christian assemblies were attached to places, as the letters of the New Testament bear witness. These assemblies were 'rooted', though not in a particular culture, but in a particular place. All the residents in that place, whatever their language, ethnicity, status and so on, were potentially members. We might call this in modern terms 'the parish principle'. The church members' ability to identify with the locality gave them an identity without giving privilege to any one local cultural or ethnic group. Equality came into this as well. Daniel Dorling has shown that heterogeneous groups tend to be more equal and also tend to identify more with the locality. He comments: 'Londoners call themselves Londoners, often in preference to British (and certainly in preference to English) because no other words describe the mix.'[18] He also points out that where inequalities are great, differences (in this case he is talking about ethnic differences) matter more. People who see themselves as significantly superior to their neighbours, for example, do not want to be put under the same umbrella. The Jewish Christians in Rome were happy to be part of the church in Rome and to be addressed by that name, because they no longer despised their fellow gentile Christians. The 'parish principle' is good for churches not only because it keeps an open door for all sorts of people, but because it fosters an identity which roots the church in the locality. A local identity ('I'm glad to call myself a...') may therefore even foster equality and justice.

We have said that postcolonialism favours a community in which all sorts of voices can be heard, voices which are otherwise in danger of being suppressed by the consensus majority. I want to take this a little further. These are not only the voices of subalterns—the minorities and the marginalised—but also voices from the past which have been lost or submerged through the overlay of other more recent voices. (We are entering here into postcolonialism's interest in cultural archaeology, or the idea of 'palimpsest', one culture overlaying another on the same site, or the general matter of 'representation'.) This is true not only in the sense that there are many things which have slipped away into the past, but in the more sinister process by which Empire exercises power in the present so that it can configure the past. Truly justice is often determined by the war of representation.

The Jews in exile in Babylon were pressed by their captors and their circumstances to forget their homeland. In the war of representation

Israel's God was portrayed as a defeated god; the gods of Babylon, Bel and Nebo and so on, had triumphed. The exiles themselves began to feel that Yahweh had forgotten them. The great prophet whom we know as Second Isaiah knew perfectly well that if ever justice was to be done (see Isaiah 42:1, 4) then this war of myths needed to be won. So, he assured the people, Yahweh had not forgotten them (40:27) and the gods of Babylon were as powerless as the idols that represented them (Isaiah 46:1). In the Roman Empire a similar process was going on. Caesar was proclaimed a god, a universal saviour, a healer and deliverer, a bringer of peace and innumerable other benefits. The small Christian communities were surrounded by imperial propaganda to this effect. They had to be reminded that the ruler of the universe was not the Roman emperor but a slaughtered lamb (Revelation 6:5). Indeed this was at the heart of Christian apologetics. A Christian evangelist like Philip understood that when the Servant Song of Isaiah 53 spoke of someone to whom justice had been denied (Acts 8:12-13) it spoke about Jesus. The nature of this injustice was partly to do with the ability to speak and to be represented by future generations. Philip and his fellow evangelists were keen to right that wrong by speaking to everyone about Jesus as Saviour and Lord, the one whom God had vindicated by raising him from the dead (Acts 2:12).

It is perhaps wise to add at this point that the justice we see here being reinstated belongs to those with whom we can easily sympathise–the exiled Jews and the persecuted early Christians, and indeed to Jesus himself. What, however, if the voice which needs to be heard is of some less attractive minority? What if in our own nation (or even our church) there are groups or individuals who are being 'submerged' and we are directly or indirectly responsible? What justice have we taken away because we have relegated them to inferior status and refused them a voice? The idea of 'subaltern studies', postcolonialism's description of allowing the underdogs their voice in history, is something that we Western Christians need to take on board. Christianity has for so long been joined to the dominant culture in the West that the voices of many other cultures have grown faint. Justice demands that we change this. One obvious response is to reject the advantages that our cultural dominance has given us. In the context of the present discussion–the subaltern's loss of voice–this would have to do with establishing a situation of dialogue, something which on the whole the established church has failed to do. We preach at people, but do not listen to them. (See below on cultural change.) More fundamentally, it means sharing power with the powerless and choosing to be on the margins ourselves rather than at the centre. As Letty M Russell has put it:

Choosing to be connected to the margin is a spiritual discipline that calls us to work for justice, beginning with the agenda of those who are marginalised or objectified as objects that can be used, abused, or thrown away. It means treating other people as subjects where particularity and difference are respected and celebrated, rather than as objects of competition and domination.[19]

> *In mission we have found the requirement to treat others as equals to be particularly challenging.*

In mission we have found this requirement to treat others as equals to be particularly challenging. We have consistently played a power game based on the claim that we need to retain our theological dominance in order to be 'true to the gospel'.

We have said that hybrid, liminal, postcolonial communities are best designed to 'give justice a chance' in our divided and polarised world which is by contrast always on the lookout for secure identities and carefully maintained boundaries. The final question I want to look at is how in fact we might create such communities. Or if that wrongly assumes that we have to begin at the beginning, how does cultural change happen in a way that might urge us in the right direction? Cultural change has so often been the near neighbour of cultural imperialism that postcolonial theorists are very cautious about prescribing structural change of any sort. The modern missionary movement, for example, has been condemned by many for bringing about change through imperialistic methods. Many of the cultural practices it stood against, such as indigenous medicine, were, it now seems, unjustly dismissed. Instead of creating open, hybrid communities, missionaries tended to reproduce the closed, hierarchical practices that they brought with them.[20]

How then do cultures change for the good, and how do the advocates of a more just world hope to bring this about, without reproducing the familiar mistakes of the colonial past? It should be said first of all that there is nothing inherently wrong or sinister about cultural change. Individuals and communities have always welcomed new ideas, inventions and improvements. Naturally the value of these will vary. Israel may have learnt the idea of an amphictyony (a collection of tribes) by looking around at its neighbours (we are not sure about this).[21] It certainly learnt some other less helpful practices—such as the introduction of a monarchy—by the same process. In the history of Western expansion communities have been enriched by the introduction of hospitals and clinics, but harmed by the introduction of firearms, to take one positive and one negative example. The idea that *nothing* new should ever be introduced, however, must surely be rejected *pace* the radical anthropologists. In any case newness is often the response to some overwhelming event or series of events that demands some response. Israel came out of the Exodus; the early church was the fruit of Pentecost.

Though there is nothing wrong with cultural change, there are dangers to be avoided:

> *There is nothing inherently wrong or sinister about cultural change.*

•   If possible there should be choice, not coercion, so that the newness is something which is on offer; people should understand what it is they are accepting or rejecting and the consequences of doing so.

•   Something new will be better accepted if it can be seen to connect with something which is already valued by the individual or community. Trying to introduce a new idea or practice will be much easier if the introducer has some knowledge of the recipient's culture. This is the well-known idea of contextualisation, not exactly the same thing as seeking hybridity, but perhaps a forerunner or near neighbour.

•   The bringers of newness are also likely to encounter newness. If they are wise they will even be on the lookout for it. Also, this may be just the beginning. When two cultures meet, there is almost always a process which leads to fusion or hybridity, and this is, according to the logic of this essay, precisely what we are looking for. New ideas may be shared; new alliances formed, old prejudices may fall away, familiar experiences may feel quite different in their new setting. Or you can wrap all these up and say that this is something which happens to people when they encounter other people—they are never the same again, as the saying goes.

•   It is still worth remembering that newness equals change and change is a threat to existing cultures because cultures are normative; they contain the rules by which we survive and thrive. Can we continue to survive and thrive if we change the rules? This question is most frequently asked by those who are the guardians of the culture, remembering that these are usually the people who benefit most from maintaining its integrity.

•   Finally it is our response to the 'threat' of change (as it is usually perceived) that may determine good and bad outcomes. As Edward Said has remarked: 'Every identity is a construction, a composite of different histories, migrations, conquests, liberations, and so on. We can deal with these either as worlds at war, or experiences to be reconciled.'[22]

Said was writing in the context of the conflict between Israel and her Arab neighbours, perhaps the most intractable conflict of modern times, a situation in which justice has been hard to discover.

There remains the Biblical, postcolonial challenge of a more equal and more just world. Israel by no means lived up to the vision of her founding fathers. The early church soon enough became hierarchical and authoritarian. The end of empire has not always led to societies that are just and equal in their arrangements. In church and state, we are still, all too often, confronted by privilege, patriarchy, prejudice, discrimination and the like. Yet the vision remains. 'Another world is possible' as the saying goes. We have these ideas in our rucksacks—to use a homely illustration. Let me list some of the ones that I have mentioned: liminality, hybridity, multivocalism, carnival, tribalism (good sense), Jubilee, *shalom*, inclusivity, children of Abraham, covenant, Sabbath economics, polyphony, a conversation of charity, holiness, non-programmatic mission, imagined communities, performance, description, imagination, magic, delegation, power-sharing, confusion (good sense), contextualisation, charisma, upside-down kingdom, 'roots down and walls down', a place to stand, the parish principle, heterogeneity, local identity, memory, subaltern studies, dialogue, on the margins, relationship, choice....

Now what we have to do is to unpack the load we carry and spread the wares out so that anybody who wants to 'buy' them may do so. If we want a name for the bundle on our backs, we could call it 'the justice pack'.

Dr Jonathan Ingleby *was a mission partner in India and subsequently Head of Mission Studies at Redcliffe College. He is author of* Beyond Empire, Christians and Catastrophe, Naming the Frame *and* Missionaries, Education and India.

Notes

1. 1 Judt, T. *Ill Fares the Land*, London: Allen Lane, 2010, p.235.

2. I am aware that not everybody follows this usage, but I have found it useful.

3. Young, Robert J. C., *Postcolonialism, A Very Short Introduction*, Oxford: Oxford University Press, 2003, p.20.

4. See further McConville, J. G. *God and Earthly Powers*, London: T & T Clark, 2006 p. 86

5. The year of Jubilee, every fiftieth year, envisaged, among other provisions, the return to their original owners of the property that had been alienated for whatever reason during the previous fifty years. It was therefore a measure which made the acquiring of large estates impossible in the long run. See Leviticus 25: 8-17.

6. Cited in Young, 2010, p.47.

7.   See Ingleby, J. *Beyond Empire, Postcolonialism and Mission in a Global Context*, Milton Keynes: Authorhouse, 2010, pp.236-7.

8.   Some recent scholars (see e.g. Brett. M.G. *Decolonizing God, The Bible in the Tides of Empire*, Sheffield: Phoenix Press, 2009, p.85) have suggested that the question of the treatment of strangers was given additional emphasis by the influx of 'northerners' into Judah after the destruction of the northern kingdom by the Assyrians in the seventh century BCE. This would again place the texts in an imperial or post-imperial context.

9.   See Bruce, F. F. *The Epistle to the Galatians NIGTC*, Exeter: Paternoster, 1982, p. 190.

10.   Myers C. *The Biblical Vision of Sabbath Economics*, Washington: Tell the Word, 2001, especially chapter 1.

11.   Bhabha, *The Location of Culture*, London: Routledge, 1994 cited by Ashcroft B., Griffiths G. and Tiffin H. *Post-Colonial Studies: The Key Concepts*, London: Routledge, 2000 p.131.

12.   Holquist, M. 'Introduction' to Mikhail Bakhtin, *Rabelais and his World*, Bloomington: Indiana University Press, 1984, p.5, cited in Ashcroft, Griffiths and Tiffin, 2000, p.118.

13.   Williams, R. *Lost Icons*, London: Continuum, 2000, p.99.

14.   'No church should isolate itself from human need' *Guardian* 18.11.2011.

15.   I have developed this a little in an article on the Occupy Movement in the British & Irish Association of Mission Studies No. 38, pp.6-10, some of the text of which I use here.

16.   Bruce, F. F. *The Spreading Flame*, Exeter: Paternoster, 1958, p.192.

17.   See Deuteronomy 11:10-12. The Deuteronomist was aware of the contrasting agricultural demands of Egypt and Palestine.

18.   Dorling, D. *Injustice*, Bristol: The Policy Press, 2011, p.164.

19.   Cited in Sørensen, J. S. *Missiological Mutilations – Prospective Paralogies*, Frankfurt am Main: Peter Lang, 2007, p.232.

20.   Ingleby, J. 2010 p.173ff.

21.   See Woustra, M.H. *The Book of Joshua*, Grand Rapids: Eerdmans, 1981, p. 145n.

22.   Said, E. The End of the Peace Process New York: Pantheon, 2000 p.142

The Influence of Religion and Culture in Development in the Philippines

If development is important to the promoting and sustaining of justice and instrumental to the well-being of community, what are the cultural and religious factors which prevent some communities from flourishing? Social anthropologist, writer and activist **Melba Padilla Maggay** *examines this question from the context of the Philippines.*

The paradox of poverty: Why are nations poor?

For more than half a century, the dominant answers to this question have been framed by what can roughly be described as the modernisation narrative. As a concept, it was first formulated in North America in the 1950s by sociologists like Talcott Parsons, who believed that the forces unleashed in highly-developed economies—industrialisation and urbanisation—would eventually engulf the whole world.[1]

Modernisation is also, before this, a historical phenomenon, rooted in the intellectual, economic and social traditions that have evolved in the West since the Industrial Revolution and the Enlightenment, hence the use of the term as if it were synonymous with 'Westernisation' or, with the advent of the American century, 'Americanisation.'

Within this narrative—which forms much of the ideological backdrop of 'development'—nations are poor because they have certain 'deficits' in those aspects that are recognised as important within this frame: deficits in capital, in technology, in the level of skill of the human resource, or in the availability of natural resources, notably in sub-Saharan Africa, for instance.

There are countries like the Philippines, however, which have none of these 'deficits,' and yet are increasingly poor. Beneath these islands are immense natural resources that are still to be mined or explored. We have a highly educated citizenry. Our professional classes serve as consultants to the development needs of the Asia region, while those at the lower end have a high level of multicultural and social skills that supply the demand for quality human touch in service industries all around the globe.

Our old *Mestizo* elite and newly-emerged Filipino-Chinese *taipans* are not without capital. They invest in China, Australia and other places, and there is a lot of old money stashed away in Swiss banks or sleeping in some financial capital somewhere else. There is no lack of savvy in accessing new technologies, as evident in our relatively competitive competencies in information technologies and business process outsourcing, not to mention that the country is reputed to be the 'texting capital' of the world.

Competing explanations are offered from social and cultural studies. In the '60s and '70s, studies showed that societies that are highly stratified tend to be trapped in poverty. Gunnar Myrdal, speaking out of the caste system in India, had found that no amount of technical solutions can work within the disincentives posed by systemic inequality. 'Greater equality,' he said, 'is a precondition for lifting a society out of poverty'.[2]

In Latin America, this line of analysis took the form of Marxist-influenced dependency theories.[3] Simply put, these theories postulated that the poor countries of the 'periphery' were being bilked by rich capitalist countries of the 'centre.' These predatory economies depressed world market prices of raw materials while inflating the prices of manu-factured goods, selling them at excessive profit to poor countries through transnational corporations.

These structural explanations cannot be dismissed out of hand in these days of over-reliance on market forces as a way of 'lifting up all boats', and with it the optimistic projection that it will also improve the plight of the poor. While highly generalised and out of fashion since the collapse of socialist regimes, these theories continue to be cogently descriptive of some of the internal and external conditions underlying underdevelop-ment in many countries, including the Philippines.

Having said this, dependency theories do not account sufficiently, however, for the laggard performance of this country in the last four decades. They do not help us very much in identifying the country-specific factors that may explain, say, the lag in growth *vis-à-vis* its neighbours in East and Southeast Asia. These 'NICs', or newly-industrialised countries, managed to overcome the shared handicap of a colonial and authoritarian history, while the Philippines continues to languish under the residue of these influences. The growth of Asian NICs has been largely fuelled by exports to the global centres. This country, once the showcase of capitalist democracy in Asia, has in the meantime shrunk its manufacturing and agricultural sectors and resorted to exporting its people instead.

A black hole exists somewhere between the highly generalised paradigms of underdevelopment and the often narrowly technical and discrete studies offered by development economists. We cast about for some coherent answers, some clarity as to why one country does well and another fails under quite similar conditions.

With the continuing poverty of at least two-thirds of the world's peoples—30 million of whom die every year of hunger and two billion suffer from malnutrition, according to the UN Food and Agriculture Organization—attention has turned to culture as an explanatory variable.

The cult of the *caudillo*, corruption in the bureaucracy, and the general softness of institutions in the Majority orld were all identified as factors causing underdevelopment which are directly attributable to culture.[4] Lawrence Harrison is one of the more visible proponents of this view: "I believe that there is no other satisfactory way to explain the deeply contrasting evolution of the North and the South in the Western hemisphere than culture—the strikingly different values, attitudes and institutions—that have flowed from the Protestant and Ibero-Catholic traditions."[5]

This line of thinking has been fiercely resisted by many sensitive anthropologists who firmly believe in cultural relativism in a rather absolute form. It is natural to feel great discomfort in the notion that some people are poor because there is something wrong with their culture. This is like 'blaming the victim', and is considered politically incorrect in a time when pluralism and diversity are sacred mantras in today's multicultural mega-societies.

Something is also amiss when it is suggested that some cultures are inherently 'development-resistant' while some are 'development-prone' and will naturally get ahead in the global race.[6] Particularly held up as examples of this were the Sinite cultures with their 'Confucian' values which were held up as a possible explanation for the rise of the Asian Tiger economies and the looming superpower status of China.

This grossly overlooks the fact that for centuries China was asleep. Confucianism as a scholarly tradition was hierarchical and elitist and did not lend itself to creating conditions for the flourishing of commercial enterprise.

Something similar could be said about the overseas Chinese contingents in Southeast Asia and elsewhere, but theirs is another story altogether. Their success as minorities may have more to do with the driving forces of migration interacting with their transported community structures and acquired competencies as a people.

With the above as a kind of caveat, there is nevertheless much to recommend the idea that culture is a critical determinant of economic success. This is so not only because there is evidence that many development initiatives fail due to lack of sensitivity to the cultural context of such interventions. Development planners have long taken account of this fact and have duly marshalled the services of anthropologists, mainly to induce acceptance of their planned change and make their work easier. The World Bank, particularly, has programmed a track called 'ethno-development' in response to the resistance of indigenous peoples and the need to accommodate and preserve local systems and structures.

On a deeper level, we submit that cultures—the patterns people historically learn for organising their life-systems in response to their environments—start out as rational and capable of sustaining their requirements for sustenance. This accounts for why there is a sense among those who have studied 'primitive' cultures that indigenous systems are self-sustaining. On the other hand, accidents of history and the trauma of disasters may cripple entire peoples psychologically and result in maladaptations.

> *Accidents of history and the trauma of disasters may cripple entire peoples psychologically and result in maladaptations*

Forcible encounters with the outside world, usually by encroachments of foreign powers, have caught many such societies unprepared for the challenges of coping with an unfamiliar world-system whose rules are stacked up against them. This seems to be the universal experience of countries once ruled by colonial empires; their relatively viable subsistence economies in the pre-colonial period collapsed and their traditional social structures were destroyed.

> *Relatively viable subsistence economies in the pre-colonial period collapsed and their traditional social structures were destroyed.*

Depending on the nature of the culture, the experience of colonisation may create a phenomenon called 'reverse ethnocentrism,' as in the Philippines, where foreign influences are deemed superior to anything within the culture and so are welcomed and embraced enthusiastically, to a fault. Alternatively, the colonisation experience may lock and isolate cultures against the stimuli of growth and innovation from the outside, as with some Arab countries that felt humiliated by the breakup and decline of the Ottoman Empire and had been frozen in time, sustaining themselves by the memory of lost grandeur as imagined from an idealized past.

Such reactions to cultural disruption have had profound implications on the economic behaviour of many nations. It is in this sense that culture plays a great explanatory role behind the relative poverty and progress of nations.

Development as a failed metanarrative

Half a century after Walt Rostow announced the inevitability of development in his 1960 landmark book, *The Stages of Economic Growth*, the optimistic projection that poverty, injustice and ignorance shall end has become a failed dream in many societies, caught in this narrative of an evolutionary progress that will universally sweep all in its path.

In spite of massive development assistance, most 'developing' countries have found themselves merely running on the spot. The World Bank estimates that the total number of poor people in developing countries has increased without interruption since the 1950s. By 1990, the poor in the Majority world numbered 1.1 billion, an increase of 0.1 billion in just five years, from 1985.[7] After four decades of development effort, the poor were still at the lowest 40 per cent of households. Three-fifths of households were in the bottom 30% of income distribution in Asia, the bottom 25% in Africa, and the bottom 20 % in Latin America.[8]

The experts had to concede that not much has happened, and global conditions may be much worse: "We live in a world of dehumanizing poverty, collapsing ecological systems, and deeply stressed social structures," thus declared one of its more prominent practitioner-theorists, David Korten, as early as the beginning of the Fourth Development Decade.[9]

Often, 'development assistance' became another form of getting poor countries perpetually indebted. Loans were tied to preferred projects of lending countries, with hefty consultancy fees for foreign 'experts' built into them. Corrupt governments entered into such contracts to line their pockets, as with the Marcos regime's mothballed Bataan Nuclear Power

Plant, which was never used because of serious safety defects and which the Filipino people ended up paying many times over at the sacrifice of more urgent social development needs.[10]

The debt crisis of the 1980s made clear that the rise in affluence of wealthy nations during this decade was inextricably linked to the further impoverishment of the poor countries. By 1992, the UNDP (United Nations Development Program) reported that "The current debt-related net transfer from the developing to the industrialized countries stands at $50 billion a year."

In other words, according to the Dutch economists Bob Goudzwaard and Harry De Lange, "since 1982, the rising standard of living of the wealthy countries has been partially subsidized by the developing countries." How else, they asked, "are we to understand the reality that every day an amount of money roughly equivalent to the total debt of the developing countries circulates uncontrollably in the 'pure' financial sphere—an amount thirty to forty times more than that which circulates in the 'direct' sphere of buying and selling goods and services?"

With a great deal of prescience, they foresaw, in the mid 90s, the financial crash that was to befall the global financial system beginning in 2008: "These uncoordinated capital movements threaten the international monetary system itself, as we saw in 1992 when Great Britain and France were forced to defend their currencies by taking them out of the European Monetary Union."[11]

Contrary to notions that the debt problem is over, they spelled out the 'three laws' that govern the dynamics of debt and its continuing impact on poor nations. The poor nations bear the brunt of external shocks in the world economy over which they have little or no control. The raising of tariff barriers or of import prices, such as that of oil, means that poor nations have no alternative but to borrow money acceptable in the international exchange from foreign banks. The UNDP estimates that this reality costs poor countries about 10 times what they receive in foreign assistance.[12]

1.   Debts increase *despite* efforts of poor nations to pay them off

Between 1982 and 1988, for example, the total debt of the South more than doubled, despite the fact that together during the same period they paid no less than $830 billion to their creditors, an amount more than they had owed in 1982! How did this happen? Because of shockingly high interest rates: "the developing countries effectively paid an average real interest rate of 17% during the 1980s, compared with 4% by the industrial nations."[11]

2.   Debts increase *because* of poor nations' efforts to pay them off

Known as the law of Irving Fischer ('the more people pay, the more they owe'), this law operates thus: in order to get out of the debt trap, poor nations increase their exports to bring in the currencies needed to pay off their debts. But in a declining world market, such as that in 1979 and now with the current global recession, every increase in the quantity of exported goods from the Majority world causes prices to plummet. As a result, export revenues fall instead of rise, and there is less money to pay off debts, which were incurred because of more production. Thus, because of their efforts to pay, poor nations find themselves more indebted to wealthy nations.

3.   Poverty increases *further* in the effort to pay off debts

The combined effects of the three laws have been more relentless poverty. In the face of their inability to pay escalating debts, poor nations have been required by creditors to structurally adjust their economies, with devastating results as we have seen.

On top of this, much of the onerous debt burden actually went to private pockets, as with the alleged $1.9 billion ill-gotten wealth of the Marcoses stashed away in Swiss bank accounts. Since the fall of the dictatorship, the Philippines has been paying on average about 25.72% of the national budget for debt servicing, money which could have gone to urgent social spending on health, education and low-income housing.[14]

Compelled by having personally witnessed the grinding poverty and the effects of the debt burden on people in the developing world, two elderly Britons—Bill Peters and Martin Dent—inspired by their Christian faith and fired by the biblical vision of debt cancellation in the Year of Jubilee, called on a network of faith-based NGOs (Non-Government Organisations) in the UK and the G-7 countries and, later, in the Majority world, to work for debt forgiveness for poor countries.

The Jubilee 2000 Campaign started in 1996 and goaded the leadership of multilateral institutions, like James Wolfensohn of the World Bank, to pose soul-searching questions to their agencies on how alternative mechanisms can be put in place to relieve the world's poor of the debt burden.

The first Heavily Indebted Poor Country (HIPC) initiative linked debt relief with progress on economic reforms, including spending for health, food security and education. Consensus was achieved to address the debt problem. However, defining sustainable debt levels and other technical questions became contentious. Of 14 countries eligible for the program in the first three years, only four—Uganda, Bolivia, Mozambique and Guyana—received debt relief.

This has raised concern among the Jubilee constituency, particularly those from the South, resulting in debates over the technicalities of the HIPC initiative and broader development issues. Progress has been painstakingly slow, and recent noises about debt caps, debt swaps for climate change initiatives, fair trade, and other such instruments have yet to yield the kind of dividends that would decisively relieve debt-burdened countries.

Nevertheless, the Jubilee 2000 Campaign built links between high-level officials and grassroots social activists. It showed the possibility of consensus among ideologically-diverse players rallying round a patent wrong. And, perhaps more important in the long run, it showed how an alternative vision sourced from a faith tradition can open windows and engage constructively with what seemed like hard-nosed financial institutions imperiously impervious to social clamour.

The global financial meltdown and the unrest in Wall Street are but signs that ethical issues cannot be side-lined in market economics. There are limits to runaway greed, and while imperfect market mechanisms are better than imperfect governments in creating wealth, we cannot merely leave the plight of the poor to market forces.

What all this tells us is that even in resurgent economies, the idea that enlarging the pie or increasing the GNP will have a 'trickle-down effect' for the poor is wishful thinking. From where I sit, 'what is good for the nation is good for the poor' has been proven again and again to be a fallacy in contexts where development initiatives only benefit a thin layer of the elite classes because the market and social structures are biased towards serving their needs rather than that of the vast poor. Even when government-sponsored growth results in unequivocal good for the modern sector of poor economies, this bypasses the survival enterprises of the poor. Experience shows that for such macroeconomic growth to benefit the poor and not be cornered by the few, it has to be of a sort that is different from the kind of development strategy that issues from the idea of modernisation:

> The benefits of economic growth in the formal sector of Third World economies tend to bypass the poor because modern-sector development projects, even those that are designated projects of national significance, do little to improve the productivity of the poor. A new power plant, a

new hospital, improved seaport facilities, a new airport terminal, or a new timber mill may augment the standard of living of bureaucrats, the captains of industry, skilled workers and professionals in the formal work force, but will make barely a difference to the value-added generated by the firms that employ the poor, produce for the poor and sell to the poor.[15]

The age of globalisation has further exacerbated this trajectory towards modernising economies which consolidate the privileges of the elite and exclude the poor. Cyberspace has democratised access to information and spawned revolutions, but the digital divide has been one factor behind the ever-increasing gap between the richest 20% and poorest 20% within and among countries. In the 1960s, we are told, the richest 20% had incomes 30 times more than that of the poorest; this doubled to 60 times by the beginning of the 1990s. By the close of the century the gap has jumped to 89 times.[16] In this country, the income disparity ratio between the very rich 150,000 families and the seven million poor families at the bottom is now calculated to be at a staggering 6,000 to one.[17]

The need to bias development towards targeting the poor spurred concern for income-generating programs that frontally attack poverty. The 1990s saw the spectacular rise in this country of microfinance as a tool for poverty alleviation. In a decade it reached more than a million families, one quarter of the country's 4.3 million poorest, and significantly raised their household incomes.[18] By 2010, it resourced the livelihood needs of at least 7 million poor households. Over time, some families have managed to break through the poverty threshold. In contrast to a command economy or state-controlled development planning, which tend to put the weight of resources into enhancing the investment ventures of those already ahead, micro-lending has reinstated the poor as the central actor and released their energy and initiative towards livelihood opportunities and small enterprises.

Micro-enterprise development (MED) held much promise to those dissatisfied with the slow pace of community development, which in its early practice was mostly focused on organizing and gaining power for poorer sectors of the community but lacked concrete achievement in facilitating village-level growth. In contrast, MED proved responsive to the immediate income needs of the poor and was also seen as an alternative 'bottom-up' process of development; a reaction to the failed 'trickle-down' approach and the ineptitude of government in compensating for market failures.

After almost another decade, however, there are signs that micro-enterprise in the country has remained at livelihood level and has yet to grow towards decisively moving the poor up the poverty line. Many microfinance organizations have grown very large, attesting to the fact that the poor can be good business. But it is not clear if access to credit has significantly improved the total output and productivity of the enterprises of the poor.

On the whole, development assistance institutions have tended to respond piecemeal to discrete parts of the problem of poverty. Now and again, development funds would be poured on the current favourite focus or the latest high-profile political concern or natural disaster: what we call locally the 'flavour of the month.'[19]

For the last fifty years, depending on the paradigms in fashion in the social landscape, institutions in the North and their conduits in the South have focused attention on land reform, community development, basic human needs, appropriate technology, devolution, and, more recently, sustainable development, gender, microfinance, empowerment and the promotion of civil society and democratic institutions.

By the beginning of the 21st century, the agenda has taken the form of a rather discrete list of 'to-do's' called the UN Millennium Development Goals (MDGs), with very concrete and countable aims and the ultimate goal of cutting by half poverty levels in all the participating countries by 2015.

These mostly technical and piecemeal solutions have had some usefulness, but fall short of decisively addressing the peculiarities of the contexts in which poverty thrives.

The NGOs themselves, primary carriers of the resources and ideological cargo of development, underwent their own crises at some point and became the subject of searching questions: 'To whom are they accountable? How effective are they? What has been their actual performance record? Why the apparent shift to economism and service delivery instead of empowerment and social transformation?'

Literature surfaced to provide answers to these questions. The answers were not very encouraging. NGOs of both North and South were found to be accountable to their donors and not to the people they served, and were not much better than government bureaucracies in providing such services as health, education, water or income opportunities in the cost-effective ways they claimed.[20] Empowering grassroots organisations or the strengthening of civil society as a whole seems to have been sidestepped in favour of the more straightforward and tractable task of service delivery.²¹

Worse, NGOs could actually do more harm than good, particularly in politically-sensitive hotspots,

> *Empowering grassroots organisations or the strengthening of civil society as a whole seems to have been sidestepped.*

paving with good intentions *The Road to Hell*—the actual title of a deeply disillusioned book on the perils of aiding a country like Somalia. High-profile disasters and famines tend to enlarge the resources of relief agencies, but may not necessarily reach their intended recipients. Food aid is a preferred intervention by rogue governments, for it can be hijacked, sold or used as political leverage as relief agencies watch helplessly.²²

What is wrong with development as theory and practice such that well-meaning efforts run themselves aground among the intended beneficiaries, with little to show for the massive aid poured into poor countries all these years?

Let me outline a way of answering this question from where I sit by telling two stories which frame my own sense of what is wrong with our idea of 'development', or, more broadly, that complex of ideas on which it is based—modernisation—and why countries labouring within this narrative cannot 'take-off' as hoped.

Development as a conundrum, or why the paradigm persists

One story took place in the USA—a country which represents to some the apex of their aspirations, bundled up in that construct called the 'American Dream', and to others, the brash symbol of the cross excesses of the logic of modernity. The other story took place at home, on my way to the airport for a trip abroad, and which to me signified a deeper failure which cannot be fixed by the usual tools of the development trade.

It was in the early 1980s when I first set foot in the fabled land of America. I had come from the UK, having spent a year in the storied university town of Cambridge, a quaint and hauntingly romantic place where much that was significant seemed to reside in the past tense, charmingly preserved in the rustic scenery as one punts along the 'backs', walks down the narrow streets of cobblestones, ancient halls and cathedrals echoing with evensong, snug in college quarters smelling of dark old wood, their creaky floorboards weighed down by centuries of historical memory.

The US, by contrast, seemed to gleam with all that is future, the streets of New York pulsated with the same vibrant vigour that I imagined must have animated the rugged pioneers who opened up the ever-receding frontier and continually drove out to the wilds of the 'West.' Everything was big and struck me as rather outsized. Perhaps, I surmised, it was a function of the primary modern value of efficiency and its impulse to maximise.

I walked into a large bookshop chain and noticed a disproportionate number of shelves devoted to 'how-tos' in every conceivable subject, including, to my surprise, things my own culture would not think of reducing into a technical manual: 'How to Conduct a Conversation,' 'How to Talk to Your Wife,' 'How to Relax,' 'How to Make Small Talk and Be the Life of the Party,' alongside the famous 'How to Win Friends and Influence People.' It struck me that these were rudimentary social skills that most of us who live in communal cultures intuitively learn as children. We grow up highly sensitised into picking up the many subtle cues that keep up the warm bubble of conviviality and steer us away from dead ends and collisions in the dense traffic of personal exchanges.

Stepping out into the sunlight, I saw a tall, obviously distraught woman with a German accent repeatedly asking the crowd who walked past her without looking, 'Can anybody help me? Can anybody help me?' She did not seem to me mad, like the many lunatics that litter the streets of the city, one of whom was a greasy, half-naked man in a black leather jacket prancing away on the sidewalk as if he were on stage. But nobody paid her any attention. I was about to ask what was the matter when a man cut into my path, wolfing down a hamburger as he ran. He was dressed for corporate America, and was hurrying away as if his life depended on it. It was my first introduction to the idea that time is money. I got carried along by the moving stream of people and lost sight of the woman.

If I had not known that the atomised individuals rushing before me were citizens of a country with the highest per capita income in the world, I would have felt quite sorry for them. As it was, something repelled me.

I was in a country that was advertised as the most powerful and successful; its businesses and military presence reached the far ends of the globe; its democratic values and institutions served as ideals for the rest of the world; its scientists and engineers are great builders and innovators, skilled in breaking down things into parts and making technologies out of them.

But then, they had to read a book just to learn how to make small talk, and the gracious communal rituals that make eating and drinking more than just feeding have been reduced to TV dinners and fast food on the run. In the things that most mattered—in those 'habits of the heart' that make us most happy and human—the country appeared to me to be sorely undeveloped.

It seemed to me that the US—like most societies heavily organized by the logic of modernity—tended to have severe deficits in spontaneous empathy, the capacity for community, and the willingness to get personally entangled in the messy task of being involved beyond purely functional relationships. The 'rugged individualism' that had built the country had been pushed to its logical extreme. Combined with such impulses as scientific detachment and bureaucratic rationality that create a sharp separation between the personal and the professional, the corollary consequence seems to be a pervasive instrumentalism and the prioritizing of individual achievement, convenience, and cost-efficiency over compassion and the shared joys and demands of community.

> *The prioritizing of individual achievement, convenience and cost-efficiency over compassion and the shared joys and demands of community.*

It is not to be wondered at that in societies we call the 'West,' crowds are said to be 'lonely' and the comfortably-sheltered feel rootless, afflicted by a 'homeless mind.' Professional networks substitute for friendships; one-night stands are confused for relationships. Those who suffer financial or other kinds of personal disasters commit suicide in spite of the safety-nets afforded by the system, perhaps for lack of secure enough personal ties that in other cultures serve as fall-back when all else fails.

People suffer and die alone and do not get discovered for weeks. Care for the elderly and the infirm and other such calls on personal compassion are relegated to institutions. East Asia and other societies vigorously on the same road to modernity are also beginning to suffer some of its social consequences, and display the same increasing depersonalisation and disruption of community.

Such modern technological societies have been penetratingly analysed and critiqued by their own sociologists and others.[23] People from non-Western societies have also written a great deal of literature on their own encounters with these technological cultures. The apparent consensus from those of us who are rooted elsewhere is that modern societies as they have developed are unliveable; they are unfit as habitations for people who prioritise being part of functioning communities. For those acquainted with the dark underside of the glitter of these societies, modernization holds no attraction.

Yet, decades later, past the 'postmodern' reassertion of ethnicity and the vernacular, past 9/11 and the rise of 'fundamentalism' in all religions and its implied civilizational contestations, the narrative of modernization persists as a compelling aspiration for societies wishing to get 'developed.'

Why, in the face of the postmodern rejection of grand narratives, has the idea of modernisation—or, in its more economic form, 'development'—remained as a metanarrative among countries playing 'catch up' with the more advanced industrial nations?

Traditional versus Modern community

People in traditional societies pray and turn to the supernatural because of a sense of helplessness before the chaotic forces of nature, the indifference of their institutions, and the hardness of the arbitrary powers that lord it over them. People in modern societies reach out for their tools and apply scientific rationalities to controlling natural diseases and disasters, solving problems of the economy and governance, and in general have a boundless confidence that with the right technologies and sufficient resources anything can be fixed.

People who retain traditional worldviews live in a bigger world, populated not just by human beings but also by spirit beings who not only influence illness, rain and crop failure, but the vagaries of human social relations and, ultimately, the fate of individuals and even of nations. Hence the one great reality is not the merely natural world but the larger cosmos; and the primary solution for disaster and disharmony is not technology but getting on the good side of the powers.

So depending on one's faith tradition, the immediate impulse when calamity strikes or despair seizes us is to get on one's hands and knees and pray to Mary and the saints, light joss sticks to the ancestors, bring out the prayer mat and bow before the inexorable will of Allah, or kill a pig or a white cock and offer its entrails in the light of the full moon to quiet the roaming restless spirits.

People in modern societies, by contrast, live in a smaller world: 'Imagine there's no heaven...,' sang the Beatle John Lennon, 'no hell below us, above us only sky.' Human beings are at the centre of this rather truncated world, a worldview which is a consequence of the Enlightenment and the 'death of God' as announced by Friedrich Nietzsche in the 'post-Christian' cultures of the West.

The one great reality is the natural world, which lately has been extended to include the vast extra-terrestrial space—the one thing which still excites primal awe in modern people. The mystery of the universe 'out there' still evokes an almost religious feeling akin to the awe that primitive peoples feel before Mother Nature. Notice movies of 'close encounters' with extra-terrestrials, and the finding in a survey that 58 per cent of American college students believe that astrological predictions are valid and that 50 per cent think the Egyptian pyramids were built with extra-terrestrial assistance.[24] Nevertheless, the language that best describes the disposition of mod-

> *The language that best describes the disposition of moderns towards space is still 'conquest' rather than reverence.*

erns towards space is still 'conquest' rather than reverence; a 'new frontier' for the exploration and expansion of human knowledge and control.

True, there is now a 'postmodern' strain in Western societies—mostly in the subjective consciousness of young people who troop to see the 'Twilight' movie saga, and in those free-wheeling baby boomers who tested the extremes of the modern temper in the 1960s and now have grown inward and gone East and found that one cannot live with 'free love' and flowers alone.

But the prevailing norms in the working world of business, governance and their global extensions—the Bretton Woods institutions—are still the values of modern secular society. By these 'values' we mean a) secularism, or the relegating of religious conviction to the private, subjective realm and the consequent belief in pluralism, or the idea that all religions ought to be tolerated and given equal space in a free society; b) absolute confidence in human rationality and in the ability of science to solve all human problems; c) egalitarianism, or a belief that all are equal—rich or poor, male or female, white or black—as against traditional notions of a hierarchy in the order of things; and d) democracy and the rule of law, as against the old monarchies and family dynasties. There is much about these values that resonate among all the peoples of the world, hence the continuing spell of wanting to become 'modern.'

Freedom is a universal value, and so is the longing for equality before the law, however hierarchical the cultural roots of a country may be. The fruits of science and technology, in so far as they make life longer, healthier, more liveable and prosperous, are welcome acquisitions. Those who know the oppressiveness of official dogma in whatever form—whether theological or ideological—flee for the chance to breathe and express freer thought.

Societies may have culturally-sanctioned rhetoric about strongman rule or female genital mutilation, but the people will 'vote with their feet', as the saying goes, wherever freedom from these repressions can be found. It is not an accident that today's mass migration is still in the direction of modern Western societies, in spite of the mounting tensions engendered by the crowding of multiple cultures in global centres that increasingly look like kitchen sinks sucking the dregs of human waste and misery.

In this country, this movement towards modern values began with the reaction against theocracy during the Spanish colonial period, which spawned a movement for the 'secularisation' of the clergy, and in later times the enshrining of the 'separation of the church and state,' a principle directly derived from the American Constitution. Freedom from the ignorance and superstition fostered by Spanish colonialism was fiercely pursued through education on the landing of the 'Thomasites,' the 600 American teachers on board the MV Thomas who volunteered to 'civilise and Christianise' these islands in the early 1900s, the precursor of the later Peace Corps.

After this country's war of independence against Spain, we declared ourselves a democratic republic in 1898, the earliest in Asia. This movement towards a self-defined democracy was ironically aborted by 50 years of American occupation. We had democratic aspirations long before the Philippines became a 'showcase of American democracy in Asia.'

It needs noting that the 'modern' values to which many countries now aspire took the West at least five centuries to evolve. Post-colonial countries, after the depredations and the shock of encounter with colonial powers, are now being asked to behave as if that process could be collapsed within 50 years.

Religion and cultural resistance

The modernisation narrative, while largely a product of the social and economic convulsions of Western history, has now been universalised as a necessary path to development for all cultures and peoples. The end results of its evolution are desired by many peoples—progressive industrial economies, democracy, a bureaucracy and a justice system that mostly works. Along with these, however, are features and by-products that cause great discomfort, even disgust in those who live in more traditional societies.

The modern secular West is perceived as libertine and decadent, lacking moral values, with an overdeveloped language for 'rights,' which issues from an overemphasis on individual autonomy and freedom of choice as against being disciplined by a sense of accountability to a community's norms and a transcendent faith tradition. The difficulty of promoting gender issues and reproductive rights, for example, is merely the tip of the iceberg; underneath are deeply cultural issues whose rock bottom has religion at its base.

In contexts like India where dowry is a 'nurtured evil', the birth of a girl-child goes to the debit side of a family's accounts, hence the preference for a male child. For the poor, not only is a large family an economic necessity; it is a way of safeguarding the generational line where children get to be the focus of curses during inter-family and inter-village hostilities.[25]

It needs to be recognised that such desired values as gender equality and the rationalities of population management are embedded in the modernity narrative of the West. They come to us within an ideological package which has secularism and individual autonomy as major touchstones. But the rest of the world is neither secularised nor individualistic, even as we value the freeing of culture and its institutions from the stranglehold of clericalism and superstition and wish for a degree of individuation from the sometimes stifling bonds of family and communal life.

The sociologist Peter Berger and his colleagues, noting the rise of religious conservatives and their politically-militant arm, the Religious Right in the US, and the renewed 'fundamentalist' fervour of all world religions, have produced a book called *The Desecularization of the World, Resurgent Religion and World Politics*.[26] While it may be true that there is a pronounced visibility among fundamentalist elements in all faith traditions, particularly Islam, this is perhaps best understood as a cultural defence, a reaction to the perceived permissiveness and hegemony of modernity. While there is a renewed religious interest in secular societies and the so-called 'Western offshoots', there is no such 'resurgence' in the rest of the world.

The reason is simple: the Majority world has always been religious. The West, with its 200 years of secularism, is a singular exception. The majority of the cultures of the world have always been shaped and continue to derive their social and ethical norms from their religious traditions. This, to me, is another case of unduly globalising a Western phenomenon.

The more accurate picture is that 'pre-modern' peoples, along with 'postmodern' people in the West, are rediscovering the power of the old religions as a buttress against the unwanted elements of modernisation as it has developed in the West and as it spreads and diffuses through the juggernaut of globalisation. In a time of moral confusion and social fragmentation, religion continues to provide a source of meaning and a basis for social integration.

While the modern West has secularised and relegated religion to a small and private compartment of life, many of the cultures of the world still find their philosophical and social centre in their religions. Until recently, this fact has been little noticed by Western development planners and their agents in the Majority world—the educated, modernised elites of these societies. Just below the radar screen of those who make decisions over the plight of the poor in the Majority world is this subterranean conflict between their society's 'traditional' values and the cultural incursions of modernising influences.

Literature in the 1960s talked of 'the passing of traditional society.' But the truer picture is that the traditional cultures of these societies have been merely submerged under the social and ideological dominance of their elites. Whether leaning towards the liberal democratic or the socialist paradigm, the post-colonial elites of these societies were all embarked on the project of modernisation, glossing over the passive and largely mute cultural resistance of their peoples.

An early warning sign of cultural resistance was the surprising swiftness with which the Shah of Iran fell, supplanted by the Ayatollahs who sought to reverse the trajectory towards secular modernity that Iran under the Shah had taken. What then followed was a wave of authoritarian governments, exposing the soft underside of merely formal democratic systems that, by and large, did not grow from the roots of these cultures but were merely transplanted wholesale, as in the Philippines. The rapid ease with which the structures of democracy were dismantled in this country shook people's confidence in the cultural viability of these institutions.

The East Asian economic miracles, led initially by Japan, put to question the inevitability of a levelling of cultures in the face of modernity. Roused to the defence of the 'strong state' and purposive command economies, the more successful leaders of this region began to make noises about 'Asian values' and an 'Asian style of modernity,' with the venerable Lee Kwan Yew of Singapore and Mahathir bin Mohamad of Malaysia as primary spokesmen.

By the beginning of this century, these signs of increasing cultural reassertion would erupt into a full-blown 'clash of civilisations' as represented by its cruder and more extreme popular symbols—MacDonald's and the late Osama bin Laden's Al Qaeda—a globalised culture war popularly dubbed as 'Jihad versus MacWorld.'

This cultural conflict, which has deep roots in both history and religion, is happening on the ground in smaller, quieter, and more incremental ways in experiences of doing 'development.' We see it in the rumblings of resistance among indigenous peoples, like the open revolt of the people of Chiapas in Mexico, or the militancy of the Cordillera peoples against projects like the Chico River Dam in this country. On a national scale, we see it in the Moro secessionist movements down South, whose long-standing war of grievance on behalf of the country's Muslim minorities has morphed into identification with the worldwide *ummah* in the jihad against the perceived decadence and global hegemony of Western democracies. On a much more subtle, grassroots level, it manifests itself in the way projects are passively embraced by the people and later allowed to die a natural death.

The Filipino culture of accommodation, for instance, is such that poor people may not articulate their sense of cynicism about new initiatives, nor mount direct and frontal resistance at first instance, like the more organised and armed elements that claim to represent them. But the passive and quiescent acceptance of interventions from the outside is often merely appearance. Soon, it becomes apparent that what seemed like willing assent in community meetings is really accommodation to the powers. Unspoken reservations soon make the rounds through gossip in the local *tiyangge,* or village store, and eventually result in lackadaisical participation and the benign neglect of community projects and initiatives.

In spite of the dominance of development as a metanarrative—an overarching story of the success of the West that has been unduly universalised as a desired future for all peoples—the instincts and values of the poor remain rooted in the indigenous culture. Much of the failure of development efforts could be accounted to this lack of congruence between the modernising values of development planners and the persistent religiosity and traditionalism of the voiceless poor.

Some modest generalisations

Based on the above observations regarding the influence of culture and religion on development, we make the following generalisations:

Sustainable change happens only within the terms determined by the narratives of a culture, which at its root is religiously-based. A fact glossed over by the secularised West is that most of our cultures are still framed by our religious traditions. We may borrow wholesale from the gleaming artefacts and tools of Western civilisation, and see rapid changes in what anthropologists call 'surface structures'—shifts in dietary patterns, building designs, even economic and political systems. But success in sustaining these changes depends on the degree of culture-fit, at the level of its 'deep structures,'—habits of consciousness, matters of worldview, and deep-seated values.

A society sustains itself by 'story', the religiously-based metanarrative which lends meaning to our fragmentary and fleeting experiences as a human community. 'Who are we? How have we come to be here? What

The myths and stories constructed by our ancestors and handed down to us...frame and control the meaning of whatever intervention comes from the outside.

is the nature of the world in which we live?' These are questions that have been answered for us by the myths and stories constructed by our ancestors and handed down to us. They frame and control the meaning of whatever intervention comes from the outside.

A story is told, for instance, of how villagers in Vietnam interpreted a Christian NGO's help in reconstructing their dikes. When asked why the NGO was helping them, they explained that Christians care about the poor. When asked why Christians care about the poor, they responded that Christians were earning merit for their next life, a Buddhist explanation.

> 'When Muslims in Mauritania were asked the same kind of question, two responses predominated. Either Christians were earning their way into paradise, a Muslim understanding of charity, or they were getting rich by working in the aid business, a secular understanding of why expatriates serve overseas.'[27]

All sustainable change begins by engaging with the stories we most believe about our lives. Until these stories are challenged or collide with other stories and adjustments are made, they will continue to shape our most entrenched beliefs about ourselves and the way the world works. The most devastating story of the poor, for instance, is what the African Augustine Musopole calls a 'poverty of being': 'this is where the African feels his poverty the most...poor Africans have come to believe they are no good and cannot get things right.'[28]

Similarly, a World Vision executive in the course of his work tells of sitting at a camp fire in the Kalahari Desert and hearing a San woman say, in response to the news that the Son of God had died for her sins, that she could believe that God would let his Son die for a white man, and that maybe she could believe that God might let his Son die for a black man, but she could never accept the idea that God would let his Son die for a San woman.[29]

Our kind of development work will either deepen this kind of disempowerment—bulldozing people into accepting the superior narrative of modernisation—or, if the organisation is faith-based, the Christian story as ethnocentrically woven from the cultural fabric of the West—backed up by technological wonders and the lure of the world's consumer goods. Or, on the other hand, we truly release people from the captivity of false stories and help them be aware of their own stories, re-connecting with what is life-giving about them and confronting that which is death-dealing.

This is best done by painstakingly entering into the stories of a people, understanding them, and sensitively affirming those cultural themes that empower people, and critiquing those that legitimise and harden structures of oppression. This kind of work is necessary for any 'institution-building' to have a measure of success. It requires long-term immersion and cannot be done within the three-year projects cycles that are part and parcel of the technologised worldview of Western aid organisations.

There is much truth to the proposition of the Harvard Symposium on culture and development that 'culture matters.' All societies, and not just Africa, need a 'cultural adjustment program' for substantial change to happen.

Structural problems often have roots in the culture. As Daniel Etounga-Mangelle phrased it, "Culture is the mother, institutions are the children."[30] Gunnar Myrdal saw the truth of this first-hand when, after ten years of study in South Asia, he concluded that cultural factors such as the caste system 'tend to make the existing inequalities particularly rigid and unyielding' and 'fortify the prevalent contempt and disgust for manual work.' The limited radius of trust and identification breeds corruption and nepotism.[31]

Political and economic systems need a corresponding infraculture in order to work. Social change needs both the 'hardware' of right economic and political institutions as well as the corresponding 'software' of subjective consciousness such as values, attitudes, beliefs and worldviews.

Most newly-emerged democracies, for instance, are having difficulties because the right systems are in place but the cultural norms that would make institutions responsive and social mobility possible are lacking. As Guatemalan sociologist Bernardo Arevalo puts it: 'We have the hardware of democracy but the software of authoritarianism.'[32]

> *"We have the hardware of democracy but the software of authoritarianism"*

Without the necessary infraculture, governance and market institutions harden into systemic disincentives to entrepreneurship, innovation and hard work. A country may have rich natural resources and a highly talented workforce, but the consequent lack of 'plausibility structures' will constrain the flourishing of enterprise. There is much micro-entrepreneurial energy in this country, for instance, but the larger social and cultural context constrains the growth of this into a force in the formal economy. Development must be contextual to be effective and sustainable. All countries have life sources, both physical and social, that were already in place long before the arrival of outside help, influence, and resources.

Cultures, for instance, have great stores of knowledge gathered from the environmental context. Depending on geography, societies develop culture-specific skills in relating to the environment or what has been termed as indigenous technical knowledge.

This culture-specific expertise shows itself, for instance, in human languages: Arabs have many words for 'horses.' Eskimos are able to finely discern at least 30 kinds of that white fluffy thing we call 'snow.' Filipinos have a host of words connected to 'coconut', which has multiple uses in the culture. Indigenous peoples of this country have a rich medical lore and can name at least 37,000 varieties of herbs and plants. Indigenous knowledge is a basic resource and should inform all interventions, particularly those from the outside.

Most development efforts fail because they do not factor in the existing local resources and merely mimic exogenous economic models. Interventions must be contextual, closely hewn out of the contours of the natural as well as human landscape, as against merely replicating what works elsewhere.

Recent massive disasters brought about by climatic changes have increasingly brought to our attention the role of geography in economic development. Jeffrey Sachs has served early notice that perhaps we don't really have a North-South divide, but a temperate-tropical zone divide in the world. He observes that the temperate regions of the world are vastly more developed than the tropics, and that geographically-remote regions—those far from the coasts or navigable rivers or mountainous states with high internal and international transport costs—are considerably less developed than societies in coastal plains or riverine communities.[33]

It is very possible that part of this country's economic lag is the lack of congruence between its development thrusts and the archipelagic nature of the islands. The economist Cielito Habito, former head of the National Economic Development Authority, has put forward the idea that development plans should take more cognisance of the business opportunities afforded by the country's extensive coastline rather than continuing to make plans that are more suited to land-based economies.

Also, besides determining the base of our economies, our habitat forms us and shapes our ideas of what the world is like. A people's sense of time, for instance, is in a measure dependent on whether seasons run a full cycle or are sharply marked. There is a difference between those who have to anticipate and contend with bitter winters and those of us who live in the tropics and merely slide from wet to dry quite seamlessly. Coastal peoples and those who live in the desert have different ideas of what constitutes scarcity. Trouble arises when those used to the uniform and linear time sequence of a modern economy have to work within settings that are still largely organized according to the rhythm of the seasons.

There is the famous story of a salmon cannery in Alaska where the Eskimos laughed when they first heard a whistle to signal the start of the day's work. They thought it was ridiculous that a man should begin or end work just because of a factory whistle, used as they were to fishing according to the seasons.

Likewise, many economies in traditional cultures seem to fail simply because there is a world of difference between their sense of time and the time requirements of an industrial economy in the passage towards modernisation. Often, this is not because of the failure to adapt but is more a backhanded resistance to the harried and grinding inexorability of mechanical life in industrial cultures. As an African once told an audience of mostly Westerners, "You may have the watches, but we have the time."[34]

> *A backhanded resistance to the harried and grinding inexorability of mechanical life in industrial cultures.*

Tying it all together: religion, culture and development

We may summarise the interrelationship of culture, religion and development in these ways:

• *Religion shapes culture; it determines the worldviews and values behind a people's relationship with the environment*

Religion is the substructure of culture. Unknown to most of us, it is the underlying presupposition behind much of our values and our

> *Religion is the substructure of culture.*

ways of relating to the material environment. It shapes our worldviews, and is the primordial vision behind the material achievements that we carve in wood or build in monuments of stone.

Social science tends to treat religion as just one compartment of life, alongside politics, economics and other spheres of human activity and thought. True enough, in secular and postmodern societies, religion can be treated as merely one of those free-floating institutions asserting their right to social space.

This is not true, however, in societies that have yet to secularise, and are in fact more deeply turning back to the psychological comfort of their religions as they navigate through the identity and other crises brought by a globalised modernity.

Religion in Asia and elsewhere in the non-Western world continues to be an architectonic structure that wields power and influence. This fact, long unnoticed, is now being forcibly brought to the attention of the secularised West and their proxies among the ruling elites in the South.

There is now some recognition that the majority of the world's poor, for good or ill, are religious, while aid agencies and their institutional extensions remain locked in their culture of secular modernity. Unless there is some congruence between the underlying worldviews of aid agencies and that of recipient communities, development interventions will remain out of context and ultimately unsustainable.

William F. Ryan, a Jesuit, inquired into the cultural portability of modern economic models. He concluded that 'Western free-market models which ignore spiritual and cultural values as "externalities"...do not work in developing countries.'[35]

• *Culture in turn determines a society's hierarchy of values, which shape patterns of consumption, investment and savings*

Values have been helpfully defined as 'a bridge between short-term and long-term expectations, decisively reinforcing distant goals in their otherwise hopeless struggle against instant gratification.'[36]

What I call 'fiesta cultures' tend to be focused on the present, immersed in the moment and are less purposive about hedging the future. More ascetic cultures tend to be driven by the future, postponing enjoyment for the sake of ensuring security.

However, recent studies on the correlation between faith and economic behaviour show that the experience of coming to some kind of encounter with transcendence tends to shift people's timeline. Poor communities move from a preoccupation with mere survival in the present to a sense of hope in the future, as indicated by increased savings and investment in more long-term goals like the education of their children. They acquire a better sense of stewardship and accountability. Money that used to go to gambling, alcohol and other vices now get saved for nutrition of the children, housing and other expenditures that indicate a growing confidence about the future.³⁷

   •   *Religion and culture pose ambiguities that can serve either as resource or as hindrance to development*

Religion provides a powerful motivational force for social compassion. Embedded in all religious traditions is some form of institutionalised concern for the poor; almsgiving or *sila*, the exercise of generosity or *dana*, the host of social legislation in early Judaism, and the communal practices of the Early Christian Churches. In various parts of the world, faith movements are involved in humanitarian support, in conflict prevention and resolution, in the fight against HIV-AIDS, the sex trade and the trafficking of girls, child soldiers, and the practice of female genital mutilation.

However, religious initiatives can also be double-edged in their effects. Faith-based organisations usually have problematic views on development, and mostly do so out of a motive to convert. Their direct engagement with the poor tends sometimes to be divisive of communities, excluding non-followers and occasioning competition for the resources they bring. They also tend to be isolationist and apolitical, rarely concerned with addressing the larger contexts of poverty.

Similarly, the idea of religion as a resource for values necessary for development has been vigorously contested. Max Weber's thesis has been questioned in the light of such facts as Sinite cultures displaying values similar to the 'Protestant social ethic' and which are considered to have fuelled the progressive economies that have emerged from them.

Peter Berger, a self-described Weberian, has called attention recently to the possibility that different stages of economic development may call for different sets of values. The kind of values articulated by Weber may be important only in the early phases of a modernising economy, as has happened in the early stages of the Industrial Revolution in a mercantile Europe with Puritan and Calvinist influences. Such values may no longer be relevant in economies driven by high consumerism. "The socio-economic effects of a religious tradition," he says, "may have an expiration date."³⁸ Frugality—whether because of an inner detachment towards worldly goods, a deep regard for the needs of the poor, or the sense of responsibility arising from knowing that one will have to make an account some day before one's Maker—is an economic value relevant to all. This is true regardless of whether one is located in societies climbing the development ladder, or in affluent societies that go on boom-and-bust cycles because of unrestrained consumerism or greed that has gone haywire.

What seems more promising as a line of analysis is the possibility that at any given point in the history of the world, some cultures may have sets of values that may be more fitted to succeed in the kind of economic system dominant at the time. Societies that tend to be rigidly organised or tightly structured to behave in linear sequence certainly have more fit in the machine age with its assembly-line systems. Japan's long expertise in metallurgy and delicately tight disciplines in both life and aesthetics was a perfect seedbed for transplanting German technology onto its shores. On the other hand, cultures that tend to be warmer and softer, with greater flexibility and more plasticity, like the Philippines, India or Brazil—countries with more mercurial tempers—may be more suited to the flux and fluidities of the information age or what has been termed as 'liquid modernity.' The British sociologist Zygmunt Bauman characterises this phase of modern life as "lived under conditions of constant uncertainty."[39] This gives an advantage to those cultures able to adapt to rapid changes with creative improvisations.

It may be that Filipinos' evident ability to adapt quickly to changing circumstances makes the country singularly poised to take advantage of this cusp in the unfolding story of a multi-focal global economy. Like the bamboo, the ability to sway and bend with the winds without breaking may be important in navigating through the clash of cultures and today's 'multiple modernities.'

This necessary collocation of a country's culture and values with the dominant shape of the global economy may account for part of the success or failure of specific societies in a given moment in history. At any rate, what seems clear at this juncture is that nations would do well to jump off the rails of 'development' as a uni-linear path to prosperity, and chart their own course based on the contours of their own unique geographical features, historical traditions and cultural resources as a people.

Today's global recession impresses anew the enduring need for culturally-embedded values that make for tight financial discipline, in whatever stage of economic development a country is in.

Dr **Melba Padilla Maggay** *is a writer and a social anthropologist, who holds a doctorate in Philippine Studies, a masters degree in English Literature, and a 1st class degree in Mass Communication. A specialist in intercultural communication, she was Research Fellow on the subject at the University of Cambridge under the auspices of Tyndale House, applying it to the question of culture and theology. She was the founder and longtime director of ISACC, a voice for conscientiousness in politics and in church-and-culture issues.*

Notes

1. Tu Wei-Ming, 'Multiple Modernities: A Preliminary Inquiry into the Implications of East Asian Modernity', in Harrison, L.G. & Huntington, S.P. (eds) *Culture Matters, How Values Shape Human Progress*, New York: Basic Books, 2000 p.257.

2. Myrdal, G. *The Challenge of World Poverty: A World Anti-Poverty Program in Outline*, New York: Random House-Vintage Books, 1970 pp.57, 101.

3. The most well-known text was perhaps *Dependency and Development in Latin America*, (trans. M. Upindi), Berkeley: University of California Press, 1979 written by Brazil's Fernando Henrique Cardoso, who in 1993 became finance minister and in the mid-90s served as President.

4. The Harvard symposium, *Cultural Values and Human Progress*, held at the American Academy of Arts and Sciences in Cambridge, Massachusetts, 23-25 April 1999 is a major example of this trend. An offshoot of this symposium was the book, *Culture Matters, How Values Shape Human Progress*, op.cit. See particularly their Foreword and Introduction.

5. Harrison, 2000. p.90.

6. Mariano Grondona, *A Cultural Typology of Economic Development*, in ibid., p.44ff.

7. World Bank, *World Development Report* 1992, p.30.

8. Remenyi, J. *Where Credit is Due: Income-generating programmes for the poor in developing countries*, Intermediate Technology Publications: London, 1991, pp.13-14.

9. Korten, D.C. *Getting to the 21st Century*, West Hartford, Connecticut: Kumarian Press Inc., 1990, p.1.

10. For a more extended account of this, the writings of Walden Bello on the subject are helpful.

11. Goudzwaard, B. & De Lange, H. *Beyond Poverty and Affluence: Toward an Economy of Care*, translated and edited by Mark R. Vander Vennen, Grand Rapids: William B. Eerdmans & Geneva: WCC Publications, 1995 pp. 11, 17.

12. Goudzwaard & De Lange, citing the *UNDP Human Development Report*, 1992, ibid., p.12.

13. Goudzwaard & De Lange, citing the *UNDP Human Development Report*, 1992, ibid., p.12.

14. Figures were supplied by studies of the Freedom from Debt Coalition. For the proposed 2010 national budget, P340.812 million or 22% was earmarked for debt servicing. See the FDC response to the Manila Times editorial, *Stimulus Measures Must not Peter Out*, 24 October 2004, p.A4.

15. Joe Remenyi, op.cit., p.34.

16. See the *UNDP Human Development Reports* starting 1992.

17. At P7,107 income per month for a poor family, and P42 million per month for a rich family, this means the disparity ratio is 1 to 6,000, as reported by Noel Alcaide, president of SUCCESS and a student of the Philippine microfinance industry.

18. See an early study by Chua, R., Reyes, C. & Carrasco, A. (eds.), *Delivering to the Poor, A Search for Successful Practices in Philippine Microfinance*, jointly published by the United Nations Development Program, National Anti-Poverty Commission, People's Credit and Finance Corporation, Asian Institute of Management, December 2003, pp. 21, 30.

19. A term borrowed from a commercial for a local ice cream, which used to invent for every month a new flavour made out of tropical fruits and other local ingredients.

20.   See Edwards, M. & Hulme, D. (eds.) *Beyond the Magic Bullet: NGO Performance and Accountability in the Post-Cold War World*, West Hartford, Connecticutt: Kumarian & Save the Children, 1996.

21.   Scogge, D. (ed.) *Compassion and Calculation: The Business of Private Foreign Aid*, London: Pluto Press and Transnational Institute, 1996.

22.   For an example of such stories, see Maren, M. *The Road to Hell, The Ravaging Effects of Foreign Aid and International Charity*, New York: The Free Press, 1997.

23.   See the works of Peter Berger, particularly *The Homeless Mind* with Brigitte Berger and Hansfried Kellner, Vintage Books: NY, 1974, and *Facing Up to Modernity: excursions in society, politics and religion*, Basic Books: NY, 1977; Jacques Ellul, *The Technological Society*, Vintage Books: NY, 1964; Robert Bellah, et al. *Habits of the Heart*, University of California Press: Berkeley, CA, 1985; and quite a few others.

24.   Gilovich, T. *How We Know What Isn't So: The Fallibility of Human Reason in Everyday Life*, NY: Free Press, 1991 cited by Edgerton, R.B. *Traditional Beliefs and Practices—Are Some Better Than Others ?* in Harrison, 2000, p.135.

25.   Christian, J. *God of the Empty-Handed, Poverty, Power and the Kingdom of God*, Monrovia, CA: MARC Books, World Vision International, 1999, p.35.

26.   *The Desecularization of the World* is a series of essays published in 1999 by the Ethics and Public Policy Center, Washington DC and Wm. B. Eerdmans, Grand Rapids, MI/ Cambridge and edited by Peter Berger.

27.   Myers, B. *Walking with the Poor: Principles and Practices of Transformational Development*, New York: World Vision International and Orbis Books, 1999, p.207.

28.   A.C. Musopole, A.C. (1997) *African World View*, presentation for *Changing the Story: Christian Witness and Transformational Development Consultation*, Pasadena California: World Vision, May 5-10, 1997. Cited by Myers, 1999, p.76.

29.   ibid.

30.   See his article, 'Does Africa Need a Cultural Adjustment Program ?' pp. 65-77, also 302, in Harrison, 2000.

31.   Myrdal, G. *Asian Drama—An Inquiry into the Poverty of Nations*, New York: Pantheon, 1968, p.104.

32.   Quoted by Samuel P. Huntington from the Guatemalan newspaper, *La Prensa Libre*, 14 December 1999, in his Introduction, *Culture Counts*, in Harrison, 2000, p.xxx.

33.   See his elaboration of this in his article, *Notes on a New Sociology of Economic Development*, in Harrison, 2000, pp.29-43.

34.   This was a quote from Richard Crabbe, head of a publishing firm in Africa, in a presentation at a LitWorld Conference of Media Associates International in England in the 1990s at which the author was present.

35.   Ryan, W.F. *Culture, Spirituality and Economic Development: Opening a Dialogue*, Ottawa: International Development Research Centre: Ottawa, 1995, p.13.

36.   Mariano Grondona, in Harrison, 2000, p.46.

37.   See, for instance, the author's *Culture and Economic Empowerment*, monograph based on *Participatory Action Research on Economic Empowerment* (PARCEE), an ICCO-funded research project done by the Institute for Studies in Asian Church and Culture, 2005.

38.   See Peter Berger's recent article, *Faith and Development*, in *Society*, 2009, Vol.46, pp.69-75.

39. Zygmunt Bauman's preferred term for 'postmodern' is 'liquid modernity'; see *Liquid Life*, Polity Press: Cambridge, 2005, p.2. Refer also to Vinoth Ramachadra's useful remarks on this in his *Church and Mission in the New Asia: New Gods, New Identities*, published by Trinity Theological College, Armor Publishing Pte Ltd: Singapore, 2009, pp.27-29.

Yeasting the Public Debate with Good News

*In an age where the public discussion is prominently located and shaped in the media, we have the opportunity to imaginatively express a timeless truth that really is good news for society. **Marijke Hoek** advocates that the creative use of the media can draw attention to structural dysfunction, raise public awareness and awaken its conscience. Critically, such public engagement is an effective way to communicate how our faith motivates us to develop a more just and compassionate way of life.*

Within the character of the citizen lies the welfare of the nation
Cicero

Sonship and citizenship

My favourite contemporary Dutch artist is the painter Ton Schulten. Following a serious car crash, he was left in a coma. When he regained consciousness, he gave up a successful career in advertising to dedicate the rest of his life to painting the beautiful array of lights he had seen whilst in the coma. His stunningly colourful landscape mosaics reflect a ray of 'the world beyond'. Walking through his gallery you sense something that is difficult to put into words; a kind of peace that seems 'otherworldly'. In a way it is. But in another, it is very much here—tangibly.

His story and paintings are a poignant metaphor for our lives. As we have glimpsed the hope for a new creation, so we can illuminate our world according to this glimpse of God's restoring reign. In fact, we have received its first fruit in the person of the Spirit, God's empowering presence who enables us to reflect 'the hope of the beyond' here and now. In his letter to the Romans, Paul appeals to us: in view of the 'bright light' we have received, let us dedicate all of our lives to God. Staying close to the original

Greek, we hear Paul move from the individual to the corporate in Romans 12:1.

> Therefore, I urge you, brothers, in view of God's mercy, to offer your bodies (plural) as a living sacrifice (singular), holy and pleasing to God— this is your spiritual act of worship.

Aware of the danger of conforming to the pattern of the world, he calls for a transformation by the renewing of our mind so that we can discern God's will. Such faithful living that reflects the transforming newness of God's good, pleasant and perfect will, develops in fellowship with the person and witness of Jesus Christ. The Church, being transformed into His image, becomes a living metaphor for the power of God (8:29). Our corporate and individual act of worship takes place in the everyday-ness of life in the sanctuary that is this world. It involves our jobs, families, relationships, gifting, time and financial management, public and private lives, passions and creativity, individual and communal responsibilities, disciplines and limitations, our desires, minds, our homes and hearts. "The community, in its corporate life, is called to embody an alternative order that stands as a sign of God's redemptive purposes in the world," writes Richard Hays in *The Moral Vision of the New Testament*.[1] The texts shape the community and the community embodies the meaning of the text.[2] That is how we communicate the gospel best.

Paul did not speak in a vacuum but connected with themes and claims in his world. His 'adoption' metaphor in Romans 8, for example, is carefully chosen, adapting a theme in Roman society to communicate the radical and comprehensive nature of his understanding of salvation. In the midst of a massive empire, the adopted family of God that lives under a new rule and according to new values proves to be a powerful display of the Spirit's liberating and restorative presence. The hope for God's reign to break increasingly into a world that is out of joint is a sustaining power that motivates a resilient and trusting people. As we connect with contemporary themes and dominant stories in our culture we can similarly subversively engage with 'the pattern of our world' and have the opportunity to imaginatively express a timeless truth that really is good news for society.

Citizens that seek the wellbeing of the city

Faithful stewardship concerns living out a vision for the good of the community:

Also, seek the peace and prosperity of the city to which I have carried you into exile. Pray to the LORD for it, because if it prospers, you too will prosper. (Jeremiah 29:7).

This small community of believers living in Babylon was to hold out a vision of wellbeing for the wider society and bring *shalom* in the place of brokenness and hopelessness. *Shalom* in the scriptures refers to God's creational intention. It includes peace, soundness, wholeness, security and fullness of life, in which our relationships with God, each other and the wider creation are thriving. It concerns the establishing of social justice and requires stewardship that causes us to live in the world in such a way that we realise its potential. As Jeremiah shows, the believers' destiny is woven together with the city's. The writer of Proverbs reflects that when God's people thrive it does society good: 'When the righteous prosper, the city rejoices.' Wise living generates blessedness, riches, peace—in other words, *shalom* (11:10; 3:13-14). And so, our influence is not so much determined by our position in the pecking order or our status, but rather by living our lives through Christ as they are founded on biblical truth.

Faithful stewardship entails work, risk, and imagination. Jesus' parable of the talents in Matthew 25:14-30 feeds our imaginative capacity and has the potential to shape business, economy, professions, community life and our households in such a way that they reflect aspects of the Father's character and plan. This parable does not merely concern the wise invest-ment of money. It has a wider agenda. Reading the parable allegorically, Jesus' teaching concerns faithful stewardship of all that is entrusted to us.

Moral behaviour, including making imaginative use of the resources entrusted to us, is directly and repeatedly connected to the invitation to eternal life (Matthew 25:46). Richard Hays asserts that the aim of Jesus' parables is to instill godly fear and motivate us to do God's will while we have the opportunity: "The New Testament writers are not concerned merely with how individuals might seek eternal life; rather, they are con-cerned with how the Church as a whole might embody the economics of the Kingdom of God."[3] The parable just mentioned links virtuous steward-ship to sharing in the Master's happiness. Faithful stewardship obligates us to shape the patterns of life, work and relationship. The Judeo-Christian concept of shalom, a wellbeing that is communal and personal, must be rediscovered in our commitment to political, economic and cultural transformation which benefits marginalised communities. Whether we are disciples in business, politics, arts, media, education, healthcare, sports, IT, or anything else, we are to seek the wellbeing of, and live out a vision for, the good of the community—a more just society.

On the other hand it is not only for exiles in Babylon or Christians in the first century Roman Empire but also for believers in the 21st century, that it proves difficult to imagine the world as if Christ is sovereign. As Walter Brueggemann observes: "The key pathology of our time, which seduces us all, is the reduction of the imagination so that we are too numbed, satiated and co-opted to do serious imaginative work."[4] And yet, when we delve into history, we see illuminating examples where the Christian faith forged an understanding of citizenship that measured success in terms of communal wellbeing. The 18th and 19th centuries contain some of the best manifestations of Christian reformation in which philanthropy and social concern permeated and shaped social and political movements and institutions in Britain. According to Harrison,[5] much of the early Victorian era was "essentially a religious age" and Christians significantly shaped its social consciousness as they contributed to factory reforms, penal reform, public health and education.[6] There can be little doubt about the progressive impulse of Christian theology in civic action and the way it "dominated British politics" at the time.[7] Reflecting on such transformative engagement, the historian David Bebbington writes:

> Evangelicals had made an impact through putting their distinctive principles into practice, through sustained use of the media, through meeting felt need, through benefiting from state toleration and through their affinity for contemporary culture. These sustained processes, rather than militant campaigns, were what transformed the land. Pondering their history may well lead Evangelicals to prefer the slower and less spectacular methods that have reaped such rewards in the past. That is the way to root the gospel in our culture....[8]

Yet, critics assert that in the goal to transform society there was too little emphasis on changing the society's patriarchal structures.[9] Also, sin was considered a personal rather than a structural evil. As James Davison Hunter has persuasively argued, our faith implies the challenge to think through in an institutional way a creative subversion of society's frameworks—thus challenging structures that dishonour God, dehumanize people and harm creation.[10] However, at times in the West we have seemed to have un-learned such hermeneutical engagement. A growing secularisation process from the 1960s onwards called for religion to be relegated to the private world. In such a paradigm, one's vocation in the 'secular' world has only 'sacred' significance in that it provides a platform for evangelism. The focus on personal piety and evangelism combined with a Christian withdrawal from significant engagement within the cultural spheres accounted for an inability to translate faith into meaningful socio-political transformation. Fortunately, contemporary scholarship on the societal, cosmic and individual aspects of the promised 'renewal of all things' has given a much-needed impulse for a faithful discipleship that also works towards a constructive reformation of the frameworks of civic life.[11]

In their book *Global Pentecostalism—the new face of Christian social engagement*, Miller and Yamamori describe a Progressive Pentecostal movement that has emerged since the 90s—a colourful array of community projects demonstrating the creativity of God's Spirit inspiring believers to build community with the marginalised. While these Christians are not trying to reform social structures or challenge government policies they are attempting to build from the ground up an alternative social reality.[12] And yet, our civic engagement does also call for ardent advocacy and structural reform. Tony Campolo, Professor Emeritus of Sociology at Eastern University, is one of many voices calling for our engagement to include the structural aspects of injustice:

> There is a reluctance to engage in advocacy, to create a public voice and insert the cause of the poor into political space. The mandate to "speak up for those who cannot speak for themselves, for the rights of all who are destitute" is clear. Yet this remains unheeded for fear of getting "too political" and stepping out of the boundary lines artificially set between church and state by secular society (Proverbs 31:8).[13]

Similarly, Joel Edwards, Director of Micah Challenge, calls for a robust theology of engagement that takes us beyond important social action to prophetic advocacy with and on behalf of the poor.[14] As anthropologist Melba Padilla Maggay writes, a key to social change is "the ability to constructively engage structures, help communities to resource their own needs within their own context, and nurture a strategic minority that will create a presence and a voice in public space on behalf of the poor."[15]

So, our sonship and our discipleship need to shape our citizenship in the social, economic, cultural, and political complexities of our world. Whereas it is commonly thought that a 'critical mass' is needed to bring about social change, most change occurs through strategically placing 'critical yeast' into the wider society.

Critical yeast

Paul's call for a transformation by the renewing of our mind is a key passage. On the basis of Christ's sacrifice, the 'Spirit of adoption' forms a new community and shapes a new communal and personal identity. This formation of a new identity 'in Christ' and a new family in which the members relate to one another in a new spirit (as we see in the thoroughly egalitarian social vision of Galatians 3:28: rich-poor, male-female, slave-free), eventually changes the socio-cultural milieu. So, the Christian impulse works as yeast that permeates all aspects of life and transforms structures from within.

In his book, *The Moral Imagination*, the peace builder John Paul Lederach introduces the concept of 'critical yeast'.

> Critical yeast asks the question in reference to social change: Who within a given setting, if brought together, would have the capacity to make things grow toward the desired end? The focus is not on the number but on the quality of people brought together, who represent a unique linkage across a wide variety of sectors and locations within the conflicted setting.[16]

In their quest to abolish the transatlantic slave trade, the Clapham sect, for example, consisted of businessmen, literary elite, aristocracy, clergy and politicians, who created strategic alliances in spheres in which the greatest possible influence in the culture could be exerted—media being one of these arenas.

Jesus reminds us that His kingdom is like a bit of yeast placed in a large amount of flour, working its way all through the dough (Matthew 13:33). Significance is not related to numbers, status or dominance. Significance has everything to do with being faithful. Living out our convictions often reminds us of our vulnerability, limitations and even powerlessness in the face of the enormity of the task, our weakness in the face of power. Weakness is a dominant theme in Paul's theology. Understandably so, for at the time the Christian community was a minority in a powerful empire. The connotations of the word are many. It refers to numerical weakness; social vulnerability and hardships of many kinds. And, poignantly, it reflects the limitations of our humanness.

Paul's 'weakness' theme is as much promising as it is realistic. For, our human weakness is the place where divine power connects best. In fact, it is the showcase for God's power. Whereas we may use 'weakness' as a term to describe our personal shortcomings—a weakness for chocolates, gadgets or fast cars—Paul uses the term in a global context. Abraham, who received such promises of fruitfulness and yet faced such barrenness, was strengthened rather than weakened in his faith (Romans 4:19). In a cosmic context, the Christian community in Rome, though aware of their vulnerability, experienced the Spirit's help in their weakness. Not always knowing what to pray for, they did however know that divine advocacy took place 'behind the scenes' by means of intercessions concerning God's purposes for his world (Romans 8:26-28). Our tenacity concerning God's redemption plan for the world is fuelled by hope. Our vision, relations and work in many different arenas contain the critical yeast that permeates the context in which we live.[17]

Novelist, journalist and leading writer of the Victorian era, George Eliot, perceived that the growing good of the world is partly dependent on unhistorical acts by people who lived faithful hidden lives. Living out the radical nature of Jesus' teaching requires a lifestyle

> *The growing good of the world is partly dependent on unhistorical acts by people who lived faithful hidden lives.*

of costly, selfless, loving acts of daily commitment to peace and justice—in the playground, workplace, family and community. It demands a daily walk of mercy, humility and justice reflecting Christ's reign that invades the world, not hindered by our 'weakness' but rather displayed in it.

And yet, the transformative elements also concern a wider stage and public role for which we have received a creative grace to seek and enact the wellbeing in our spheres of influence. In ancient Greece, the *oikos* referred to the house and everything included, such as the extended family, slaves and farmland. *Nomos* means act, law, or principle. The ancient Greeks first combined these two roots to form *oikonomia*. Eventually, the word 'economy' was born, which literally means 'the principles to maintain our house'. Whether that 'house' is government, classroom, boardroom or family is secondary. The household of faith lives out an alternative imagined reality and so contributes to a more just society. Once the focus is on seeking the wellbeing of the place and sphere to which God has called us, the evaluative questions concerning 'success' focuses on the creation of opportunities for the hopeless; the increase of wellbeing to the oppressed.

The prophet Isaiah describes the shape of worship that God intends. He addresses a form of religion that is unconcerned about the vulnerable members of society and maintains that the right kind of worship—the true fast—concerns a sacrificial lifestyle for the sake of others and breaking structures that are oppressive. It is a radical form of 'whole life stewardship'. Such worship that satisfies the needs of the marginalised causes the Christian community to 'glow in the darkness': 'You'll be known as those who can fix anything, restore old ruins, rebuild and renovate, make the community livable again.' (Isaiah 58: 9-12, The Message translation).

> *You will be known as those who can fix anything, restore old ruins, rebuild and renovate, make the community livable again (Isaiah 58:9-12)*

The transforming vision for society found in the scriptures is so elaborate it has the potential to shape our industrial disputes, asylum debate, education, media engagement, budgets, NHS, housing, international relations and beyond. It is a vision that sketches both the broad brush strokes of life and the daily, personal, colourful contours of our family, community, vocation and leisure, in order to build a community reflective of God's will.

Advocacy with, and on behalf of, the marginalised

The message of the prophets concerns injustice with regard to the marginalised, and calls rulers to account. Social change has to be built and worked out through policies and mechanisms that contribute towards eliminating injustice. Moreover, true advocacy is combined with the empowerment of those who are on the margins. Rather than being excluded from the decision-making process, they need to find channels for their opinions and exercise influence in order to change mechanisms that are hindering the common good and their own wellbeing.[18] As Luke Bretherton outlines in his book *Christianity and Contemporary Politics*, community organising is an important avenue for creating a healthier common life amidst our fragmented civic society and its inherent injustices. It gives the marginalised a place from which to act within a political arena, thus seeking to restore the democracy that enables just decisions to be made and resources to be allocated appropriately for the benefit of all, and those on the margin in particular.[19]

Such community work concerns a process whereby people become aware of the social, political, economic and cultural reality and injustices that shape their lives. Furthermore, it causes an awareness of their ability to transform that reality.[20] The conscientisation movement, significantly developed by Latin American Christians such as the Brazilian Roman Catholic Paulo Freire, has critically influenced wider developmental thinking. While such pedagogy includes cognitive-critical reflection it "goes beyond this to the telling of God's actions and purposes and the testifying of how humans can join in these actions for the transformation of the world."[21] Brueggemann speaks in terms of 'prophetic imagination': "The prophetic imagination knows that the real world is the one that has its beginning and dynamic in the promising speech of God and that this is true even in a world where kings have tried to banish all speech but their own."[22]

All issues of apparent need provide an opportunity to forge links with those who feel deeply excluded. And all kinds of communities contain the capacity to bring about significant change, be it a friendship circle, a neighbourhood centre, a trade union, a vocational network, an arts collective and so on. As Christians, we are not alone in our concern for the marginalised, and we should work in partnership with those who also seek the common good but do not share our faith. Ardent advocacy involves all parties.

To illustrate this, we can focus on the advocacy for, and with, the asylum seeking community. An example of effective community organising is found in the Refugee Charter launched by the Refugee & Migrant Forum Manchester. The Charter is a unique statement of rights and entitlements written by refugees and asylum seekers that is endorsed by more than 100 individuals and organisations including Manchester City Council. The Charter lists the issues of housing, education, healthcare, and legal representation. The Forum promotes the principles within the Charter by creating channels of participation so that its members can access decision-makers and influence policy. In this way, they develop solutions to the problems they face and raise awareness amongst the general public of issues facing refugees and migrants.[23] In other words, a city of refuge is built by all involved. It requires a process of intentional seeking and aiming for the wellbeing of all.

Secondly, building community with people of various backgrounds is vital in reweaving civic life. The Christian story is most powerful when it is lived out. Having been born in a refugee family, which escaped Herod's regime when the child of the family was in danger, it may be no coincidence that Jesus' final instruction revisits loving hospitality to strangers (Matthew 25:34). Thus the destitute living conditions in which parts of the asylum seeking community found themselves, in Manchester, called for the need to recover a compassion for the persecuted. While aiming to adhere to the nation's legal procedures, it was evident that structural legal and civic inadequacies were causing desperate predicaments. An extensive network of Christian households[24] which offered hospitality to the destitute asylum seekers echoed virtues that characterised the early Church (Romans 12:13). The new friendships that grew through this shared life changed both parties as the host and the refugee established a mutual relationship in which they gave and received while seeking a common good. As Bretherton points out: 'However, such mutual transformation necessarily involves loss, as the familiair and what counts as 'home' is renegotiated.'[25]

While a greater level of justice has to be worked out through policies, we can only be good stewards

'The gospel is not so much heard as it is overheard.'

if we model the alternative vision. 'The gospel is not so much heard as it is overheard,' as Søren Kierkegaard rightly states. Costly hospitality is not merely a compassionate, humanitarian and pastoral expression; it is also a political statement.

We delve into a rich history of God's people responding compassionately to the huge human costs attached to the twists and turns of their times. In an era of widespread dislocation and economic deprivation in the late 19th and early 20th centuries in the United States, the Christian community provided 'islands of humanity' in which care was given, and the power of expression restored, to people without identity and powers of speech.[26] In our time of sea change, we need similar islands of humanity. In view of the sharpening antithesis that at times will occur between God's requirements and the civic dysfunctional procedures, faithful Christian living is worked out in conflicting arenas, both through dialogue and subversive resistance, leading us at times to civil disobedience.

While building an alternative social reality from the ground up fosters a 'trickle up' model of social change—a quiet revolution—parts of the Church have been reluctant to be involved in political activism, thus offering little inspiration for systemic social change, as Miller and Yamamori observe. In civic society, it is vital that the Christian perspective shapes the public debate, whether that takes place on a local or national level. In the pub, workplace, classroom or civic forum, the asylum debate, for example, continually needs to be salted with truth to preserve health and add flavor. Recently, children at an Anglican primary school proved to be powerful advocates for their fellow pupil threatened with deportation. Taking their case to the local media and to 10 Downing Street, they were part of an educative process that shaped their citizenship and character, not merely their league tables. Our classrooms, homes and cities can be places of refuge in a lost and hostile world. Our 'citizenship in heaven' prominently shapes our citizenship on earth.

While part of our work remains 'under the radar', it also has a public face. Creative use of the media is a crucial way to draw attention to structural dysfunction, raise public awareness and awaken its conscience. Critically, such public engagement is an effective way to communicate how our faith motivates us to develop a more just and compassionate way of life. In the above examples, the media were crucial in reporting the launch of the Refugee Charter, highlighting the destitute conditions of asylum seekers hosted in Christian homes, and in broadcasting the concerns of children for their friend. This public advocacy role of the Christian community in the media needs to be developed at the grassroots, national and international levels, in order to influence the powerful to act in ways that benefit the marginalised. Seeking society's wellbeing involves policy, hospitality, mercy and advocacy, as the above examples illustrate.

In an age where the public discussion is prominently located and shaped in the media, it is vital that the Christian voice is heard on a local and national level, expressing the gospel as an aspirational narrative and exercising our advocacy in the public domain. After all, we can commend this gospel to the wider world, appealing to its conscience, inspiring its response and providing the hopeful dynamics for transformation.

> *If* you want to learn about a culture, listen to the stories.
> If you want to change a culture, change the stories.
> Michael Margolis

Media: Narrative and Counter-narrative

The world is made up of stories. The family of God is a story-formed community. Story is all about character and relationship. We are told time and time again that we worship a God who… 'heals you', 'sees you', 'brought you out of Egypt', and so on. The Israelites told their children and each other stories of what God had done. As they recount the stories of His intervention in their lives and that of their forefathers, they are reminded of their identity. Retelling the history of Abraham, Isaac and Jacob reminds them also of the kind of God they are praying to: the one who has shown Himself faithful throughout time and will act again on their behalf. Later, the sermons of Peter and Stephen recite the events and purposes in the history of the people of God, placing their lives in a larger context.

Anthropologists, philosophers, historians and theologians agree that we experience our lives and the world around us narratively. We seek beginnings and endings, climax and conclusion. We also weave our own personal stories into larger ones. For we do not live in a vacuum. There are powerful, dominant narratives such as the meta-narrative of progress; the predominance of global capitalism, or the class culture. Similarly, there are dominant narratives in our localities, such as hopelessness, fatalism, status, survival-of-the-fittest, and so forth. Whether this narrative is explicit or held below the level of consciousness, it shapes the communal life as well as that of the individual.

As James Davison Hunter poignantly states, culture is most powerful when it is self-evident.[27] As long as each (sub-)culture tells and lives out a world-story that is to some degree incompatible with the gospel, Harvey

Gallagher Cox calls for our Christian theology and our storytelling to constantly expose the false and unjust values that prevent human flourishing and are destructive to God's will.[28] Theologian Stanley Hauerwas describes the social-ethical task of the Church as being 'the kind of community that tells and tells rightly the story of Jesus. We continue this truth when we see the struggle of each to be faithful to the gospel as essential to each of our lives'.[29]

Jesus' parables are provocative stories, inviting the hearers to leave conventional understanding and encounter new and potentially transformative views. The point of a parable is to transform how we intersect with the world. It is designed to rupture, to shake up and reconfigure. Jesus' challenge is not to hide our light but, rather, to raise it on a stand so that people may see and praise God. It motivates us to tell the tales publicly (Matthew 5:15). In his book, *Disciples and Citizens*, Bishop Graham Cray writes:

> Jesus was a storyteller. He taught in parables. Many of the parables retold Israel's story in ways that seemed familiar when they began, but brought the listener to a conclusion they did not expect. In this way, he gave his listeners the opportunity to see their assumptions and worldviews differently and to respond accordingly... God's power was as much in action in the telling of parables as in the healing of the sick. In the parables, the kingdom demands a response. They are a call to discipleship. This was subversive engagement with Israel's understanding of its story. We need to find similar, imaginative ways to retell, subvert and challenge our nation's stories.[30]

We need to find imaginative ways to retell, subvert and challenge our nation's stories.

The Christian story is able to awaken a consciousness in society and subvert the cultural dominant narratives. An historical glance demonstrating the power of story can be found in the struggle against the transatlantic slave trade in Britain, which in the early 1780s was still an accepted social institution. Within two decades a social movement turned a large proportion of the British public against slavery. Research shows that this shift that led to the abolition of the trade can partly be explained by the critical role of empathy generated by stories. These were generated by a variety of means such as the public talks by former slaves, the use of posters, and reports, all of which educated people about the slaves' plight and caused an upwelling of empathy for their suffering. Empathy can prove to have a major social impact and can be a significant policy tool as it contributes to a revolution of human relationships.[31]

We see this also exemplified through the work of Charles Dickens—a primary storyteller who addressed injustice in his time. He wrote *A Christmas Carol* in the context of the reform of the English Poor Laws. The New Law concerned orphanages, workhouses and debtors' prisons. While on the surface The Poor Law Act appeared to provide for the poor, Dickens challenges the poor stewardship of the ecclesiastical boards who governed with harshness rather than kindness, compassion and mercy. His *Carol* is undergirded by his critique of society and of a form of Christianity that lacks mercy and contains an ardent advocacy concerning the oppression of the weak. So, it's a carol with a bite.[32] As his readers see the change in Scrooge, so they may find a shift in their own hearts.

Dickens is considered to be one of the most persuasive advocates for the poor of his time. His style of writing belongs to Realism. Contrary to the Romantic Movement of the 18th century that gave an idealistic representation of life in literature and the arts, Dickens' novels vividly describe the world as he knew it, shining a light on dark realities such as the destitution and exploitation of children and the oppression of women.[33] Capturing the imagination across social classes, his books raised awareness and created a vein of sentiment, not merely entertaining Victorian society but giving it a progressive impulse for change. For, as the upwelling of empathy shapes individuals, so also it is a significant force in wider societal reform. Over time, various Acts would, among other things, reduce the working hours of children, improve their education and ultimately lead to the end of child labour. Dickens' novels were one of the major driving forces in the social reforms in England.

> *Dickens is considered to be one of the most persuasive advocates for the poor of his time.*

This brief historical glance shows that Christian transformative engagement in Dickens' time included extensive use of the media, aiming to permeate the popular consciousness and contributing to legislative reform. Media is a primary storyteller in our time, and thus, very influential in shaping the culture. Any focus on a more just society must be a multi-lateral vision that includes a creative and pro-active media engagement. In *The Practice of Prophetic Imagination*, Brueggemann provocatively states that the biblical narrative is rarely recognised as a genuine alternative to the dominant narrative. Rather, it is more often reckoned as 'a footnote or a pin prick

> *Any focus on a more just society must be a multi-lateral vision that includes a creative and pro-active media engagement.*

to the dominant narrative but not the real alternative'.[34] The telling of alternative tales is like the 'salting and yeasting' of the public debate. As social anthropologist Melba Padilla Maggay rightly asserts:

> Artists, writers, journalists, social scientists and others with similar gifts for analysis and articulation must be inspired with a vision that will challenge and give them a missional sense of their significance in a post-modern world. It is now through the imagination rather than through reason that the Word breaks through to people. It is time to anoint these underutilised gifts in the Body of Christ and release them to the wider world.[35]

While much Christian public engagement is marked by criticism and negation, James Davison Hunter calls for affirmation to be our starting point:

> Theologically, affirmation must be the starting point because the story of life begins with God's creative initiative and the affirmation He declares on it at each moment of creation... The public witness of Christianity has for too long, shared in, contributed to, and deepened the negational character of this culture. Affirmation is based on the recognition that culture and culture-making have their own validity before God that is not nullified by the fall.[36]

As the prophets of old were social commentators in their time, their critique was not merely characterised by what they were against, but by what they were for. The Church Fathers developed their thinking concerning social consciousness and justice in the light of the Scriptures and applied it to the circumstances of the time, affecting not only the individual but also socio-economic and political dimensions. In the third century, the African author Lactantius describes the perfect justice that sustains human society in which wealth is used 'not for present profit but for justice, which alone endures forever' (*The Divine Institutes*, 6.12). Advocacy and policy went hand in hand.

> *Advocacy and policy went hand in hand.*

In his book *God's Politics*, Jim Wallis advocates the need to move beyond the politics of complaint and offer alternatives in order to change the political framework of debate: 'Clear and compelling alternatives are needed in every area: in education, health care, housing, and economic development and in personal, family, and community renewal.'[37]

The recent Robin Hood Tax campaign is an example of a constructive critique on banking by offering an alternative. Church leaders and Christians in various vocations (economy, arts) champion this cause that works as a double-edged sword. For besides the just redistribution of wealth, the tax proposal is a constructive engagement with our present banking crises. The money raised through the taxation of transactions between financial institutions would be allocated to fund domestic programmes of poverty reduction as well as combat global poverty, thus increasing the chance of delivering the Millennium Development Goals. This note of redemptive activism is reminiscent of the moral imagination of those who initiated the Jubilee 2000 and Make Poverty History campaigns that galvanised wide public support. Again, creative media engagement proved the key.

Abraham Kuyper (1837-1920) articulated implications of a Christian worldview for all spheres. "In the total expanse of human life there is not a single square inch of which the Christ, who alone is sovereign, does not declare, 'That is mine!'" He had a clear missional intent as he expressed his comprehensive view in his multifaceted life as journalist, theologian, politician, prime minister and founder of the Free University in Amsterdam, seeking the *shalom* that is a comprehensive restoration, not merely of individuals but cultural and social life. The commitment to a renewed critical and creative engagement with the media as part of making the case for the truth of Christ in our cultures is included in *The Cape Town Commitment* following the Third Lausanne Congress on Word Evangelization in 2010.[38] The development of an authentic and credible Christian media presence; the commendation of media careers as influential Christian vocations; and the development of a creative use of 'old' and 'new' media to communicate the gospel are significant commitments for our time to tell the life-giving stories that are already pulsing among us.

Producing material such as documentaries, films, books and radio shows that engages the issue of justice is a powerful means of influencing public debate and mobilising people. In his mission to encourage empathy, Muhtar Bakare, founder of an independent publishing house in Nigeria, believes in the quietest of revolutions, convinced that what we read can change people: "Respect comes from understanding each other's stories. But we shout over each other and forget to listen. If we listened, we would find that what the other person was saying is an echo of what we are saying ourselves."[39] Besides publishing, training the next generation of journalists and resourcing media practitioners are crucial in our long-term commitment to a just society. An example of such work is found in the World Media Trust which provides training, consultancy and resources to professional and aspiring media practitioners in order to develop a strong, vibrant, diverse, responsible and free independent media, crucial to the development and sustaining of democratic societies. This faith-based educational charity states: 'The existence of an independent press makes a major contribution to the alleviation of poverty and the upholding of basic human rights, with particular emphasis on the equality of every person, with particular concern for the needs of marginalised and 'at risk' communities'.[40]

Anglican scholar John Stott laid out the concept of 'double listening' as indispensable to discipleship and mission:[41]

> Double listening is vital if we are ever to communicate the gospel, to speak God's Word to God's world with a necessary combination of faithfulness and sensitivity. Not of course that we listen to the Word and the world with an equal degree of respect. We listen to God to believe and obey. We listen to the world rather in order to understand and feel its predicament.

As we listen to what the local community is talking about—through its local paper or radio station, for example—we begin to mingle in the debate. We place the Christian witness as 'salt' in the mix, for without it such debates become corrupt. When the media features youth as 'a lost generation', we respond with hope. When they discuss asylum, we talk about the need to recover compassion for the persecuted. When they speak about the penal system, we speak about restorative justice. A wide variety of Christian spokespeople representing a huge diversity in age, background, and expertise, are needed to help reshape the image people have of 'church', that it is Asian, black, female, youthful, aged, learned, as well as streetwise. And, significantly, the Christian voice needs to be heard in philosophical reflection, in artistic and literary expressions such as poetry, rap, lyrics, comedy, story, paintings, prose, and film. Thus, we creatively mix and mingle with the discussion. As the late Bishop of Liverpool, David Sheppard, rightly argued, if we do not take part in the public debate, the debate will go on without us.[42] By opting in we communicate our worldview, offer an alternative, speak on behalf of the voiceless and hold out a hope for a better tomorrow.

The Christian community has the best stories. Moreover, as we learn to engage hermeneutically bringing faith and the network of opinions and structures that make up society together, we have access to a colourful array of media channels to 'spread the gospel as a rumour'. We whisper in emails, blogs, books, media interviews, articles, conversations, tweets, and videos—a myriad of opportunities to exercise our citizenship. The speed by which our whispers travel is potentially fast and the number of recipients frequently beyond count. A convergence of mobile technology, social media and satellite TV may even cause news to go 'viral', as the dynamics of 'the Arab Spring' clearly show. Nobel prize winner Amartya Sen argues that a free press is key to avoiding famines due to its informative function to government and the opposition as well as the mobilisation of citizens. In *Democracy as a Universal Value* he claims:

> Famines are easy to prevent if there is a serious effort to do so, and a democratic government, facing elections and criticisms from opposition parties and independent newspapers, cannot help but make such an effort. Not surprisingly, while India continued to have famines under British rule right up to independence... they disappeared suddenly with the establishment of a multiparty democracy and a free press.[43]

Famines, after all, are less about food and more about power, caused by bad politics. "Famines are allowed to happen in monochrome regimes that permit no dissent and that brook no argument in a plural press. A democracy is an early warning system in the form of an opposition and vigorous independent press," wrote columnist Phillip Collins in the Times.[44]

Noam Chomsky, Professor of Linguistics and Philosophy, argues that in a fractured society the creation of more open public spaces is vital in the growing of communities of mutual support and democratic interchange. The reconstruction of local media is a critical avenue for such reform. Community-based media outlets engage the broader sectors and give people a reason to feel that they can be a part of the formation of communities, dealing with interesting topics that are part of their lives, giving them an opportunity to give their view.[45] Whether that is a local radio in inner city Moss Side or in the suburbs of Rio, the inclusion of all voices is vital in shaping a just society. An un-free press in undemocratic regimes causes the suppression of a wide range of voices. But also, the narrow social layer of the upper echelons that most UK journalists belong to, distorts the media coverage.[46] The socio-political implication of Christianity with its egalitarian view of the value of each person—regardless of social class, gender, ethnicity or familial lineage—is a subversive political force since such egalitarianism is profoundly democratic.[47] It is therefore vital that a wide array of voices is heard in the public debate.

The effective use of 'new' and 'old' media is vital to create a healthier climate and vibrant debate that includes the previously voiceless. Being heard is crucial in a person's identity formation and the formation of the community's character. David Augsburger, Professor of Pastoral Care and Counseling at the School of Theology at Fuller's Theological Seminary, reminds us that being heard is so close to being loved that they are almost indistinguishable. Furthermore, stories enable decision-making and help us to understand the depth of human nature, causing us to know ourselves in a transformative way and understand how God is at work in the world, giving the community and ourselves "the courage to go on and the will to live in a transformative way," according to Hauerwas.[48]

In our aim to be a prophetic voice and a catalyst for change, the Christian community needs to imaginatively create acts that can be storied. The Archbishop of York, Dr John Sentamu who cut up his clerical collar on live television in protest at the injustice the people of Zimbabwe suffer under its leader Robert Mugabe, created such a dramatic act. So also was his week-long fast and prayer vigil for those caught up in the Israel-Hezbollah conflict. The visual dimension of a tent set up in York Minster was part of a public rallying call for many others to join him in prayer for peace. And thus, our advocacy has not merely a public face, but, significantly, in prayer represents the people before the throne of God, for *shalom* remains a gift from Him.

Conclusion

Our shared sonship and brotherhood with Christ places a responsibility on us to uphold the honour of the Father's house, glorifying Him in the character of our stewardship and community life. Our prophetic role involves the affirmation of what is good, the critiquing of what is bad and the proposition of a more just alternative. While that is best lived out, our voice needs to be heard publicly, reflecting the diversity in our vocations to seek society's wellbeing and address structural dynamics which hinder the flourishing of all, and the poor in particular. Blessed are the *shalom* seekers, the peacemakers. Blessed are they who have a glimpse of the renewed earth they will inherit, the first rays of which already illuminate their lives. For it disturbs, challenges and inspires them today, invites to new frontiers, awakens the hopeful imagination and makes them gloriously creative.

*M*arijke Hoek *is co-ordinator of the Forum for Change, which explores how the Christian community can be active in key change drivers in our culture such as education, politics, media, arts, business, and sports and can thereby contribute to society's wellbeing. She is a regular contributor on BBC Manchester and part of the adjunct faculty of Regents Theological College. Marijke co-edited the book* Micah's Challenge: The Church's Responsibility to the Global Poor *(Paternoster, 2008).*

Notes

1.   Hays, R.B., *The Moral Vision of the New Testament. A Contemporary Introduction to New Testament Ethics*, Edinburgh: T&T Clark, 1996, p.196.

2.   Hays, 1996, p.304.

3. Hays, 1996, p.107.

4. Brueggemann, W., *Interpretation and Obedience*, Minneapolis: Fortress Press, 1991, p.199.

5. Harrison, J.F.C., *Early Victorian Britain, 1832-5*, Suffolk: Fontana, 1979, p.150.

6. Bebbington, D. W., *Evangelicalism in Modern Britain: A History from the 1730s to the 1980s*, London: Unwin Hyman Ltd., 1989, p.19.

7. Hilton, B., *The Age of Atonement: The Influence of Evangelicalism on Social and Economic Thought, 1785-1865*, New York: Oxford University Press, 1988, p.7.

8. Bebbington, D., "Evangelicals, Theology and Social Transformation", in Hilborn, D. (ed.), *Movement for Change. Evangelical Perspectives on Social Transformation*, Carlisle: Paternoster, 2004, p.19.

9. Smith, D.W., *Transforming the World? The Social Impact of British Evangelicalism*, Milton Keynes: Paternoster, 2005, p.18.

10. Hunter, J.D., *To Change the World: The Irony, Tragedy, and Possibility of Christianity in the Late Modern World*, New York: Oxford University Press, 2010, p. 236.

11. Dover, C., "Eschatology and the Workplace", *Journal European Pentecostal Theological Association* 2, 2011, pp.185-197.

12. Miller, D. and Yamamori, T., *Global Pentecostalism. The new face of Christian social engagement*, Berkeley: University of California Press, 2007, p.2.

13. Campolo, T., "Isaiah 58, The Fast that God Requires" in Hoek, M. and Thacker, J. (eds.), *Micah's Challenge. The Church's Responsibility to the Global Poor*, Milton Keynes: Paternoster, 2008, p.93.

14. Edwards, J., "Justice and Pentecostals" JEPTA 1, 2011, pp.5-16.

15. Padilla Maggay, M., "Justice and Approaches to Social Change", in Hoek and Thacker, 2008, p.132.

16. Lederach, J.P., *The Moral Imagination, The Art and Soul of Building Peace*, New York: Oxford University Press, 2005, p.181.

17. See further, Hoek, M., "Divine Power in Human Weakness", in Hoek & Thacker, 2008, pp.48-64.

18. Bretherton, L., *Christianity and Contemporary Politics*, Oxford: Blackwell, 2010, p.73.

19. Bretherton, 2010, p.104.

20. Johns, C.B., *Pentecostal Formation. A Pedagogy among the Oppressed*. JPTSS 2, Sheffield: Sheffield Academic Press, 1993, p.13.

21. Johns, 1993, pp.109-110.

22. Brueggemann, W., *The Prophetic Imagination*, Minneapolis: Fortress, 2001, pp.66-67.

23. http://www.communitynw.org.uk/cgi-bin/viewnews.cgi?article=40

24. "Our guest the asylum seeker", *Guardian* 25/6/2010, accessed 6 May 2012. http://www.guardian.co.uk/uk/2010/jun/25/giving-asylum-seekers-a-bed

25. Bretherton, 2010, p.151.

26. Hollenweger, W., *The Pentecostals*, Minneapolis: Augsburg Publishing House, 1972, p.457.

27. Hunter, 2010, p.211.

28. Cox, H.G., " 'Pentecostalism and Global Market Culture': A Response to Issues Facing Pentecostalism in a Postmodern World" in Dempster, M., Klaus, B.D., Petersen, D.

(eds.) *The Globalization of Pentecostalism. A Religion Made to Travel*, Carlisle: Regnum, 1999, pp.387-8.

29. Hauerwas, S., "Jesus: The Story of the kingdom", *Theology Digest*, 26:4 (winter 1978), pp.302-324.

30. Cray, G., *Disciples & Citizens. A vision for distinctive living*, Nottingham: IVP, 2007, p.178.

31. Krznaric, R., "Empathy and Climate Change. Proposals for a Revolution of Human Relationships", accessed at http://www.romankrznaric.com/Empathy/Empathy.htm#3 on 1/9/09.

32. Kincaid, C.A., *Hearing the Gospel through Charles Dickens's "A Christmas Carol"* Second Edition, Newcastle upon Tyne: Cambridge Scholars Publishing, 2011, p.7.

33. Makati, P., "A Critical Study of Charles Dickens' Representation of the Socially Disadvantaged" (Unpublished paper, University Fort Hare), 2008. Accessed via http://ufh.netd.ac.za/jspui/bitstream/10353/173/1/Makati%20thesis.pdf

34. Brueggemann, W., *The Practice of Prophetic Imagination: Preaching an Emancipating Word*, Minneapolis: Fortress, 2012, p.4.

35. Padilla Maggai, 2008, p.132.

36. Hunter, 2010, pp.231-254.

37. Wallis, J., *God's Politics. Why the Right Gets It Wrong and the Left Doesn't Get It*, New York: Harper Collins, 2005, p.48.

38. Cape Town Commitment 2011 http://www.lausanne.org/ctcommitment, accessed 4 May 2012.

39. http://www.guardian.co.uk/media/2012/aug/26/new-africa-nigeria-leading-publisher

40. http://www.worldmediatrust.org/

41. Stott, J., *The Contemporary Christian: An Urgent Plea for Double Listening*, Nottingham: IVP, 1992.

42. Sheppard, D., *Bias to the Poor,* London: Hodder & Stoughton, 1983.

43. Sen, A., "Democracy as a Universal Value", *Journal of Democracy*, 10:3, 1999, pp.3-17.

44. http://www.thetimes.co.uk/tto/opinion/columnists/.../article3087658.ece accessed 8/7/11.

45. Chomsky, N., "What next for Occupy?" *Guardian*, accessed 30/4/2012. http://www.guardian.co.uk/world/2012/apr/30/noam-chomsky-what-next-occupy?newsfeed=true

46. The Sutton Trust—a British charity working for social equality—published research which demonstrated that journalism is one of the few professions which is actually becoming more unrepresentative of its society in terms of the social/educational background of its professionals. They rightly asked the question whether it is "...healthy that those who are most influential in determining and interpreting the news agenda have educational backgrounds that are so different to the vast majority of the population?" See http://www.suttontrust.com/about-us/annual-reports/annual-report-2006. (accessed 3/5/2012).

47. Miller and Yamamori, 2007, pp.4, 34, 177-179.

48. Hauerwas, quoted in David Johns, J., "Yielding to the Spirit: The Dynamics of a Pentecostal Model of Praxis" in Dempster, M., Klaus, B.D., Petersen, D. (eds.) *The Globalization of Pentecostalism. A Religion Made to Travel*, Carlisle: Regnum, 1999. p.88.

Business as Mission, Justice and Human Dignity

Mats Tunehag explores how the entrepreneurial gift has the potential to bring social reform, model justice and equality, and reduce poverty. Amid complex historic, ethnic, climactic, economic and social dynamics of communities, biblically shaped enterprise holds the capacity to serve God and the common good. Historic and contemporary vignettes highlight the vitality of the entrepreneurial strands in our re-imagining and re-weaving of society.

It was a warm and humid day in June 2012. One may say almost too hot for a Swede. But the story that emerged was more than cool. I listened to the mayor of a small Muslim village. We sat outside his house, drank tea and nibbled on fruit, nuts and sweets. He was enthusiastic and composed. As a devout Muslim he had come to appreciate Christian business people in a way that surprised him. There is a long and sometimes violent history of severe distrust and tension between Muslims and Christians in Indonesia.

The village used to be quite poor. Rats ate 40 percent of the crops every year. These creatures also spread disease. Collaboration for irrigation was non-existent. There was a lack of entrepreneurial spirit and seemingly no-one thought about praying for a difference.

But some good friends and colleagues of mine visited the mayor and his village. They were Christian business people, they wanted to help and they wanted to build bridges across a religious divide. At first the mayor declined. Why did business people come, and not charity workers or government people? On top of that, these people were Christians—not Muslims. But one Christian businesswoman suggested that they at least could pray. She said that prayers make a difference; yes, God can make a difference. It was agreed. Something happened and it became a turning point. The mayor invited them to come back and they did.

The mayor could see me sweating profusely and he kindly turned on a fan and turned it towards me. But he didn't stop telling the story, a story of transformation. The team of Christian business people did research and explored ways to kill the rats in an environmentally-friendly way. They also researched how one could increase the agricultural production and start profitable businesses. They found an owl called *Tyto alba* (Common Barn Owl) that eats rats, but is very hard to breed. Some told them it was impossible. But they prayed, researched and it worked. I could see birdhouses everywhere on the fields. The loss of crops has decreased from 40 to 2 percent per year. Through new wells and irrigation the annual yield of rice has doubled.

I asked the mayor why they didn't dig wells and develop irrigation before the business people came. He said that the Christians changed their mindset regarding work and working together, and first and foremost taught them the importance of prayer, to always start with prayer. "Now we are open to change and we take action. But we always start with prayer," said the mayor.

My Indonesian business friends have started business training courses in the village—based on Biblical principles. They have also helped start small manufacturing businesses, helped with marketing and sales, and local infrastructure. This small village with 2320 people has now become a model village in Indonesia. National television has portrayed this as a model on how to build bridges between Muslims and Christians, and on how to develop transformational businesses. The village is now a national learning center on how to breed owls that kill rats.

I heard several testimonies on how concrete prayers had led to concrete answers, related to rain, a paved road, a job, a motorcycle, and so forth. As we left the village I was encouraged and felt privileged. I had witnessed significant indicators of economic, social, environmental and spiritual transformation. The key contributing factors were: prayers, Christian business people and owls. One might say that this was an expression of Business as Mission.

Business as Mission

Did Christopher Columbus discover America? Not really. The Vikings were there many centuries earlier. So one might say that Columbus *re-discovered* America. Business as Mission is not a new discovery—it is a rediscovery of Biblical truths and practices. In one sense it is like the Reformation and its rallying cry: *ad fontes*—back to the sources.

Business as Mission, BAM, is a term widely used today. The term is new but the underpinning concept is nothing new. During the Reformation old truths were highlighted and contemporary assumptions were challenged. This is what the global BAM movement is doing today. We are revisiting Scripture, questioning jargon and traditions, and assessing the situation in the world. We are also revisiting history and highlighting untold stories of Christians who were instrumental in societal transformation as they engaged in business. Here's one example from Norway:

> Hans Nielsen Hauge was born in the late 1700s in a poor, underdeveloped agricultural society in Norway. There was no democracy and limited religious freedom. When Hauge was 25 years old he had an encounter with God. Hauge's life motto became: Love God and fellow men. He traveled extensively throughout Norway and did what we in modern day terminology would call church planting and business as mission.

> He started 30 businesses, including fishing industries, brickyards, spinning mills, shipping yards, salt & mineral mines, paper mills, and printing plants. He was an entrepreneur and a catalyst. Many others were inspired to read the Bible, to meet with other believers for prayer and fellowship, and various businesses were started and developed.

> Even secular historians today acknowledge Hauge's legacy and contribution to the development of modern Norway. He is sometimes called "the Father of democracy in Norway". He facilitated equality between men and women and his work led to a spiritual awakening and an entrepreneurship movement. Hauge's legacy is thus one of spiritual, economic and social transformation. His life and work illustrates some of the BAM goals, principles and outcomes.

Three Biblical Mandates

Many Evangelicals often put an emphasis on the Great Commission, but sometimes make a great omission. This is only one of three mandates we have. The first one God gave us is the *creation mandate*, Genesis 1-3: we are to be creative and create good things, for ourselves and others, being good stewards of all things entrusted to us—even in the physical arena. This of course includes being creative in business—to create wealth. Wealth creation is a godly talent: "Remember the LORD your God, for it is he who gives you the ability to produce wealth." (Deuteronomy 8:18) As Christians we often focus

> "Remember the LORD your God, for it is he who gives you the ability to produce wealth." (Deuteronomy 8:18)

more on wealth distribution, but there is no wealth to distribute unless it has been created.

The second mandate is the *great commandment* which includes loving your neighbor. In the first and second mandates you find a basis for what modern day economists call Corporate Social Responsibility (CSR). It is about creating wealth and producing products and services in ways that consider 'your neighbor'. CSR recognizes the importance of serving several constituencies through business—not just the owners, but also staff, suppliers, clients, community and the physical environment. CSR includes three bottom lines and looks at the impact businesses have economically, socially and environmentally for the various stakeholders.

BAM also recognizes the importance of the triple bottom line as it is based on the God given mandates about being a creative steward and serving people. But BAM goes beyond this, to CSR+, as we include the third mandate—the *Great Commission*. We are to glorify God and make Christ known among all peoples. This is the fourth bottom line. As we integrate the Great Commission into our business goals, we develop a global and missional perspective. BAM is CSR+, where the + can also be seen as a cross—putting everything under the Lordship of Christ.

We need to re-discover our three Biblical mandates and review their implications on church, business and our global mission. But there are of course many other issues and aspects as well. During this much needed re-discovery process we need to ask ourselves:

- Why do we seem to value the calling to be a pastor and a missionary over the calling to be an entrepreneur or accounting executive?

- Why do we tend to focus on non-profit mechanisms to alleviate poverty, when for-profit businesses are a natural and biblical mechanism for creating wealth?

- Why do we tend to value wealth distribution and often neglect wealth creation?

- Why do we tend to limit the contribution of Christian business people to donating money to ministry programs?

- Why do we often settle for doing good business—triple bottom line—and forget the fourth bottom line: glorify God and make Christ known among all peoples as we do business.

- Why are so few seminaries and Bible colleges providing courses on the theology of work and business?

Can you mix God and business?

If business was only about maximizing profit, it would be acceptable to get involved in human trafficking, which is relatively low risk (few traffickers are caught and sentenced) and it has a relative high profit margin. If job creation was the only purpose of business, one could commend the Mafia for the jobs they create.

Businesses should serve various groups through their products, services, relationships and conduct: employees, owners, suppliers, customers, families, communities, and others.

Businesses should strive towards having a positive impact on individuals and societies, not only economically but also socially and environmentally.

Businesses should embrace a godly ethical framework to shape all aspects of the business. Good corporate values will also help build healthy societies.

Businesses need to make a profit to survive but they should also look beyond that. Pope John Paul II wrote: "The purpose of a business firm is not simply to make a profit, but is to be found in its very existence as a community of persons who in various ways are endeavouring to satisfy their basic needs, and who form a particular group at the service of the *whole of society.*"

This was even understood by a so called capitalist like David Rockefeller:

"The old concept that the owner of a business had a right to use his property as he pleased to maximize profits has evolved into the belief that ownership carries certain binding social obligations. Today's manager serves as trustee not only for the owners but for the workers and, indeed, for our entire society."

> **T**oday's manager serves as trustee not only for the owners but for the workers and, indeed, for our entire society.

John Paul II says that the Church "recognises the fundamental and positive role of business, the market, private property and the resulting responsibility for the means of production, as well as free human creativity in the economic sector". However, he adds that there must be a strong juridical framework, which at its core is ethical and religious.

But can ethically-run businesses survive in a today's tough global market? Can a business have Christian values and be profitable at the same time? Yes, and here follows one example.

The R.W. Beckett Corporation was founded 1937 and is now a third generation family business which "endeavors to apply a biblically-based philosophy throughout every phase of its operations". Its mission is: "By God's grace we will grow, relentlessly improve and passionately serve our customers and fellow employees."

Here are some of the values guiding the business:

- Our intention is to be a Christ-centered company.

- We will conduct ourselves with dignity, adhering to the highest ethical and moral standards.

- We desire to be known as honourable, reliable and trustworthy, always willing to go the extra mile for something we believe in.

- Profits are important and necessary, but never at the expense of good, long-term business judgment.

- Recognising that there are business cycles, we have a high priority to provide employment stability.

- We want to be good "corporate citizens"—active in serving others, helping meet human needs in the community and beyond.

- We realize we are not an end in ourselves, but a part of God's larger purposes. As such, we are called upon to work as "unto Him," to view our business as a trust and to be wise and able stewards of the trust He has placed with us.

So can a business have Christian values and be profitable at the same time? Yes! Beckett has 75 years of experience.

A God-Pleasing Capitalism

Some of us grew up during the Cold War, and in Sweden the dividing line was often described as two economic systems. But in actual fact the dividing line was rather about human rights and freedoms, and thus about human dignity. The centrally-planned command economy in communist countries was disastrous for people, societies and the environment. But does that mean that capitalism is the answer? Pope John Paul II addressed that issue:

> Can it perhaps be said that, after the failure of Communism, capitalism is the victorious social system, and that capitalism should be the goal of the

countries now making efforts to rebuild their economies and societies? Is this the model which ought to be proposed to the countries of the Third World which are searching for the path to true economic and civil progress?

The answer is obviously complex. If by "capitalism" is meant an economic system which recognizes the fundamental and positive role of business, the market, private property and the resulting responsibility for the means of production, as well as free human creativity in the economic sector, then the answer is certainly in the affirmative, even though it would perhaps be more appropriate to speak of a "business economy", "market economy" or simply "free economy".

But if by "capitalism" is meant a system in which freedom in the economic sector is not circumscribed within a strong juridical framework which places it at the service of human freedom in its totality, and which sees it as a particular aspect of that freedom, the core of which is ethical and religious, then the reply is certainly negative."[1]

Godly wealth creation

Political processes and legislation often determine the framework for economic relations and business development. We may of course take issue with some policies of some politicians, but it is nevertheless good to note that the former UK Prime Minister Margaret Thatcher addressed these kinds of issues in a speech to the General Assembly of the Church of Scotland on 21 May 1988. Here are some excerpts:

The Old Testament lays down in Exodus the Ten Commandments as given to Moses, the injunction in Leviticus to love our neighbour as ourselves and generally the importance of observing a strict code of law. The New Testament is a record of the Incarnation, the teachings of Christ and the establishment of the Kingdom of God. Again we have the emphasis on loving our neighbour as ourselves and to "Do-as-you-would-be-done-by".

I believe that by taking together these key elements from the Old and New Testaments, we gain: a view of the universe, a proper attitude to work, and principles to shape economic and social life. We are told we must work and use our talents to create wealth. "If a man will not work he shall not eat," wrote St. Paul to the Thessalonians. Indeed, abundance rather than poverty has a legitimacy which derives from the very nature of Creation.

Nevertheless, the Tenth Commandment—"Thou shalt not covet"—recognises that making money and owning things could become selfish activities. But it is not the creation of wealth that is wrong but love of money for its own sake. The spiritual dimension comes in deciding what one does with the wealth. How could we respond to the many calls for help, or invest for the future, or support the wonderful artists and craftsmen whose work also glorifies God, unless we had first worked hard and used our talents to create the necessary wealth?

A businesswoman from the Middle East as a role model

John Paul II and Margaret Thatcher have made some valuable observations, but the Business as Mission concept and praxis is much older. The Bible portrays a businesswoman as a godly example of how to serve others and meet various needs. Let's briefly look at a few

She sees that her trading is profitable.
(Proverbs 31:18)

verses of Proverbs chapter 31 and translate these into modern day business language:

Proverbs chapter 31	*What does that mean?*
16 She considers a field and buys it.	She does a market assessment and invests.
Out of her earnings, she buys a vineyard.	She makes a profit and reinvests.
18 She sees that her trading is profitable.	She keeps books and manages cash flow.
24 She makes linen garments and sells them	She is involved in manufacturing and retail.
and supplies the merchant with sashes.	She has set up a supply chain.
20 She opens her arms to the poor and extends her hands to the needy.	She uses part of the profit for charitable work.
15 She provides food for her family	She is the breadwinner of the family.
and portions for her servant girls.	She provides employment.
31 Give her the reward she has earned, and let her works bring her praise at the city gate.	Her work in business should be recognised and is certainly commendable.

Moose hunting and Business as Mission

9 million people live in Sweden. Approximately 300,000 Swedes go hunting every year and they shoot 100,000 moose. Moose hunters need to know what a moose looks like. If they do not know, you certainly do not want to be around during hunting season. Your success as a hunter depends

on knowing your target. One can only succeed—or fail—in relationship to a target, a defined purpose, and specific objectives.

The same applies to Business as Mission, BAM. We can only determine success or failure based on our purpose. So what is the purpose of BAM? A key word is transformation.

From church planting success to genocide

In just 100 years, this country went from 'unreached' to 'churched', with approximately 90 percent of the population attending church as members. It is the ultimate success story in the history of Christian mission—if the success criteria are church planting and church growth.

In just over 100 days, nearly one million citizens (and church members) were killed—by other citizens and church members—in a brutal genocide in the spring of 1994. The country? Rwanda. It had seen tremendous success in evangelism and church planting but little penetration of the Gospel in ethnic relationships—it had people in church, but not church in people.

How we define our mission has both short and long-term implications. Church planting and growth is not wrong, but clearly insufficient as a success criterion.

As we look at sub-Saharan Africa today, it has some of the most Christian countries in the world (percentage of Christians), some of the poorest countries in the world, and some of the most corrupt countries in the world. What is wrong with this picture? Is this success? Is this in line with our mission as Christians? Is this what God wants?

Our mission and success criteria must include *transformation*. We want people and societies to be transformed—holistically. The global Business as Mission (BAM) movement is aiming at *transformed lives around the world through ethical business with integrity*. This sounds grand, but what does it mean?

Transformation: It is about a good and lasting change. And that takes time; we need to have an inter-generational perspective. BAM is an intentional praxis of faith at work in all relationships in and through business. BAM is about practicing business based on ethical principles. It is about following Jesus in the market place to see people and societies transformed.

We also need to give priority to small and medium size businesses (SMEs). They are strong *transformational* agents—not only economically. They are, in many ways, the backbone of developed economies. SMEs are often missing to a large extent in poor countries and regions.

Lives: We are all people with physical, social, spiritual, emotional, economical and other needs, operating in a political and cultural context. So transformation must be holistic—for people and societies. This is also what the word 'integrity' means—something whole and complete. Our mission is and must be more than evangelism and church planting—we do not want to create another Rwanda!

Around the World: The BAM movement can never be true to God and our mission if we limit ourselves to a local outlook. We must be a part of God's centrifugal force, moving out and beyond our immediate comfort zones to all peoples and nations.

BAM and the challenge before us

A focus for the global BAM movement is the Arab world & Asia. Why? There is a concentration of many needs in this region.

a) The name of Jesus is rarely heard in the Muslim, Hindu, and Buddhist worlds.

b) This is where you find up to 80% of the world's poorest.

c) Unemployment and underemployment in many of these countries ranges from 30% - 80%.

d) These nations have the fastest population growth, with hundreds of millions of young people coming into the labour market looking for jobs.

e) These are also often high-risk areas for trafficking and prostitution. Unemployment makes people vulnerable.

We can take a closer look at a couple of these points: unemployment and human trafficking.

1.8 billion jobs needed

There is a global shortfall of about 1.8 billion good formal jobs, according to Jim Clifton, CEO of Gallup.[2] That is nearly a quarter of the world's population.

Many people live and work in the insecure, informal job sector, which is often filled with survival activities in the form of subsistence businesses. Most people hope for a formal job, but many have little or no prospect of finding one. And the problem is increasing.

50 million new jobs need to be created in the Arab world alone by 2020 and there is no indication of that happening. According to the Economist,

unemployment rates are 24% in Egypt, 27% in Jordan, 30% in Tunisia, 39% in Saudi Arabia and 46% in Gaza.[3]

44 million people in the so-called rich world are unemployed and another 11 million are underemployed. The human costs are enormous, for joblessness increases depression, divorce, substance abuse, etc.

Youth are disproportionately affected and this goes for both rich and poor countries. In Spain, for example, 46 percent of young people under the age of 25 are out of work. In South Africa it is over 50 percent.

The challenge is huge and global. What must be done?

Handouts do not give dignity—jobs do. To illustrate: In May 2012 I met a former soldier in Cambodia. A landmine took his arm and killed his friend, and he also lost every family member in the war. He told me: "After the war the church became my family, and a job gave me dignity." I warmly recommend the encyclical letter by John Paul II, which deals with work and human dignity.[4]

Aid can ease problems temporarily but cannot create 1.8 billion new jobs. We know, for example, that aid has not lifted Africa out of poverty, as the international economist Dambisa Moyo has clearly demonstrated in her book *Dead Aid*.

Micro-loan programmes can help, but tend to build the informal economy and thus run the risk of cementing people and nations in poverty. More than 80 per cent of African jobs are created by small and medium businesses, according to World Bank surveys, yet those businesses are neglected by traditional aid agencies.

Jim Clifton writes: "The demands of leadership have changed. The highest levels of leadership require mastery of a new task: job creation."

> *The demands of leadership have changed. The highest levels of leadership require mastery of a new task: job creation*

But as we stress again and again in the global business as mission movement: We don't want just any kind of jobs. The Mafia also creates jobs. The traffickers put people to work in the sex industry. No, we want to create jobs with dignity that add value to life, which bring good and holistic transformation to people and societies.

To this end we need innovators, entrepreneurs and mentors. One study referred to in The Economist (10 Sep 2011) "shows that between 1980 and 2005 all net new private-sector jobs in America were created by companies less than five years old".

As stated in the Business as Mission Manifesto, from the Lausanne paper on BAM 2004:

> We call upon the Church worldwide to identify, affirm, pray for, commission and release business people and entrepreneurs to exercise their gifts and calling as business people in the world—among all peoples and to the ends of the earth.

> We call upon business people globally to receive this affirmation and to consider how their gifts and experience might be used to help meet the world's most pressing spiritual and physical needs through Business as Mission.

Human Trafficking

One can make two observations about big, organised crime: Firstly, it is big. Secondly, it is organised.

Human trafficking, modern day slavery, is the second biggest organised crime in the world. It is worth many billions of dollars and involves very sophisticated transnational operations. Some estimates indicate that about 27 million people have been tricked, shipped, deployed to slave-like work and are held against their will. This is happening all over the world. It is big business. It is organised. The trafficking operations involve all kinds of professions and skills and they are very interconnected; think of it as a multi-national company with all levels, from janitors to high-flying CEOs.

Unfortunately, anti-human-trafficking initiatives can be labeled as small and disorganised in comparison. To adequately address and combat human trafficking we need to build critical mass (become big) and build strategic alliances (become organised).

I see two major challenges for anti-trafficking initiatives. One problem is that it is mainly two categories of people and groups who are involved: Firstly, legislators, policy makers, and government agencies. Secondly, NGOs, non-profit and volunteer based organisations. These people and groups are good and needed. They are not the problem. The problem is the people and groups who are *not* involved or not even invited to combat this evil.

We know that unemployment makes people vulnerable to traffickers. It is also a fact that we cannot talk about restoration of victims of human trafficking unless we can offer them jobs with dignity. Thus adequate prevention and restoration must include job creation. This means that business people must be a part of anti-trafficking networks as we try to get big and organised.

The second problem is disconnectedness. Local and national disconnected anti-trafficking measures are not sufficient to tackle big, organised crime, to initiate preventative steps and to plan and effect rescue and restoration of the victims of these criminal gangs.

In short: we need to get more professions and skills involved and we need to build international strategic alliances. Is that a pipe dream? No!

Let me briefly mention two significant initiatives, one regional and one global.

The European Freedom Network, EFN, facilitates information sharing, coordination and cooperation among over one hundred partners in over 30 countries. They are working together to prevent human trafficking and provide restorative processes for its victims. EFN is an important step in the right direction of building critical mass and getting organised transnationally.[5]

The global think tank on Business as Mission has a working group dealing with these issues, and pro-actively inviting business people to be a part of the solution.[6]

Think beyond micro[7]

Why is Bangladesh poor and Taiwan rich? This admittedly provocative question is intended to help us drill down into important questions: how and where might we most effectively apply resources for the extension of the Kingdom of God through business?

The definition of Medium Sized Businesses (SME) varies, but most would accept that a business of moderate capitalisation requirements, employing perhaps 20-250 employees or so, would be a typically acceptable description; such is the case here.

It is a fact that SMEs are the backbone of economically-healthy countries, be they so-called "developed" or "developing". It is beyond dispute, and true anywhere in the world, across a long historical timeline, that countries with vibrant and numerous SMEs tend to experience a number of positive socio-economic changes. Apart from the relatively large number of jobs created, SMEs also help bring larger segments of the economy into the formal sector. This in turn contributes to the creation and growth of an essential tax base from which other socially desirable outcomes can be supported, such as hospitals, schools, roads and other infrastructure.

There is generally a desirable association between a robust taxpayer base and the development of participatory ("democratic") institutions associated with justice and good government. Conversely, any failed or failing state (economically, socially, politically) will show unmistakable signs of the SME sector being under attack or largely absent.

SMEs also seem to fare better even in times of economic crisis, as the *The Economist* reports:[8]

> In contrast to the doom and gloom coming from Europe's biggest firms, many SMEs are cautiously optimistic. The main umbrella organisation for Germany's more than 4m SMEs predicts that its members' sales will contract by only 2% this year. The country's renowned Mittelstand will therefore outperform the economy as a whole, which the government expects to shrink by 6%. A survey last month of 804 French SMEs found that just over half of them expected revenues to either stay flat or increase in 2009.

> Europe's SMEs, defined as firms with fewer than 250 employees, collectively employ 88m people and account for two-thirds of private-sector employment. As big companies send jobs out of the country in an effort to reduce costs, smaller firms are becoming increasingly important as domestic employers. And although most SMEs are tiny mom-and-pop operations, with little capacity or desire to grow, their number also includes fast-growing, innovative firms which, if properly nourished, could become tomorrow's champions.

These perspectives need to be put alongside the pervasive, increasingly popular, and often unquestioning effort to promote micro-enterprise, both through NGOs and even commercial interests. Will micro-enterprise really help poor nations in the long-term? How is it that Bangladesh (famous as a micro-enterprise country) is still endemically poor and Taiwan (a country of SMEs) is rich? How might a more intentional focus on SMEs in countries like the first have a more effective impact?

Professor Milford Bateman wrote in *The Financial Times* about the danger of micro-enterprise as a big picture strategy, over the long-term.[9]

> Put simply, to the extent that local savings are intermediated through microfinance institutions, the more that country or region or locality will be left behind in a state of poverty and under-development. This is an "iron law of microfinance". Focusing on isolated cases of micro-enterprise success simply does not add up to economic development. The reason microfinance is supported is overwhelmingly political/ideological—the economic rationale is simply not there.

Professor Bateman contrasts Bangladesh with other relatively rich countries, also in Asia:

> The East Asian countries managed to develop brilliantly through channelling much, if not most, of their savings into serious growth-oriented

sustainable business projects. This is the reason many East Asian countries may have started at similar GDP levels as Bangladesh in the 1970s, but have since then massively outpaced Bangladesh in terms of growth and development. Economics 101 shows conclusively how critical savings are to development, but only if intermediated into growth- and productivity-enhancing projects. If it all goes into rickshaws, kiosks, 30 chicken farms, traders, and so on, then that country simply will not develop and sustainably reduce poverty.

Dr. Peter Heslam, at Cambridge University comments further on the issue:

> Some may wonder whether entrepreneurship has biblical warrant. But if entrepreneurship is about innovation, judgment and risk-taking, archetypal figures such as Abraham, Jacob and David reflect, despite their faults, strong entrepreneurial traits. Yet the primary model of entrepreneurship occurs at the very start of the Hebrew Scriptures, where the curtains open on a God who overflows with innovation, wise judgment and the willingness to take risks—especially the risk of creating human beings and inviting them to join his start-up as stewards of the earth.

On the basis of these reasons, we call the church and the global BAM movement to place greater emphasis on cultivating and enabling entrepreneurs and the SMEs of which they have been made stewards.

Business as Mission is bigger than you think

Business as Mission is sometimes a tricky term, but it is an important concept and an essential praxis. But BAM it is not a silver bullet; it is not the ultimate strategy. It is, however, a growing global movement of Christians in the market place asking: How can we shape business to serve *people*, align with God's *purposes*, be good stewards of the *planet* and make a *profit?*

Business as Mission is not trying to replace traditional means of serving God and people among

People, purpose, planet, profit.

all nations. Business as Mission is not a fundraising method. Nor is it about attaching some church-like activities to a business. It recognises the importance of and embraces Corporate Social Responsibility, CSR. But it goes beyond as well: BAM is CSR+.

We are on a mission in and through business. It is for example a mission of justice. One could even say 'Business as Justice'. This and other terms may help us understand the holistic and transformational nature of Business as Mission. Let me give 12 brief examples. The list could be made longer, but these 12 will hopefully show that Business as Mission is not just doing business with a touch of "churchianity."

1. Business as Justice

God loves justice and hates injustice. God sent prophets again and again who spoke out against injustice, and they demanded change and correction. Injustice often manifested itself in the market place: it was corruption, labour exploitation and abuse of vulnerable people like immigrants.

To pursue honest business and care for staff is *Business as Justice*. To treat customers and suppliers well is also a part of this God-honouring pursuit. *Business as Justice* includes fighting corruption and bribery.

2. Business as True Religion

True worship is to take care of widows and orphans (James 1:27). These are two vulnerable groups, who are often exploited in the market place today. Human traffickers often target lonely children. Circumstances and cunning people may force widows into prostitution.

These are realities in many parts of the world. Who will offer orphans and widows a future; give them jobs with dignity, so they can support themselves and others? That would be *Business as True Religion*.

3. Business as *Shalom*

Shalom is a Biblical concept of good and harmonious relationships. But relationships were damaged and broken through the fall as described in Genesis chapter 3. Through Christ there is a way to restored relationship with God, with one another, and with creation.

Business is so much about relationships, with staff, colleagues, peers, customers, clients, suppliers, family, community, tax authorities, and so forth. How can we as Christians in business strive towards *Shalom*; *Business as Shalom?*

4. Business as Stewardship

Every human being has been entrusted with gifts and talents. In business we also talk about assets. Stewardship is another important Biblical concept. How can we use what we have to serve? What does stewardship mean when we own and/or run a business?

God has given some people strong entrepreneurial gifts. They can be used for God and for the common good through business. It is the same with managerial gifts or gifts of bookkeeping or sales. We should encourage people with business skills to be good stewards—*Business as Stewardship*.

5. Business as Servant Leadership

Jesus came to serve. He was an example of good and godly leadership. Many books are written on this topic and it indicates the importance of the very concept of servant leadership.

Doing business as unto the Lord means that we also explore what servant leadership means in the business context. It is not a simple formula or a cookie-cutter approach. It may look differently in different industries and cultures. But the key underlying principle is to serve people, communities, nations, and God. We are too often reminded about the lack of good leadership in the business world. *Business as Servant Leadership* is more than needed.

6. Business as Human Dignity

Every person on this planet is created in God's image. We all have value and dignity linked to the Creator. He created us to be creative, and to create good things for others and ourselves. It is deeply human and divine to create; it is an intrinsic part of human dignity. This creativity process, and thus human dignity, has been partly broken, but there is restoration power through Jesus Christ.

It is not a sin to be unemployed, but unemployment and the inability to work and support oneself and family, is a consequence of the fall. It is a loss of human dignity. Putting people to work, providing jobs with dignity, is a godly act—it is *Business as Human Dignity.*

*P*utting people to work is a godly act.

7. Business as Reconciliation

The Apostle Paul writes that we are agents of reconciliation. Broken relationships and conflicts are common, even in the market place. We also witness tension and violence between ethnic and religious groups. Can businesses provide a forum for reconciliation? Can business people bridge ethnic and religious divides?

There is a long and sometimes violent history of severe distrust and tension between Muslims and Christians in Indonesia. But I have seen first-hand how Chinese Christian business people in Indonesia have changed interethnic dynamics and transformed interreligious relationships by intentionally doing business as justice, stewardship, *shalom,* servant leadership, and so forth. This chapter started with such a story or case study. As God's ambassadors, we can be business people on a mission to do *Business as Reconciliation.*

243

8.   Business as Creation Care

During the creation days, God did a daily evaluation, he exercised quality control on the products he produced. His verdict was "these are good". He has entrusted us to be stewards also of creation. Like God we can rejoice in being creative in the physical arena and produce goods and services that are good for people and the creation. This is the first Biblical mandate we have—to be creative and to work, also in the business world.

The importance of environmentally-friendly businesses is included in the triple bottom line, striving to have a positive impact economically, socially and environmentally. Profit, people, planet.

On a visit to South Asia in 2012, I met a couple who are working as management consultants to major manufacturing companies. This couple had a clear BAM mission, and were able to help these companies to become more profitable, improve working condition, save energy and clean up huge amounts of water. Access to and preservation of clean water is one of the biggest challenges we face globally. *Business as Creation Care* is essential.

9.   Business as Loving Your Neighbour

The second scriptural mandate is the great commandment and includes to "love your neighbour as yourself". We know that business can and should serve people and meet various needs. For example: unemployment is a major underlying cause of malnourishment and starvation, homelessness, human trafficking, disease and limited access to medical treatment, as well as to debt and crime. Providing people with jobs is alleviating and preventing these dire conditions.

Human resource management (a term which sounds too impersonal and technical to me) should be an expression of loving your neighbour. Taking our neighbors' physical environment into consideration as we run businesses is also a part of this responsibility. CSR is thus not a new thing; it is based on Biblical principles.

We can also study and learn from history. For example, the Quakers in England and Hans Nielsen Hauge in Norway were agents of holistic transformation through business already a few hundred years ago. They did *Business as Loving Your Neighbour.*

10.   Business as Great Commission

The third Biblical mandate is the global centrifugal thrust: to all peoples, to all nations. This is a major theme in the global BAM movement. How can we serve in and through business, empowered by the Holy Spirit, "in Jerusalem, and in all Judea and Samaria, and to the ends of the earth"?

Business as Mission is about being a follower of Jesus, in business and to the whole world, especially in areas with dire economic, social and spiritual needs.

This is CSR+ and this dimension is not an elective. We want to see the Kingdom of God demonstrated among all peoples. It is *Business as Great Commission.*

11. Business as Body of Christ

God calls and equips some people to business. We need to affirm and encourage business people to exercise their calling with professionalism, excellence and integrity. Martin Luther puts it this way:

> A cobbler, a smith, a farmer, each has the work and the office of his trade, and they are all alike consecrated priests and bishops, and every one by means of his own work or office must benefit and serve every other, that in this way many kinds of work may be done for the bodily and spiritual welfare of the community, even as all the members of the body serve one another.[10]

12. Business as Glorifying God

BAM is the acronym for Business as Mission. Another relevant acronym is AMDG. The ultimate bottom line of Business as Mission is AMDG—*ad maiorem Dei gloriam*—for the greater glory of God.

Mats Tunehag is a freelance consultant, speaker and writer from Sweden. (http://www.matstunehag.com/) He has worked in nearly half of the countries of the world, developing global strategic alliances for various constituencies, including Business as Mission. He is a senior Associate on Business as Mission for both the Lausanne Movement and World Evangelical Alliance Mission Commission, and has lectured widely on Business as Mission as well as published numerous articles and papers on the topic. He initiated and co-led the first global think tank on Business as Mission (BAM) 2002 – 2004, and he is now co-chairing the second global think tank on BAM: http://www.bamthinktank.org He also serves with a global investment fund based on Christian values that helps SMEs to grow in size and holistic impact in the Arab world and Asia, by providing financial, intellectual and human capital. He is also a global spokesperson on Religious Liberty & Freedom of Speech for the World Evangelical Alliance. He serves on the Global Council of Advocates International, a global network of 30,000 lawyers in over 120 countries. He has lectured to lawyers in Europe, Latin America and North America on Human Rights issues and lessons learned in building strategic and influential alliances shaping public opinion and legislation. He wrote editorials on international affairs for ten years for a national newspaper in Sweden.

Notes

1. *Centesimus annus*, 1991.

2. Clifton, J., The Coming Jobs War, New York: Gallup Press, 2011.

3. *The Economist*, 10 September 2011.

4. *Laborem Exercens*, 1981.

5. http://www.europeanfreedomnetwork.org

6. See http://www.BAMThinkTank.org

7. This piece on SMEs and micro-enterprises is excerpted from an article I co-wrote with Peter Shaukat in 2009, called "Think beyond micro".

8. May 21, 2009.

9. 26 December 2008.

10. *An Open Letter to the Christian Nobility.*

Afterword: A New Day

Life happens amid great gaping gulfs of inequality. Huge, impersonal social forces all too often intersect with human fragility. Injustice comes with a massive price tag, not merely in depriving us of opportunities but also in taking captive our personal and communal imagination. Society is after all a complex network of mutuality. We are actually in this together - "tied in a single garment of destiny", as Martin Luther King Jr. would say.

The civil rights movement shows that the friction caused by gross injustice can create social sparks that torch a transformative movement. It's one of the many historic examples that can inspire us in the challenges and the turbulence of our times. The previous chapters have touched upon other examples, reminding us that our work stands in a long tradition of the people of God whose faith stimulated a commitment to the politics of justice; the business of justice; the stories of justice; or the art of justice. And all testify to the capacity to overcome. Their commitment to a greater liberty, equality and compassion transformed their world. It demonstrates that a movement of people who face up to injustice and pay the price can bring about a seismic shift in their time, affecting moral, social, historical, economic, spiritual and legal dynamics in society.

When the streets and public squares were filled with misery, the prophets' visions for restored community life lit up the world as they knew it. And they still do. Zechariah, Joel, Isaiah... they not only help us to lament but also to glimpse again this vibrant hope for rebuilding a flourishing community. For they offer an alternative vision for the future. They also point to our personal responsibility and remind us of the price tag: spending ourselves on behalf of others. Isaiah actually uses the Hebrew word for 'soul', our whole persona (Isaiah 58:10). In whatever capacity – banker, community leader, teacher, police officer, journalist, shop owner, academic, pastor, pensioner or parent – we are called 'repairers of broken walls, restorers of streets with dwellings'.

So, God is after a radical form of 'whole life stewardship'. We see that best lived out in Jesus' life and teaching. Standing on a hill in Galilee, He pronounces people with an aching hunger for justice blessed (Matthew 5:6). Where ever we are placed in society and whatever country we live in, we need to become mindful of cultural and religious factors that prevent communities from flourishing and develop a critical theology of culture. In all our vocations we need a pursuit of craftsmanship that has its home in faith and virtue and is concerned with the wellbeing God intended for the wider community.

Since God is just, the 'justice' theme resonates prominently in His conversation with us. We can read it in the Bible, in books such as this, in our prayers and, poignantly, we need to see it reflected in our communities. For we won't be known by our theology or by our theories but by our fruit. The gospel contains a radical critique of injustice and inspires a new imagination and expectation. Times of carnival offer the possibility for creativity and critique of power, but, as explored in the various chapters in this volume, so do times of austerity, forced migration, poverty and marginalisation, climate change and social unrest. All provide the occasion to subversively create an alternative reality and provide sparks to consider a more compassionate and just response, whether personally, locally or globally.

Ultimately the palpable outworking of this great conversation continues best in the kind of communities that embody the love and justice of God. A city on a hill constitutes, after all, a community of people, the character of which is pure, merciful, humble, peace-building and mournful over the world's pain. Living in a fractured world, we not only share in the pain but also share in the promise that we shall be satisfied (Matthew 5:6). Aching visionaries have caught a glimpse of God's new day. Jesus' call to understand the times and follow Him is a vital way to bring the love and purposes of God into the ordering of collective life. In the harsh reality of the present and the misery that weighs heavily upon people, we are challenged to live wisely as we are part of the move of God to bring in his wisdom (Ecclesiastes 8:5-6).

In Proverbs wisdom is personified in a woman. She is described as 'calling aloud' from the streets. Out in the open, she raises her voice in the public square, the city gates and at the busiest street corner (1:21). Wisdom emerges from the marginal districts of Villa María del Triunfo in Lima, the poorest provinces in the Philippines, or the makeshift Occupy camps across many Western cities. Wisdom calls out in song, poetry, literature, enterprise, protest... Wisdom speaks from the heart of the community and invites us to come and learn. We do well to heed the invitation and create space for imagination.

In his book The Prophetic Imagination Walter Brueggemann writes, 'The prophet engages in future fantasy. The prophet does not ask if the vision can be implemented... The imagination must come before the implementation. Our culture is competent to implement almost anything and to imagine almost nothing... It is the vocation of the prophet to keep alive the ministry of imagination, to keep conjuring and proposing alternative futures'.

While the enormity of the task could reduce us to spectators, the Scripture calls us forth as spect-actors; transmitting rays of the sacred in our own state of play today. We hope this book will have inspired you and further moved you to thresholds of change you may not have anticipated as you recognise the opportune times in your community. As the political activist Helen Keller said: 'Although the world is full of suffering, it is also full of the overcoming of it.' We hope that it may cause you to explore new frontiers and has given you an impulse of courage. For there are new horizons that want to be seen. There are vibrant alternatives to be developed, there are dominant narratives to be subverted and new ones to be told and embodied. As followers of the Way, the Truth and the Life, there is a brave agenda to be lived out that invites us all to a new future.

So, let's conclude with a blessing for a new day.

May my mind come alive today
To the invisible geography
That invites me to new frontiers
To break the dead shell of yesterdays
To risk being disturbed and changed.

May I have the courage today
To live the life that I would love,
To postpone my dream no longer
But do at last what I came here for
And waste my heart on fear no more.

(A Morning Offering by John O'Donohue)

Marijke Hoek

Lightning Source UK Ltd.
Milton Keynes UK
UKOW032217310113

205675UK00006B/78/P